Targeting Iraq

Other Books by Geoff Simons

Geoff Simons

TARGETING IRAQ

Sanctions and Bombing in US Policy

Saqi Books

For Chris
who, as always, helped greatly
and understands it all

British Library Cataloguing-in-Publication Data
A catalogue for this book is available from the
British Library

ISBN 0 86356 527 1

this edition first published 2002

Saqi Books
26 Westbourne Grove
London W2 5RH
www.saqibooks.com

Contents

Contents

Contents

Contents

Figure and Tables

Figure

Tables

The Chronology of Genocide

'. . . nothing that we had seen or read had quite prepared us for the particular form of devastation which has now befallen the country [Iraq]. *The recent conflict has wrought near-apocalyptic results . . . Many food prices are already beyond the purchasing reach of most Iraqi families . . .'*

Report of mission (March 1991) led by Martti Ahtisaari, UN Under-Secretary-General for Administration and Management

'. . . the continued sanctions . . . have virtually paralysed the whole economy and generated persistent deprivation, chronic hunger, endemic undernutrition, massive unemployment and widespread human suffering . . . a vast majority of the Iraqi population is living under most deplorable conditions and is simply engaged in a struggle for survival . . . a grave humanitarian tragedy is unfolding . . .'

UN Food and Agricultural Organization, World Food Programme, Special Alert No. 237, July 1993

'Alarming food shortages are causing irreparable damage to an entire generation of Iraqi children . . . "I didn't think anything could shock me, but this was comparable to the worst scenarios I have ever seen" (Dieter Hannusch, WFP's Chief Emergency Support Officer). 70 per cent of the population has little or no access to food . . . nearly everyone seems to be emaciated . . .'

UN World Food Programme, *News Update*, 26 September 1995

'. . . findings illustrate a strong association between economic sanctions and increase in child mortality . . . since August 1990, 567,000 children in Iraq have died . . .'

Sarah Zaidi and Mary C. Smith Fawzi, *The Lancet,* 2 December 1995

'The Red Cross has criticised the "dire effects" of sanctions on civilians . . . There is chronic hunger . . . with 20,000 new cases of child malnutrition every month.'

Victoria Brittain, *The Independent,* London, 4 December 1995

'. . . health conditions are deteriorating at an alarming rate under the sanctions regime . . . the vast majority of Iraqis continue to survive on a semi-starvation diet . . . The most visible impact of these problems is . . . the dramatic rise of mortality rates among infants and children.'

UN World Health Organization, 25 March 1996

The food ration was continuing to fall "far short of meeting the nutritional needs of the Iraqi population", with UN observers now reporting "an exceptionally serious deterioration in the health infrastructure, a high infant mortality rate and high rates of morbidity and mortality in general".'

Report of the UN Secretary-General, S/1997/935, 28 November 1997

'What we are seeing is a dramatic deterioration in the nutritional well-being of Iraqi children since 1991. And what concerns us now is that there is no sign of any improvement since Security Council Resolutions 986 (1995) and 1111 (1997) came into force.'

Philippe Heffinck, UNICEF representative in Baghdad,
26 November 1997

The country is presently in a situation where a whole new generation of citizens was born and is growing up in an environment of comprehensive deprivation'

Special Topics on Social Conditions in Iraq, UN overview, 24 March 1999

The Chronology of Genocide

'I will briefly speak to the issue of United Nations economic sanctions on the people of Iraq as a case of genocide – a crime against humanity . . . men and women of conscience, with moral posture and integrity, will continue to demand the termination of crimes against humanity, indeed genocide, in respect of Iraq.'

Denis Halliday, International Conference, Madrid, 20–21 November 1999

'Iraq's Health Ministry has said that more than 10,000 Iraqis, mainly young children, died in July because of the international sanctions . . . "Some 7457 children under five years of age and 2843 adults died in July . . .".'

Middle East News Online, Monday Morning (Beirut), 30 August 2000

'Since 1991: Over 2 million Iraqi civilians have died. An average of 5000 children per month have died of hunger and disease. Cancer has reached epidemic proportions . . . People have been forced to sell their body organs to get enough to eat . . . We call on our good fellow citizens to wake up to the realities of the tragedy in Iraq, and to pressure our government to lift the sanctions on this dying nation.'

Islamic Association for Palestine, Chicago, 17 January 2001

*   *   *

'Our policy is to keep Iraq in its box.'

Western diplomat, The Guardian, London, 18 October 1995

'What we have done is put him [Saddam] back firmly in the cage.'

Prime Minister Tony Blair, 20 December 1998

'Saddam Hussein is bottled up.'

US Vice-President Dick Cheney, 20 September 2001

Introduction

Iraq, in official American and British propaganda, has long been a problem in the Middle East – with Iraq generally identified with Saddam Hussein, the demonized leader routinely excluded from all negotiation. (No matter that Washington, the CIA and American businessmen found it convenient to be friendly with Saddam for well over a decade.) This was the Arab head of state who had to be kept 'in a box', 'in a cage', 'bottled up' or, in subsequent US–UK thinking, overthrown to remove the alleged threat that he posed to his neighbours, the West and the world.

The Washington strategists judged that to combat their nominated Demon King, the 'Beast of Baghdad', and to further a range of covert agendas, any action against Iraq was permissible. Over more than a decade Iraq suffered cruise missile strikes, endless bombing, Iranian attacks in the south, Turkish invasions in the north, terrorist sabotage, anti-Saddam coup attempts, remorseless black propaganda, and a continuous sanctions regime, which even the most measured UN officials acknowledged had assumed a genocidal scale.

The events of 11 September 2001 (Chapter 1) heightened the focus on Iraq, even while the US-led war on Afghanistan was being planned and prosecuted. The United States, despite prodigious effort, was unable to find any convincing links between Saddam Hussein and Osama bin Laden or the al-Qa'ida terrorist network, but it remained essential in Washington strategy that Iraq be targeted. It was partly a matter of 'unfinished business': Bush II had resolved to complete the job that Bush I had begun. But the idea of toppling Saddam did not begin with the George W. Bush administration. Madeleine Albright, Secretary of State under Clinton, had frequently asserted that the economic sanctions on Iraq were intended in part to achieve 'regime change', an illegal policy for which there was no UN mandate. On 6 December 1999, after almost a decade of bombing and blockade, the American Under Secretary of State, Thomas Pickering, declared that Washington's policy on Iraq rested on three pillars: containment, humanitarian relief and regime change – which in reality meant punitive sanctions, illegal air patrols over the 'no-fly' zones, an aggressive US military presence in the region, and support for anti-Saddam terrorists ('We do not rule out providing lethal assistance').

In the same vein, on 15 March 2000, nine months before the election of George W. Bush, Assistant Secretary Edward Walker reported that the threat posed by Iraq had been managed 'using diplomacy backed by the credible use of force, pending a change of regime in Baghdad',[1] as if Washington were entitled to overthrow a national government. On 21 May, Robert Zoellick, an advisor to George W. Bush, suggested that the Iraq problem might be solved by dismembering the country, by splitting Iraq into different states: 'That means that we essentially undermine his [Saddam's] position within his own country, also with the Russians, the French and others, and that means slowly taking away pieces of his territory. We have started that in the north. I believe we could do that in the south. I believe that in part this involves air power. In part it involves more.'[2] Hence the US would continue to bomb Iraq, would threaten additional force, would encourage domestic terrorism, would maintain the genocidal sanctions regime, and would work to dismember the country – none of this, as perpetrated in American policy, with any authorization in UN resolutions or international law.

On 7 June 1999, Iraq was making one of its many complaints to the United Nations about US support for terrorism against the country.[3] On 6 July, Iraq complained about UN staff depositing locust eggs as part of a biological attack on Iraqi agriculture.[4] Such matters, along with the incessant American bombing campaign and the merciless sanctions regime were provoking widespread outrage in the international community and even in the United States. In June 2000, Fadia Rafeedie, a Palestinian student, replied to Madeleine Albright who had addressed an audience at the University of California, Berkeley. Rafeedie accused Albright

> of lying by omission, of responsibility via UN sanctions for the deaths of thousands of innocent Iraqi civilians, of failing to tell her audience that it was an American company that had supplied Saddam Hussein with his chemical weapons and the CIA that had earlier funded him.[5]

Then, 'to the horror of the university authorities, who thought that they had control of her address, Fadia Rafeedie even mentioned the unmentionable: that US-made depleted-uranium (DU) munitions fired by the Americans in the 1991 Gulf War may be destroying the lives of thousands more Iraqis'.[6]

The US-sustained economic sanctions (Chapter 2), maintained against a country already polluted by the radioactive and chemical detritus of war, were widely being perceived as a 'weapon of mass destruction'. Senior UN officials were resigning in protest at the impact of sanctions; Scott Ritter, once head of the UN weapons inspectors, returned to Baghdad to film the social devastation that the embargo was causing; and in London hundreds of protesters 'died' outside Downing Street to highlight the US-contrived genocide in Iraq. On 7 September 2000, Tariq Aziz, Iraq's Deputy Prime Minister, noted the irony of the UN's alleged protection of human rights set against the suffering caused by UN-mandated sanctions: 'The Iraqi victims of these unjust and unrestricted sanctions amount to more than a million children, women and elderly people during the past ten years.'

The lethal impact of sanctions has been compounded by the deadly war residues, not least those associated with DU ordnance. Few serious observers doubted that the allied use of a million DU munitions, known to produce swathes of radioactive contamination, was associated with soaring cancer rates and fetal deformities among the Iraqi civilian population. On 4 March 1998 the journalist Robert Fisk reported the 'nightmare "epidemic" of leukaemia and stomach cancer . . . claiming the lives of thousands of Iraqi civilians who live near the former war zone, including children so young that they were not even born when hostilities ended'.[7] (And what else did the allied aircraft drop in Iraqi civilians? A mother of an eight-year-old dying child recalled 'a burning, choking smell, something like insecticide' after the aircraft had bombed near their home.) The human tragedies were appearing in their thousands. Dr Jawad al-Ali, a cancer specialist in Basra, reported the soaring cancer rates and expressed his fear that he too would soon develop a cancer.[8]

The ten-year-old Faisal Abbas, one of thousands, bled to death in a paediatric cancer ward – a way-station for dying children – from the leukaemia that would have been treatable with the drugs that were denied to Iraqi civilians by the sanctions regime. Moor Mohammed Younis, two-and-a-half years old, had one eye removed, and then the other, to stop the cancer reaching her brain. Another child, Ahmed Fleah, began bleeding from his mouth, eyes, ears, nose and rectum – and took two weeks to die. And the unborn were ravaged too, with one doctor, Ala Bashir, and many others noting 'an astonishing rise in congenital abnormalities'.

Dr Jenan Ali, working in Basra, photographed full-term babies to record the 'bunch of grapes' syndrome, reminiscent of what happened in the Pacific islands after nuclear weapons testing in the 1950s. Some of the babies had no brain, no face, no eyes; others had limbs fused together. Dr Ali showed the British journalist Felicity Arbuthnot a tiny baby that was making small bleating noises. The baby had no genitalia, no eyes, nose, tongue, hands or oesophagus; and its twisted legs were joined by a thick web of flesh from the knees. Ali said that many babies were being born in such a condition, and that the radiation levels in the region were alarming.

The journalist Maggie O'Kane described a typical scene in an Iraqi maternity ward as a mother nervously awaited the birth of her child. Dr Haifa Ashahine observed, of one new-born baby: 'See, the spine ends here. There is no head.' He had seen it all before: 'If it is not a child without a brain, then maybe it's one with a giant head, stumpy arms like those of a thalidomide victim, two fingers instead of five, a heart with missing valves, missing ears.' On 13 February 2000 the Bishop of Coventry, England, recalled the 'hideous physical deformities' that he had seen in Iraqi hospitals. Many of the children were suffering from infantile leukaemia: 'There is very strong evidence to suggest that all this was caused by the depleted uranium in our weapons.'[9] Even in these circumstances the sanctions had been upheld throughout the 1990s and well into the 21st century – and in such a way that the nominal humanitarian provisions in the embargo were deliberately sabotaged by the US and UK representatives on the UN Sanctions Committee (Chapter 3).

Washington and London had always maintained that Iraq was in violation of United Nations resolutions – which evidently served as justification for the endless US–UK punishment of helpless Iraqi civilians. It is useful in this context to look at the most important Security Council resolutions on Iraq (Chapter 4) and to profile the American attitude to the United Nations over the decades (Chapter 5). In particular, it is important to acknowledge the US indifference to Security Council decisions and other aspects of international law when these do not accord with American foreign policy – as graphically shown by the crucial US support for a criminally derelict Israel over many years (Chapter 6).

In early April 2002, a massively-armed Israel waged a fresh war on the Palestinians of Gaza and the West Bank. This blatant aggression, launched by Prime Minister Ariel Sharon on the pretext of Palestinian suicide bombings in Israel, wrecked much of the administrative machinery of the Palestinian Authority, destroyed homes and utility services, and caused thousands of Palestinian casualties. This was the same Ariel Sharon who, when Israeli Minister of Defence, was deemed *personally responsible* for the massacres of thousands of Palestinians at the Sabra and Chatila refugee camps in Beirut in 1982 – a judgement that was made not only by Israel's enemies and victims but also by an official Israeli Commission of Inquiry into the crimes:

We have found, as has been detailed in this report, that the Minister of Defence [Ariel Sharon] bears personal responsibility. In our opinion, it is fitting that the Minister of Defence draw the appropriate personal conclusions arising out of the defects revealed with regard to the manner in which he discharged the duties of his office – and if necessary, that the Prime Minister consider whether he should exercise his authority under Section 21-A(a) of the Basic Law: the Government, according to which "the Prime Minister may, after informing the Cabinet of his intention to do so, remove a minister from office".[10]

Hence Ariel Sharon, responsible for massacres, was made to relinquish his post by an Israeli commission in 1983, though he stayed in the Cabinet. In February 2002 he became Israeli Prime Minister – and again behaved in the manner for which he had been rightly and universally condemned two decades earlier.

The Arab states have responded to Western policies on Iraq and Palestine with an inevitable disunity of purpose, though the current US belligerence over Iraq and the criminal excesses of Sharon have generated an unprecedented degree of Arab solidarity. The Arabs in general, not only the Iraqis and the Palestinians, have many problems – often caused by the debilitating residue of their colonial past: the Ottoman Turks, the British in Palestine, the French in Lebanon, the Italians in Libya, etc. – leaving, in much of the region, a confusing mix of residual monarchies, feudal barbarisms, suborned autocrats, secular socialists and business interests. Today the Arab response to their history and present situation is deeply influenced by how efficiently the various regimes have been bribed, cajoled and intimidated into serving the current regional hegemony, that of the United States.

It is unfortunate that neither the Arab ethnic identity nor Islam (variously interpreted, not only by Arabs) has proved sufficient to give a solidarity of purpose to what some Arab optimists choose to call 'the Arab Nation'. Such Arab fragmentation has been very unhelpful to Iraq and the Palestinians, not least because various US-managed feudalists were partly responsible for provoking the Iraqi invasion of Kuwait in 1990. The resulting Arab confusion and disunity has been only partly dispelled by recent events.

The belligerent plans and rhetoric of the current Bush administration, together with the criminal outrages of the Sharon government, have encouraged a movement towards Arab solidarity (Chapter 7) that was already under way before the events of 11 September 2001. On 9 August the Saudi Prince Sultan bin Abdul Aziz, Second Deputy Premier, commented: 'We are ready to forget the past to overcome the present difficulties and welcome Iraq's return into the Arab fold. We do not have anything against Iraq.' On 6 October, in the same spirit, Ahmed Mahir, Egypt's foreign minister, appealed to Washington to stop the bombing campaign against Iraq. At the end of March 2002, the Arab

Summit in Beirut consolidated much of the progress that had already been made towards Arab solidarity. Here the final communiqué:

- affirmed the right of Arabs to resist Israeli occupation and aggression;

- welcomed Iraq's confirmation that it would respect Kuwait's 'independence, sovereignty and security';

- rejected the use of force against Iraq;

- reaffirmed calls for the lifting of sanctions on Iraq;

- expressed satisfaction over progress towards an Arab free-trade zone.

These statements, and others in the communiqué, showed an important degree of Arab consensus, unlike some earlier summits that had ended in acrimony. At the same time, there were few practical suggestions on how to combat the Bush and Sharon excesses. Some $55 million would be donated monthly over the next six months to help the Palestinians, renewable if the violence continued, with $150 million added to two pro-Palestinian funds set up in 2000. No new relations with Israel would be established as long as the current situation continued to deteriorate. But, it was left to Iraq to adopt practical measures to address the Arab predicament in Gaza and the West Bank. Where Egypt proposed no more than a cooling of diplomatic relations with Israel, Saddam Hussein declared that Iraqi oil supplies to the United States would be blocked for 30 days, after which the situation would be reviewed.

President Bush and Secretary of State Colin Powell protested at Israeli aggression in the Occupied Territories, but were not prepared to force an Israeli withdrawal. Powell concluded his abortive (and artificially delayed) visit to Israel in April 2002, but nothing was done to stop the copious flow of US armaments and other war aid to the Israeli aggressors. And Washington indicated that it would continue the illegal bombing of Iraq (Chapter 8), while planning a fresh military onslaught to topple the Saddam regime. British aircraft were also flying bombing and reconnaissance missions, and Washington was continuing to approve the frequent bombing by Turkey, a key American NATO ally, of Kurdish targets in northern Iraq. The US–UK air patrols stand down when the Turkish raids are in prospect, with the Turks allowed to use US-supplied equipment and training in their frequent land and air attacks on sovereign Iraqi territory. The Turks bomb the very areas that the US–UK-patrolled 'no-fly' zones are supposed to protect. Turkey, like Israel, has been decisively inoculated against the unhelpful demands of international law.

Despite all this, the United States had been forced to acknowledge that its Iraq policies have failed to impress an increasingly sceptical international community. The US propaganda war over sanctions, remorselessly punishing millions of human beings, has proved to be a public relations disaster – forcing Washington to agree a package of so-called 'smart' sanctions (Chapter 9) whereby the innocent would be protected while the Iraqi regime would be targeted more effectively. No independent observers were convinced by this fresh attempt to give genocide a makeover.

There are many reasons why Washington wanted to maintain an endless embargo on the Iraqi nation, not least the attraction of a 'compensation' system providing a massive 'gravy train' for hosts of US-friendly claimants (Chapter 10). The present system channels billions of dollars to hundreds of thousands of grateful anti-Iraq recipients – with all the cash being paid out of Iraqi oil revenues over which Baghdad is allowed no control. At the present rate of payment this bounty will be distributed to the United States and its mercenary friends for more than a century. It is a neat system. The United States receives Iraqi oil while a substantial part of the oil revenues are channelled 'in compensation' to US and US-friendly companies, groups and individuals. At the same time, the Washington propagandists proclaim, with straight faces, that the entire 'oil for food' system has been devised out of genuine concern for the plight of the Iraqi people.

In fact, more than 100 countries have lodged 2.6 million separate claims for compensation, on their own behalf and on behalf of companies and individuals. Hence the sanctions regime denies the Iraqi people the right to benefit fully from their prodigious natural resource, while the oil revenues are fed elsewhere in vast amounts. As one example among thousands, in September 2000, the appropriate UN committee approved a Kuwait Petroleum Corporation claim of $15.9 billion at Iraq's expense. We can only speculate at the analogous claims that Iraq itself could lodge against Washington for the needless destruction of the entire civil infrastructure and the massive losses to the national economy caused by twelve years of economic sanctions.

There are many reasons why Washington and London find the war against Iraq – and the prospect of a larger military onslaught – very congenial. It offers 'live-fire' practice for military personnel – a point that has been conceded in the Western media. A wide range of military systems can be tested in real-world conditions, rather than via computer simulations. In May 2002, it was known that the US had a new generation of cruise missiles, the Tactical Tomahawk, that it wanted to test, and a new generation of atomic-scale thermobaric bombs as yet untested in the field. The improved cruise missiles could be fired in real-world test conditions to examine the performance of new electronic systems, enhanced range capabilities and new warheads.

The incessant military activity, *with production increased in preparation for the new war on Iraq*, keeps arms factories humming, corporate shareholders content and the national arms budgets intact. The symbiotic relationship between the US armaments corporations and the communications conglomerates thrives, and the prospect of a second Bush II term is enhanced.

In this congenial atmosphere US virtue and Iraqi perfidy are assumed and rarely challenged with any enthusiasm. The reality is that Iraq's poor human rights record is no worse than that of any other state in the region, and Washington chooses to ignore its own derelictions in this area. We should remember that there is religious freedom in Iraq where there is none in Saudi Arabia. Saddam's killing of Kurds and Shi'as, some during a war supported by the United States, is matched by the late President Assad's slaughter of members of the Muslim Brotherhood in the Syrian town of Hama.[11] Moreover, we may expect Western approval of such Saddam innovations as a minimum wage, substantial support for public health and education (before war and sanctions wrecked the entire social infrastructure), support for the emancipation of women against Muslim prejudice, and the multifaceted funding of cultural development.[12] Western governments certainly rejoiced when Saddam Hussein robustly opposed the efforts of left-wing groups to take over the Iraqi Ba'thist Party.[13] It is useful also to consider the moral credentials of Iraq's principal accuser.

The United States, like Iraq but without the pressures of war, has used some chemical weapons against its own citizens;[14] allows the torture of prisoners in jail;[15] denies suspects legal protection; allows the rape of captive females;[16] summarily executes members of ethnic minorities;[17] encourages commercial firms to exploit prison inmates;[18] and executes juveniles and mental defectives.[19] We should consider the many alleged members of the Taliban and al-Qa'ida held by the Americans in wire cages open to the weather at Guantanamo Bay, Cuba[20] – a compound abuse of human rights and international law that has generated a copious literature in the general and legal press.

At the same time it should be emphasized that none of the above, or anything else in this book, is intended to exculpate the Saddam regime for any of the many human rights abuses committed over the years.[21] However, it does not help the cause of human rights when the United States, Iraq's main accuser, can be seen to be acting from *realpolitik* calculation with little genuine concern for human welfare. Here we can recast the celebrated Juvenal tag, *quis custodiet ipsos custodes* ('who will guard the guardians?'), to ask the equally important question, *quis iudicabit ipsos iudices?* ('who will judge the judges?'). It is important that the credentials of the United States, self-appointed to be judge and executioner, are carefully considered in connection with American foreign policy on Iraq or any other state. When this is done – as demonstrated in Chapter 5 and elsewhere – it is obvious that the United States does not act as an accountable international policeman but as a global gangster outside the law.

ONE

The September 11 Pretext

The Unfinished War

The long war on Iraq, through sanctions and bombing, over the entire decade of the 1990s and beyond, had done nothing to end the debate about whether even more should be done to topple the Saddam regime. There were always those in the United States and elsewhere prepared to argue that the Coalition forces should have moved on Baghdad in 1991 to overthrow the Iraqi leadership and to end the alleged threat from Saddam Hussein once and for all. But the situation was always more complicated than the simple rhetoric suggested. Who would have replaced Saddam? Would there have been a permanent American occupation of an Arab land? What would have happened to Washington's relations with the entire Muslim world? Would the pro-West Arab regimes have been destabilized? And in particular, what would the real American agenda have been in prosecuting an expanded military campaign 'to finish the job'? Total US control of Iraqi oil? A massive expansion of US hegemony in the region? A tightening of the US noose around Kuwait, Saudi Arabia and other Muslim states?

President Bill Clinton had no interest in finishing the job that George Bush had begun in 1990–91 with sanctions and military force. Clinton was prepared to continue the bombing of Iraq with manned aircraft and cruise missiles over the years, and to maintain the harsh sanctions regime, but he was not prepared to act decisively to accomplish 'regime change'. Clinton's political behaviour, in part shaped by sexual scandal, did not quell the growing American clamour for a final onslaught on Saddam Hussein. There would be heavy civilian casualties, 'collateral damage', but – as Madeleine Albright had declared in 1996 when considering the 500,000 Iraqi children killed by sanctions – the price would be worth it.

On 26 January 1998 a group of influential Americans wrote an open letter to the Honorable William J. Clinton ('Dear Mr President') urging the adoption of a strategy that would aim 'above all, at the removal of Saddam Hussein's regime from power'. The letter observed that the United States could 'no longer depend on our partners in the Gulf war coalition to continue to uphold the sanctions or to punish Saddam when he blocks or evades UN inspectors'; and noted that in consequence the US ability 'to ensure that Saddam is not producing weapons of mass destruction . . . has substantially diminished'. If Saddam were to acquire the capacity to deliver such weapons, 'the safety of American troops in the region, of our friends and allies like Israel and the moderate Arab states, and a significant portion of the world's supply of oil will all be put at hazard . . . *the security of the world in the first part of the 21st century will be determined largely by how we handle this threat'* [my italics]. This meant that the United States President should demonstrate a willingness 'to undertake military action as diplomacy is clearly failing . . . it means removing Saddam and his regime from power'. That, declared the signatories to the letter, 'needs to become the aim of American foreign policy'.

The letter is of interest because, written during the Clinton era, it prefigured the post-September 11 bellicosity of a nation. But perhaps it was of more interest because the people who signed it were destined to become leading figures in the administration of George W. Bush (Table 1). The agitation, unsuccessful under Clinton, for a decisive military initiative against Saddam Hussein gained immense impetus with the election, through questionable tactics,[1] of Bush II to the presidency in December 2000.

Table 1
Senior Bush administration officials; 1998 signatories of open letter to Clinton

Donald Rumsfeld	Secretary of Defence
Paul Wolfowitz	Deputy Secretary of Defence
Robert Zoellick	US Trade Representative
Richard Armitage	Deputy Secretary of State
John Bolton	Under Secretary of State
Paula Dobriansky	Under Secretary of State
Peter Rodman	Assistant Secretary of Defence
Elliott Abrams	senior NSC official
Zalmay Khalilzad	senior NSC official
Richard Perle	senior Bush advisor

It was quickly made plain that Bush would not be diverted from taking a tough line on Iraq. Even without the trauma and fury generated by 11 September, it had seemed likely that Bush would be highly receptive to

American pressure for action to topple Saddam Hussein. Soon after assuming office, he authorized more bombing raids on Iraq, though not enough to threaten the survival of the regime. The bombing continued through 2001 until there was a further escalation on 11 August. In a substantial operation, some 20 bombers, supported by 30 reconnaissance, electronic counter-measures, air defence and tanker aircraft, attacked three targets at Numaniyah, 70 miles south-east of Baghdad, and Naziriyah, 170 miles south-east of the capital. Bush was making it plain that his policies on Iraq would not be affected by difficulties over Israel, but the size of the operation was reportedly scaled back for fear of causing serious reactions in Arab countries. The targets, according to US sources, were a fibre-optics communications node, a surface-to-air missile site and a long-range early warning radar.

The punishment of Iraq was continuing but it seemed that Bush, despite all the rhetoric, had not yet opted for decisive action that would accomplish 'regime change' in Iraq. There was growing international hostility to the US bombing campaign and the genocidal sanctions regime: Washington was losing the endless propaganda war. Bush officials were complaining that not enough was being done about the Saddam problem, that it was time to finish the job begun more than a decade ago. Few can have imagined the imminent terrorist outrage that was set to impinge so dramatically on their strategic calculations.

The Terrorist Prelude

The words 'terrorism' and 'terrorist' are of relatively recent origin, though the use of coercive intimidation and violence to achieve political goals is age-old. In 1795 Edmund Burke, British statesman and political philosopher, said in reference to the French Revolution, that 'thousands of those hell hounds called terrorist' had been let loose on the French people, and it has been suggested that the Jacobins would not have minded calling themselves 'terrorists'.[2] In more recent times, the United States has defined 'international terrorism' as 'acts dangerous to human life . . . that appear intended to coerce a civilian population or to influence the policy of a government by intimidation or coercion'.[3] Today 'terrorist' is universally regarded as a pejorative term, used by people to denounce those prepared to employ violence against them. The friends of the terrorist prefer to talk of heroic allies, courageous martyrs and freedom fighters.

The United States was no stranger to terrorism before 11 September. Washington has supported countless pro-West terrorist movements and itself has worked hard to intimidate and coerce weaker states around the world. And it is true also that America has suffered many terrorist attacks, a relatively small proportion launched by al-Qa'ida. The United States has sired dozens of terrorist groups, many of which are active today. We need mention only the Ku Klux Klan, the Black Panthers, the Weathermen, the League of the South, Christian Identity, Aryan Nations and the many private right-wing militia organizations. (For example, the Michigan Militia Corps Wolverines comprises a 15,000-strong private army that successive US administrations have been loath to disturb.) Terrorist groups, domestic and foreign, have attacked a wide range of American targets, at home and abroad, including the World Trade Centre before 11 September (Table 2).

Table 2
Terrorist attacks against US targets at home and abroad

November 1979	Islamic students storm the US embassy in Tehran; 52 American hostages held for 444 days.
April 1983	Suicide car-bomber blows up the US embassy in Beirut, killing 63 people, including 17 Americans.
October 1983	Shi'ite suicide bombers blow up a US Marine barracks in Beirut, killing 241 US servicemen.
December 1983	Shi'ite Muslims set off car bombs in front of the US and French embassies in Kuwait, killing five people and wounding 86.
September 1984	Car bomb at US embassy annex in east Beirut kills 16 and wounds the ambassador.
November 1984	Bomb attack on the US embassy in Bogota kills one passer-by, following death threats against US officials.
April 1985	Bomb explodes in restaurant near an American airbase in Madrid, killing 18 Spaniards and wounding 15 Americans.
June 1985	Shi'ite Muslims hijack TWA Boeing 727 in Mediterranean and force it to fly to Beirut; US Navy diver killed and 39 other Americans are held until July after Syrian mediation.
August 1985	Car bomb kills two and injures 20 at a US base in Frankfurt; one US soldier killed for his identity papers.
October 1985:	Palestinian militants seize the Italian cruise liner *Achille Lauro*; kill a disabled American, Leon Klinghoffer.
November 1985	Hijackers of Egypt Air plane kill a US passenger.
December 1985	Arab suicide squad attacks US and Israeli check-in desks at airports in Rome and Vienna; four guerrillas and 16 others killed.

April 1986	Bomb explosion on TWA plane approaching Athens airport causes four people to be sucked out of the plane; bomb explosion in La Belle Discothèque, Berlin, kills a US citizen and a German woman and wounds 150, 44 of them Americans.
December 1988	Bomb explodes on Pan Am Boeing over Lockerbie, killing 259 passengers and eleven people on the ground.
February 1993	Bomb explodes in garage under World Trade Centre, killing six and wounding more than 1000.
April 1995	Bomb destroys Federal Building in Oklahoma City, killing 168 people and wounding more than 500. Timothy McVeigh found guilty and executed in 2001.
November 1995	Bomb at Riyadh base kills seven, including five Americans.
June 1996	Truck bomb at Khobar Towers, Dhahran, kills 19 US personnel and wounds nearly 400 people.
June 1998	Rocket-propelled grenades explode near US embassy in Beirut.
August 1998	Lorry bombs explode at the US embassies in Nairobi and Dar es Salaam, killing 224 people, including 12 Americans, and injuring thousands; all but ten of the deaths are in Nairobi.
October 2000	Bomb kills 17 US sailors aboard the US destroyer *Cole* as it refuels in the Yemeni port of Aden; the US calls the Saudi exile Osama bin Laden the prime suspect.

By the start of the 21st century the United States had become well acquainted with terrorist attacks on its personnel and property. There was worse to come.

11 September 2001

In a totally unprecedented type of terrorist attack, the huge twin towers of the World Trade Centre in New York and parts of the Pentagon in Washington were destroyed by hijacked aircraft, causing thousands of fatalities.[*] American Airlines Flight 11, carrying 81 passengers, nine flight attendants and two pilots, had taken off at 8.02 am from Boston's Logan Airport bound for Los Angeles. At 8.45 it crashed into the 1368-foot tall north tower of the World Trade Centre in Manhattan. Some eighteen minutes later, another Boeing 767, United Airlines

---

[*] On 16 May 2002, a scandal erupted in the US when it emerged that the Bush administration had known before 11 September of planned al-Qa'ida hijackings.

Flight 175, flew straight into the World Trade Centre's south tower. At 9.30 yet another United Airlines Flight, carrying 65 people from Boston to Los Angeles, crashed into the Pentagon.[4] A Boeing 747, with 45 passengers, also crashed near Pittsburgh airport and a car bomb exploded outside the State Department in Washington. Within hours both the World Trade Centre towers had collapsed, sending clouds of dust billowing through New York.

After some confusion, not least about the location of President Bush, the United States was placed on a war footing. The United States closed its borders, evacuated other buildings across the country and grounded all aircraft. In Britain, Docklands and the Stock Exchange were evacuated in case of further attacks, and throughout the world national leaders rushed to express their shock and horror at what had happened. Russian President Vladimir Putin referred to 'barbarous terrorist acts' and called for an international campaign against terrorism. The Palestinian leader Yasser Arafat condemned the attacks as 'unbelievable and terrible', offered his condolences to the American people, and was photographed donating blood.

The United States had been deeply traumatized by an act of aggression that many observers compared to the Japanese attack on Pearl Harbour in December 1941 when more than 2000 American service personnel were killed, a similar number to those people killed on 11 September 2001.[5] Another precedent springs to mind – that of Vietnam. Here, too, with total neglect of the fathomless pain of the Vietnamese, there was much Western commentary on the psychiatric state of an American nation afflicted by the catastrophe of national humiliation and defeat. The American experience of the Vietnam debacle has been described in terms of paranoia, trauma, shock, amnesia, megalomania, frustration, confusion and behavioural paralysis. Elsewhere I wrote about the psychiatry of the Vietnam Syndrome: 'The shock to the American psyche had been profound, not least because of the arrogant assumptions of US omnipotence.'[6] Much the same could be said about the American trauma caused by the events of September 11. Here, too, the American people experienced bewilderment and incomprehension[7]

On 12 September, President Bush declared that the attacks on the United States were 'acts of war', while Osama bin Laden was denying any involvement. Then Bush, seemingly not noticing dozens of other conflicts around the world, announced that the world was facing 'the first war of the 21st century', a 'war against terrorism'. On 15 September Bush named bin Laden as the prime suspect and told the American people: 'You will be asked for your patience, for the conflict will not be short.' It was obvious that the Washington strategists, industrious long before 11 September 2001, had been preparing the ground for a military campaign.

Preparing the Ground – the UN

The United Nations was already a useful American ally in the battle against international terrorism: UN Secretary-General Kofi Annan would be unlikely to question American assertions as to which individuals, groups or states should be properly regarded as *terrorist*, and the United Nations had already developed a wide range of legal instruments that could be invoked to buttress the American war against terrorism (Table 3). In addition to its involvement in developing specific UN Conventions, the General Assembly had also adopted the Declaration on Measures to Eliminate International Terrorism (1994) and the Declaration to supplement the 1994 Declaration (1996). The Declaration and supplement condemn all acts of terrorism as criminal and unjustifiable, whoever is responsible, and urge all states to take measures to eliminate international terrorism.

The UN Security Council had also been active, before the attacks on Washington and New York, in adopting resolutions that were highly supportive of the fresh US military campaign being planned:

- SCR 1267 (1999), demanding that the Taliban turn over Osama bin Laden so that he could be brought to justice;

- SCR 1269 (1999), condemning all acts of terrorism as criminal and unjustifiable, and calling on Member States to adopt specific measures;

- SCR 1333 (2000), demanding that the Taliban authorities in Afghanistan act swiftly to close all camps where terrorists are trained.

Table 3

UN Conventions against international terrorism

Convention on Offences and Certain Other Acts Committed on Board Aircraft, adopted in Tokyo, 1963

Convention for the Suppression of Unlawful Seizure of Aircraft, The Hague, 1970

Convention for the Suppression of Unlawful Acts against the Safety of Civil Aviation, Montreal, 1971

Convention on the Prevention and Punishment of Crimes Against Internationally Protected Persons, including Diplomatic Agents, New York, 1973, adopted by the General Assembly

Convention against the Taking of Hostages, New York 1979, adopted by the General Assembly

Convention on the Physical Protection of Nuclear Material, Vienna, 1980

Convention for the Suppression of Unlawful Acts against the Safety of Maritime Navigation, Rome, 1988

Convention on the Marking of Plastic Explosives for the Purpose of Detection, Montreal, 1991

International Convention for the Suppression of Terrorist Bombings, New York, 1997, adopted by the General Assembly

International Convention for the Suppression of the Financing of Terrorism, New York, 1999, adopted by the General Assembly

---

On 12 September 2001, immediately after the terrorist attacks on Washington and New York, the Security Council adopted Resolution 1368 (2001), condemning the terrorist attacks on the United States on 11 September, and calling on all states to work together urgently to bring the perpetrators to justice. Here it is stressed 'that those responsible for aiding, supporting or harbouring the perpetrators, organizers and sponsors of these acts will be held accountable'. The Security Council was ready *to take all necessary steps to respond to the terrorist attacks* – the manifest blank cheque that Washington wanted. The United States had contrived a resolution, adopted at the height of international revulsion at the terrorist acts, that would seemingly serve to authorize *any* US military action anywhere in the world.[8] It was obvious that the first target would be Afghanistan, but Iraq was already in the frame.

The Iraq Option

On 20 August 1998 the United States launched between 75 and 100 Tomahawk cruise missiles from six US warships and a submarine at 'terrorist facilities' in Afghanistan and Sudan, opening what President Bill Clinton called a 'long war' against terrorism: 'Our target was terror. Our mission was clear. The countries that persistently host terrorism have no right to be safe havens.' At the same time it was emphasized that the attacks were not an isolated raid but part of an ongoing assault against the resurgence of anti-American acts around the world. Secretary of State Madeleine Albright declared: 'We are not going to take an *ad hoc* approach to this. This is a very serious battle . . . We have to organize in the long run to confront a serious threat to our way of life.' The Bush 'war against terrorism' in which Afghanistan was selected as a primary target was begun by his Democratic predecessors.

The Afghan target chosen by the Clinton strategists was a compound of six buildings at Khost, near the Pakistani border, allegedly comprising training camps and a military arsenal. The site, operated with the blessing of Afghanistan's Taliban regime, was part of what US propagandists were calling the most extensive Sunni Muslim 'terrorist university' in the world. The Republican leadership in Washington supported the Clinton initiative, despite accusations that the President was trying to distract attention from the Lewinsky scandal.[9] The bombing of Afghanistan failed to kill Osama bin Laden, a presumed target.

After the September 11 attacks on Washington and New York, Afghanistan was again chosen for a US military assault, but this time as a target for a prolonged bombing campaign designed to overthrow the Taliban regime and to disrupt the al-Qa'ida terrorist network. On 7 October 2001 the United States began what would be a months-long bombing onslaught on one of the poorest and most war-ravaged countries of the world.[10] But, throughout this period, the Bush administration never lost sight of the fact that the Iraqi regime of Saddam Hussein was a principal irritant to Washington, a painful thorn in the side of the behemoth. It seemed likely that as soon as the Afghanistan business had been settled, Iraq – already copiously bombed for more than a decade – would be given particular attention by the Washington military planners.

In its response to the September 11 attacks, Iraq stood alone among the Arab regimes. Where commentary in Jordan, Egypt, Lebanon, Saudi Arabia and elsewhere, while suggesting causes for the attacks, was broadly condemnatory of the terrorist actions, only Iraq (and some Palestinians) was prepared to voice what many Arabs were feeling. On 12 September 2001, Iraqi television declared:

> The American cowboy is reaping the fruits of his crimes against humanity. It is a black day in the history of America, which is tasting the bitter defeat of its crimes and disregard for the people's will to lead a free, decent life. The massive explosions in the centres of power in America are a painful slap in the face of US politicians to stop their illegitimate hegemony and attempts to impose custodianship on peoples.

Whatever the justice of such charges, they served simply to inflame the already massive anti-Saddam feeling in the Bush administration. Few observers could doubt that the option of a fresh military campaign against Saddam Hussein, with the objective of 'regime change', was moving up the American agenda. Western intelligence agencies were reportedly scrutinizing every scrap of information to see whether Saddam had any involvement in the September 11 attacks. It was plain that even the most tenuous links between the Iraqi regime and the perpetrators of the terrorist strike on Washington and New York would be used by the Bush administration to justify a massive escalation in the war against Iraq.

American intelligence experts were quick to declare that a Saddam involvement should not be ruled out, that he had the motive, the experience and the resources to help the hijackers who launched the terrorist attacks. On 14 September 2001, James Woolsey, Director of the CIA in 1993–95, said that there was considerable circumstantial evidence that Saddam Hussein may have cooperated with Osama bin Laden in the past, but Woolsey's comments seemed to be no more than speculation: 'It could be a very fruitful marriage between Saddam and bin Laden. Bin Laden gets the publicity he wants, while Saddam is the sleeping partner who gets revenge and causes disruption, while still selling his oil and keeping the support of Russia and China.'

It was now being suggested that Ramzi Yousef, convicted of organising the first bombing of the World Trade Centre in 1993, may have had ties with Iraqi intelligence; and Saddam's own observations were doing little to deflect consideration of a possible Iraqi complicity. Soon after the September 11 attacks, Saddam reportedly commented: 'Irrespective of the conflicting human feelings about what happened, America is reaping the thorns planted by its rulers in the world. There is hardly a place that does not have a memorial symbolizing the criminal actions committed by America against its natives.' He cited America's record in the 1991 Gulf War, its behaviour in Vietnam and its use of nuclear weapons against Japan: 'He who does not want to reap evil should not sow evil, and he who considers the lives of his people precious must remember that the lives of the people in the world are precious also.'[11]

Few commentators doubted that in the post-September 11 political climate Iraq would be a 'prime candidate' for American attention.[12] Saddam was fanning the flames. On 15 September 2001 he acknowledged the large number of victims of the terrorist attacks, but pointed out that

> Many countries of the world have suffered from America's technological might, and many peoples do recognize that America has killed thousands or even millions of human beings in their countries.

America, he suggested, was always keen to experiment with new weapons,[13] and pointed out that Muslims were often the victims of such tests. Moreover, one and a half million Iraqis had been killed by sanctions and aggression, according to Western documents – which meant that Iraq had lost one twentieth of its population:

> And just as your beautiful skyscrapers were destroyed and caused your grief, beautiful buildings and precious homes crumbled over their owners in Lebanon, Palestine and Iraq as a result of American weapons . . . In a single place, a civilian shelter, the Amiriyah Shelter, more than 400 children, young and old men and women were killed in Iraq by American bombs . . . *Americans should feel the pain they have inflicted on other peoples of the world, so that when they suffer, they will find the right solution and the right path* [my italics].

On 15 September, a Bush advisor acknowledged that Iraqi targets were being considered for a bombing campaign, and two days later James Woolsey was suggesting that Saddam may be the target the 'Americans are looking for'.[14] Woolsey proposed Iraqi complicity in the 1993 bombing of the World Trade Centre, but even he was driven to admit the paucity of the evidence: 'One can only speculate.'[15] There was, he conceded, 'no evidence of explicit state sponsorship of the September 11 attacks', but then Woolsey emphasized that absence of evidence did not mean that such sponsorship had not occurred. Was such speculation an adequate ground for a massive bombing campaign against Iraq? Some influential figures in the Bush administration certainly seemed to think so.

Paul Wolfowitz, Deputy Secretary of Defence, had chillingly advocated 'ending states' that sponsor terrorism, and Iraq was at the head of his list of regimes deserving termination. He, with Vice-President Dick Cheney and Donald Rumsfeld, Defence Secretary, had consistently urged a more forceful policy against Iraq; and Richard Perle, head of the Defence Advisory Board, rushed to declare that the United States should take the opportunity afforded by September 11 to remove Saddam from power *even if he had played no part in the terrorist attacks.* 'We want to choose targets very carefully and, when we have chosen them, we want to be devastatingly effective. We have the capacity to make the costs of supporting terrorism extremely high.'

Implicating Iraq

The Bush administration, nursing its grievances against Iraq, was continuing to suggest a Saddam involvement in the attacks on Washington and New York. It seemed increasingly clear that leading figures in the administration were keen to exploit September 11 as a pretext for finally toppling the Iraqi regime. In the week after the attacks, American intelligence officials were claiming that Mohammed Atta, believed to have flown the Boeing into the north tower of the World Trade Centre, had met the head of Iraqi intelligence earlier in 2001. At the same time it was acknowledged that this alleged meeting did not necessarily prove an Iraqi link with the terrorist attacks. Rumsfeld was refusing to rule out the possibility of state involvement, Cheney was saying that the US would have no hesitation in pursuing Saddam if he was harbouring terrorists, and Perle was declaring that a 'primary goal' of the war on terrorism should be to overthrow Saddam.

Much of the Arab world, unconvinced even that a link between the terrorist attacks and Osama bin Laden had been established, refused to countenance September 11 as a pretext for bombing Iraq. In Kuwait, still smarting from the 1990 Iraqi invasion, it was easier to find support for a Bush policy of toppling the Iraqi leadership. Thus Abdulaziz al-Awadi, a Kuwaiti businessman, commented: 'I can't help but think that all this will lead back to Baghdad, and it will mean the end of Saddam Hussein at last. There is unfinished business to do, and the world will not be safe until Saddam goes forever.' Anwar al-Madina, another Kuwaiti, wondered who was behind the group that had carried out the attacks in America: when the Western intelligence services had done their work 'the trail will lead back to one place . . . Baghdad'.

A senior Western diplomat commented that the Kuwaitis would love Saddam to put his head above the parapet, 'so the US and its allies can blow it off'. The Bush administration, however, was having to admit that as yet it had no evidence to link Iraq with the terrorist attacks. The Iraqi Deputy Prime Minister, Tariq Aziz, declared in a telegram to the Voices in the Wilderness activist group his 'sincere condolences for the American victims' of the September 11 attacks. On 18 September, in a second open letter, Saddam Hussein claimed that Washington was using the crisis to get back at old enemies and had yet to prove who was responsible: 'The United States has made the accusation before possessing the minimum evidence. Could this mean other than a desire to settle old accounts?' Naji Sabir, the Iraqi foreign minister, denied that Baghdad had 'any connection whatever' to the attacks launched on America: 'The US administration and its allies know very well that we have no relation whatsoever with groups that are being accused now by the US of committing what happened.'

The Bush administration, unlikely to be impressed by Iraqi protestations of innocence, seemed uncertain how to proceed. The preparations for war against Afghanistan were proceeding according to plan, but what then was to be done about Saddam? Pundits such as Woolsey had offered nothing more than empty speculation, Rumsfeld was claiming to 'know' that states were supporting 'these people', and Cheney was denying any link to Baghdad ('Saddam Hussein is bottled up'). Moreover, there were many signs that Saddam remained deeply hostile to Islamic fundamentalism, the stock-in-trade of Osama bin Laden. Thus a former CIA official, not identified, commented to the *Wall Street Journal*:

> The reality is that Osama bin Laden doesn't like Saddam Hussein. Saddam is a secularist who has killed more Islamic clergy than he has Americans. They share almost nothing in common, except a hatred for the United States. Saddam is the ultimate control freak and, for him, terrorists are the ultimate loose cannon.

The US cabinet was divided. Figures such as Rumsfeld and Wolfowitz assumed a connection between Baghdad and the September 11 attacks, but Cheney was continuing to assert that the administration had no evidence. A consensus for action had still to emerge.

On 23 September 2001 *The Sunday Telegraph* (London) reported that Saddam Hussein put his troops on high military alert two weeks before the attacks on America, providing 'the strongest indication yet that the Iraqi dictator knew an atrocity was planned'. One intelligence official said that there had been nothing obvious to warrant Saddam's declaration of 'Alert G', Iraq's highest state of readiness: 'He was clearly expecting a massive attack and it leads you to wonder why.' It was further claimed that three high-ranking Iraqi intelligence officials, among them the notorious Hassan Ezba Thalaj, had visited Pakistan to meet al-Qa'ida representatives; and that earlier Iraqi visitors, including Ahmed al-Jafari, a senior Iraqi intelligence officer, had taken large sums of money with them.[16] By contrast, Major-General Amos Malka, the chief of Israeli military intelligence, told Israel's *Yedioth Ahronoth* newspaper that there was no evidence of a direct link between Iraq and the terrorist attacks in the United States.

Amr Moussa, the Arab League chief, was now warning that any US strikes against an Arab state would be 'unacceptable', although it was far from clear how the League would respond to an American bombing campaign against Iraq. There was no doubt that the Bush administration was working hard to find links between the Iraqi regime and terrorism, though on 24 September Secretary of State Colin Powell was forced to admit that 'no clear link' had been found. By the end of September 2001, there was mounting agitation in the United States for a strike to end the Saddam regime once and for all, though the growing bellicosity alarmed some of America's strategic allies:

Bite the bullet and target Iraq[17]

Washington's hawk trains sight on Iraq ('Hawk doesn't do him [Paul Wolfowitz] justice. What about velociraptor?')[18]

Turkey signs up, but fears Iraq is next US target[19]

It was obvious that the Washington hawks were committed to the overthrow of Saddam Hussein, irrespective of any evidence linking him to the September 11 attacks. Such evidence, useful in the propaganda war, might help to sway international opinion but it seemed increasingly likely that the United States would launch a decisive onslaught on Iraq, whatever the pretext.

Preparing for Phase Two

Phase One of President Bush's alleged war against terrorism – the targeting of Afghanistan – was proceeding apace. Most of the US military assets were in place and in a few days' time, on 7 October 2001, the bombs would start falling, wrecking the remains of Afghanistan's war-torn social infrastructure, curtailing the aid efforts upon which millions of people depended for their survival, and killing – in one estimate – around 10,000 civilians. All this was insufficient for the Washington strategists. Already Phase Two of the Bush war was being planned and advertized. Many countries were being cited as meriting the sort of treatment that would soon be meted out to Afghanistan. Bush had not yet delivered his absurd 'axis of evil' (Iraq, Iran and North Korea) speech, but the various 'rogue states', the 'states of concern', were being lined up for attention. Iran, Iraq, North Korea, Syria, Sudan, Somalia, Yemen, Cuba – the world was certainly a target-rich zone. Afghanistan, declared the propagandists, would soon be dealt with. Where next for the forces of righteousness? Iraq remained the most likely option.

Baghdad was again bracing itself for an American onslaught, with officials conceding that they were taking a number of unspecified 'precautions'. Military units were being deployed around the country and food was being stockpiled in government warehouses. One Ba'th official, speaking over a sound system to an assembled crowd, denounced America for its international crusade against Arabs and Muslims. At the same time officials were stressing that Iraq had no links with al-Qa'ida, a claim that was endorsed by at least one Western diplomat: 'This regime, and its leader, never fail to surprise me, but I just don't see how Saddam could work with bin Laden.' Iraq is largely a secular country where women enjoy the same rights as men. There is nothing in this of the culture of Islamic fundamentalism

On 7 October 2001 President Bush was again declaring that other countries would be targeted after the first phase of the war against terrorism: 'Today we focus on Afghanistan, but the battle is broader. Every nation has a choice to make. In this conflict, there is no neutral ground.' The Republican Trent Lott, the Senate Minority Leader, was saying that an attack against Saddam could follow the military operation against the Taliban and Osama bin Laden:

> Somewhere down the line we're going to have to deal with Iraq. Clearly, they have their own form of terrorism, and they still have Saddam Hussein. So we're going to have to contend with that problem, but probably a little later down the line.

Saddam Hussein made his own contribution to the debate:

> They [the Americans] claim to have evidence [about Osama bin Laden's culpability] that they have showed Pakistan . . . If they have evidence, why don't they let the whole world see it to make their stand and rationale strong? Is just saying they have evidence enough . . . to start a war against a country? [If the suspects had been from a Western country, the Americans] would have denied it even if all the angels came. But when the accusation points at a Muslim or Arab country, they would believe it even if the accusation is made by one of the earth's devils.

It was plain, in early October 2001, that the US intelligence services were not managing to uncover evidence linking Saddam to the September 11 attacks, an obvious failure that was reflected in much American political commentary. Thus Democratic Senator Joseph Lieberman argued that possible links might justify US action against Baghdad in the future: 'It depends, frankly, on what the evidence is. *If* the trail leads in this case to Iraq . . . we have to go at them' (my italics). Again it was being claimed that Mohammed Atta, the suspected mastermind of the terrorist attacks on America, had met Ahmed Khalil Ibrahim Samir al-Ani, a former consul and second secretary at the Iraqi embassy in Prague, in June 2000. Al-Ani was later expelled from the Czech Republic for spying. Was this the sort of material that Washington intended to use in justification of a massive new bombing campaign against the Iraqi nation?

The Western media were in no doubt that the Bush administration was itching to bomb Iraq and to topple the Saddam regime:

America turns sights on Iraq[20]

Bombing goes on as US hints at attack on Iraq[21]

The real threat is Iraq – as Bush's men have said for years[22]

Iraq, it was being proclaimed would 'indeed be the next target', and this was not 'mere speculation' because 'we have it from the horse's mouth'.[23] Stephen Pollard, a senior fellow at the Centre for the New Europe, a Brussels-based think-tank, was happy to echo the view of the American Right: 'Iraq must be the next target. The point of a war on terrorism is, surely, to stamp it out – not to build a coalition that includes its most prominent sponsors and that ignores the single greatest threat – Iraq.'[24]

But all the inconvenient uncertainties about Iraq's terrorist involvement remained. The links with Osama bin Laden had not been demonstrated, and nor could it be shown that Saddam Hussein had had a hand in anthrax attacks within the United States. Donald Rumsfeld declared that, *if* evidence was found to link Saddam with the anthrax outbreaks then direct action would be taken against Iraq. It was familiar rhetoric but Washington seemed at a loss about how to proceed. Judith Kipper, Council on Foreign Relations, summarized a widespread perception: 'The truth is that nobody knows how to go after that regime [Iraq] and bombing won't do the job.'

On 10 October 2001 the 57-member Islamic Conference Organization, whilst neither supporting nor condemning the air strikes in Afghanistan, warned the United States that it would not accept attacks against any 'Arab or Islamic state under the pretext of the fight against terrorism'. There seemed to be little chance that Washington would be able to organize an international coalition for a new military campaign against the Saddam regime. At the same time John Negroponte, the US Ambassador to the United Nations, had reportedly told Mohammed Douri, his Iraqi counterpart, that Iraq would be attacked if it tried to exploit the situation in Afghanistan to further its interests: 'There will be a military strike against you and you will be defeated.'

A spate of inexplicable anthrax outbreaks in the United States was then stimulating fresh consideration of possible Iraqi involvement, with former weapons inspectors divided on the issue.[25] James Woolsey, former CIA chief, had claimed that Iraq was a prime suspect behind the anthrax terror, 'the leading rogue state in the world in their capabilities for biological warfare'. On 23 October Tariq Aziz, Iraq's Deputy Prime Minister, denied that his country had anything to do with the September 11 atrocities or the spate of anthrax attacks in the United States: 'Iraq has nothing to do with what happened in America in September. We worked on anthrax in the '80s and, in the '90s we destroyed all our anthrax assets.' Also, UN weapons inspectors would not be allowed back into the country: 'We proved our good intentions for seven-and-a-half years . . . They were here for a purpose and their goal was to finish the job and lift the sanctions. They finished their job, but the sanctions were not lifted.'

The Bush administration was working to build a case against Iraq, but with few results to show. James Woolsey had met with the exiled Iraqi National Congress, the main opposition group, in London on a trip funded and approved by Paul Wolfowitz, Deputy Secretary of Defence. Woolsey, sensitive to the nature of his mission ('I was in London, and that's it'), had been given the job of building a propaganda justification for a fresh war on Iraq. Already there was further damning evidence: on 25 April 1998 an al-Qa'ida delegation had journeyed to Baghdad to attend Saddam's birthday celebrations. With this the best that the US intelligence services could manage, it was unsurprising to hear Woolsey denying the need for proof that would be admissible in a court of law ('Evidentiary standards are the wrong standards'). It was enough that there was some available hearsay ('almost all intelligence is hearsay'). But the absence of relevant evidence would not be allowed to limit the scale of the envisaged onslaught on Iraq. Woolsey said: 'If the government chooses . . . to take military action against any other state outside Afghanistan, I believe that the world will see our reaction in that case will be ruthless, relentless and devastating' (Woolsey).

Tariq Aziz, in interview with the journalist Hala Jaber in Baghdad, declared that Iraq was aware of American plans to strike 300 Iraqi targets with 1000 missiles. It was 'just a matter of time' before 'such an attack' began, though it would be a grave mistake: 'The Arab world is not going to tolerate that at all because they know that this is unjust and is sheer aggression.'[26] On 28 October Donald Rumsfeld announced that the Bush administration was not afraid of saying the word 'Iraq', that Iraq had been on the terrorist list for years, and that Iraq was a threat to other countries in the world including the United States.

The Propaganda War

Towards the end of 2001 the United States was engaged in a massive propaganda campaign, designed to prepare international opinion for a military onslaught on Iraq to topple President Saddam Hussein. The Western media was then carrying a torrent of innuendo, accusation and threat – much of it in violation of the UN Charter – creating the impression that a new war was inevitable.[27] Washington and London were outraged that Russia's President Putin planned to visit Saddam, and continuous efforts were being made to stress the need to address the Iraq Problem once and for all. Iraqi defectors, with much to gain from graphic tales, were describing Saddam's terrorist training camps and his continuing development of prohibited weapons. Martin Woolacott, writing from America, observed that Saddam would be the next US target, 'one way or another'. The US war lobby was recognising the need 'for a period of diplomatic preparation',[28] signalling the uncomfortable awareness in America and elsewhere that the case for war was still unconvincing. It would be necessary to redouble the propaganda efforts, or perhaps Washington, increasingly impatient with international doubts, would decide to take unilateral action.

Pliant Western journalists, happy to work as Bush foot soldiers in the media war, were variously proclaiming that 'Saddam must go' (Finkelstein) and that 'Saddam also can be forced out' (Godson). There was no reference here to the legality of using military force to depose the leader of a sovereign member of the United Nations, and no attempt to analyse the political consequences for the region and the wider world. On 19 November 2001 John Bolton, the US Under Secretary for Arms Control and International Security, told an arms conference in Geneva that he suspected Iraq had 'developed, produced and stockpiled biological warfare agents and weapons', taking advantage of the absence of UN weapons inspectors: 'The existence of Iraq's programme is beyond dispute.' It was plain that, as always, the Washington hawks had Saddam in their sights. On 25 November President Bush warned that Saddam Hussein could face the sort of destruction visited on Afghanistan unless he opened up his country to international inspection: 'Saddam is evil. I think he's got weapons of mass destruction . . .' Asked if he would set a deadline for inspections, Bush replied: 'I just told him.'

The US military was now running live-fire war games, Operation Desert Spring, in Kuwait within 30 miles of the Iraqi border. The manoeuvres, long planned, had been inflated to involve some 3000 American troops following the September 11 attacks – a signal that Washington was determined to turn up the heat on the Saddam regime. The US propaganda strategy was plain. The hunt for links between Saddam and al-Qa'ida had been a dismal failure, and the US intelligence services had failed to find a Saddam thumbprint on a single anthrax spore, so it had become necessary to shift the propaganda war to weapons of mass destruction and the return of UN inspectors. Suddenly the Bush 'war on terrorism' had been converted to a potential 'war about UN weapons inspectors'. There was ample right-wing opinion that favoured such a ploy. Even the British Tory leader, Iain Duncan Smith, was visiting Washington to proclaim his enthusiasm for an extension of the war on terrorism to topple the Saddam regime. Said a Duncan Smith aide obliquely: 'His instincts are strongly on the side of those who say the war does not stop in Afghanistan.'

On 27 November 2001, Baghdad rejected a demand from George Bush for UN weapons inspectors to be allowed back into the country. By this time, Bush was asserting that the anti-terror campaign was also aimed at 'those who make weapons of mass destruction and terrorize the world'. Secretary of State Colin Powell, rapidly abandoning his alleged dove-like instincts, commented to CNN that Bush's words were 'a very sober, chilling message'. Baghdad, long accustomed to the bullying posture of the United States, declared that Iraq would not bow to threats: the American position was 'arrogant and unilateral' and, before asking Iraq to allow weapons inspectors to return, the United Nations should lift sanctions and the US should abolish the illegal no-fly zones. On the following day, the United States was warned by both Russia and Germany not to make Iraq its next target in the war against terrorism. Russia would pull out of the anti-terror coalition, and Berlin urged the US to be very cautious about widening the campaign. At the same time Israeli military intelligence was telling its government that it expected an American attack on Iraq within three months. On 29 November, following an Anglo-French summit in London, Tony Blair and President Jacques Chirac proclaimed their demand for 'incontrovertible evidence' of Iraqi complicity in the attacks on America before they would support a new war against the Saddam regime. Two days later, Blair emphasized that it was important first to complete the military action in Afghanistan, while a Downing Street source was emphasizing that there was no evidence at that stage that Iraq was involved in the September 11 attacks.

Again the focus in the propaganda war was shifting. American opinion was divided on Saddam's terrorist culpability, though European commentary tended to discount a connection between Iraq and al-Qa'ida. The journalist Philip Johnston, writing in *The Daily Telegraph* (London) suggested in December 2001 that the evidence was growing of a link between Saddam and the attacks in the United States. ('This is precisely what opponents of Saddam and some in Western security agencies are now starting to believe . . . ') Richard Butler, reliably anti-Iraq as always, was urging the Bush administration to secure the full backing of the UN Security Council 'to hold Saddam's feet to the fire': Iraq had 'a whole cocktail cabinet' of chemical and nerve agents, 'and the [Bush] administration knows this very well'.

Planning for War

The military plans for the overthrow of Saddam were being openly discussed in the Western media, though Washington was not giving precise details or any indication of when the campaign would start. It was generally assumed that the vast missile onslaught expected by Tariq Aziz would be the precursor to action on the ground involving either a massive American-led invasion, as in 1991, or at least substantial military aid to opposition groups inside Iraq. In early December 2001 *The Observer* (London) reported that President Bush had ordered the CIA and his senior military commanders to draw up the detailed plans for a military operation that could begin within months. Key planners were former CIA chief James Woolsey and General Tommy Franks, the US Central Command head who was leading the war against Afghanistan. Again, less attention was being given to Iraq's imagined links with al-Qa'ida than to Saddam's alleged arsenals of prohibited weapons. 'Iraqmania' was said to be gripping the United States, with public discussion degenerating into jingoistic rhetoric: 'Do we take out Saddam this week or next? Do we attack one country or five? Shall we wipe out everyone who disagrees with us, or just most of them?'[29]

Few observers doubted that Tony Blair would agree to function as a minor cog in the Bush war machine. On 3 December, a Downing Street source, while emphasizing that no decision had been taken on widening the military campaign, emphasized that the war against terrorism would take two phases. Only two? And two days later, Jack Straw, the British foreign secretary, declared that 'action must be taken' to counter the threat posed by Saddam's alleged weapons of mass destruction. *Any* country, said Geoff Hoon, defence secretary,

ʻ

was entitled to take pre-emptive military action in self-defence – *a principle that presumably entitled Saddam Hussein to take a military initiative, for no country was under greater threat of imminent military action than Iraq.*

The Pentagon had removed its 3rd Army headquarters from America to Kuwait, a sure sign of plans to expand the war on terrorism. Military experts commented that the move of several hundred headquarters staff from Fort MacPherson, Georgia, to an undisclosed location in the Gulf was 'significant', facilitating – according to a US Central Command spokesman – support for the American ground forces 'for the ongoing war against terrorism'. Other reports suggested that thousands of moth-balled military vehicles in Kuwait were being prepared for action, and that substantial US military forces were being transferred from an unhelpful Saudi Arabia to more sympathetic Gulf states. Ryan Crocker, the US Under Secretary of State for Near East affairs, was heading an American delegation to northern Iraq to prepare the ground for possible military action. Kurdish rebel leaders were warned not to deal with Saddam Hussein, following November meetings between the Iraqi leadership and the Kurdish Democratic Party (KDP). The US State Department, seemingly not yet ready for an American military strike against Iraq, had refused to allow Pentagon officials to take part in the visit to Kurdish Iraq.

The Iraqi authorities, in anticipation of massive US air strikes, were detaining scores of people they deemed a possible threat to the regime. In oil-rich Kirkuk more than 100 people were detained, and then released after giving written pledges not to hide information on activities hostile to the regime. Kirkuk's new security chief, a replacement for his corrupt predecessor, had reportedly summoned tribal leaders in the city and threatened them with execution if their areas were ever used by anti-Saddam factions to hide weapons, to hold meetings or to conduct other hostile activities. More than 50 people in areas bordering Syria and Jordan had been arrested, and the governor of Missan, having detained scores of young people, wrested a pledge from the elders of the Bani Kaab and Bani Lam tribes to cooperate with the authorities in the fight against opposition groups.

On 11 December 2001 President Bush warned that 'rogue states' with weapons of mass destruction would be his next priority in the war against terrorism, a clear sign – if any were needed – that he intended to target Iraq:

America's next priority in the war on terrorism is to protect against the proliferation of weapons of mass destruction and the means to deliver them. Every nation now knows that we cannot accept and we will not accept states that harbour, finance, train or equip the agents of terror. Those nations that violate this principle will be regarded as hostile regimes. They have been warned. They are being watched, and they will be held to account.

Iraqi opposition groups, heartened by the Bush posture, had lobbied the American government with a war plan calling for an air assault and the deployment of US special forces. Seymour Hersh, writing in the *New Yorker* (17 December), claimed that America's success in routing the Taliban had improved the standing of Ahmed Chalabi, leader of the main Iraqi opposition grouping. The Afghanistan experience, according to one defence analyst, had revealed to Washington 'the perfect model' – 'bombing, a modest insertion of special forces plus an uprising'. But in fact no analysts believed that the ineffectual Chalabi faction was analogous to the Northern Alliance in Afghanistan. One senior US official, talking of Chalabi and his supporters, summarized the general American attitude: the administration had no intention of allowing 'a bunch of half-assed people to send foreigners into combat', adding: 'Who among them have ever smelled cordite? These are pissants [non-entities] who can't get the President's ear and have to blame someone else. We're not going to let them lead others down the garden path.' The Bush administration was determined to target Saddam but in its own way and in its own time.

It was unhelpful to the US propagandists when an alleged link between Saddam and the September 11 attacks collapsed. On 17 December 2001, the Czech police announced that they had no evidence that Mohammed Atta, the ringleader of the suicide attacks, had met an Iraqi intelligence officer earlier in the year. It was this alleged meeting, between Atta and Ahmed al-Ani, constantly regurgitated in Western reports, that had served as supposed evidence for Iraqi involvement in the attacks on America. Now even this feeble evidence was in shreds.[30]

In mid-December Saddam Hussein was urging Arab solidarity in defiance of 'our faithful struggling people in plundered Palestine' and to prevent yet more 'American-Zionist' aggressions. At the same time it was reported that in excess of 20,000 American troops had been moved into Qatar and Kuwait amid mounting speculation of US plans to invade Iraq. The Pentagon insisted that it was merely rotating troops but defence analysts claimed that perhaps as many as 24,000 troops had been moved in with barely a brigade, around 4000, moving out. In addition, the Czech Republic announced that 400 troops it had committed to the US-led war on terrorism were being sent to Kuwait. Thus Miroslav Titz, the Deputy Chairman of the Czech parliament's Defence and Security Committee, said that an anti-chemical warfare unit and a field hospital could be deployed at an American military base in the Gulf: 'A joint contingent

. . . might be deployed at a US base in Kuwait where it would have logistics support.'

An Iraqi defector, Adnan Ihsan Saeed al-Haideri, a civil engineer, was claiming that Saddam Hussein had rebuilt some of his capability to make nuclear, chemical and biological weapons, though such testimony was proving insufficient to generate an international pro-Bush consensus for war on Iraq. Mandela had condemned the prospect of a new war, Putin was declaring that a fresh military campaign against Iraq would demolish the anti-terrorist coalition, and even Tony Blair seemed ambivalent ('Saddam Hussein is next— and Tony Blair must grin and bear it'[31]). On 21 December Hubert Vedrine, French foreign minister, said that a war against Iraq could not be justified under the terms of the American campaign against terrorism: 'No European country believes that it is in the logic of the anti-terrorist drive to undertake something against Iraq.' Even US Secretary of State Colin Powell was suggesting that the American success in Afghanistan could not be repeated in Iraq:

> They're two different countries with two different regimes, two different military capabilities. They are so significantly different that you can't take the Afghan model and immediately apply it to Iraq.

Despite all this, the US strategists continued to plan for war on Iraq. In early 2002, President Bush was scheduled to receive three military options prepared by the CIA and the Pentagon. Said one observer: 'You'll see the pace of administration decisions pick up in January.' The Chalabi plan was to be considered, along with the possibility of a US-orchestrated *coup d'état* against the Iraqi leadership and the option of a massive US-led ground invasion. But again the Washington case was not helped by the 'clearing' of Saddam of links to the anthrax and aircraft attacks.

The Isolation of Washington

The Bush administration was as committed as ever to a fresh military campaign to topple Saddam Hussein, but there was ever-diminishing international support for such an enterprise. Even the Blair government, pressured by elements of Cabinet dissent and wider British opposition to a new war on Iraq, seemed to be increasingly unreliable. On 23 December 2001 Peter Hain, British foreign minister, speaking on BBC radio, warned the United States against taking military action against Iraq under cover of the war on terrorism. There was 'not a shred of evidence', he asserted, to link Iraq to the September 11 attacks, and the war in Afghanistan had relied upon a consensus that would be shattered by a strike on Iraq: any action had to proceed 'with the full involvement of the United Nations'. In the same vein Lord Robertson, NATO Secretary-General, said that there was no justification for action against Iraq under the auspices of the war against terrorism: 'Iraq is not in NATO's backyard in any event. So far, the US itself has publicly said that it doesn't see evidence linking bin Laden to Saddam Hussein's regime.' On 26 December, leading political and military figures in Turkey, a key American ally, declared themselves opposed to a fresh war against Iraq.

The political constraints on an American military initiative were compounded by matters of logistic requirement. The US military plans had been thrown into disarray by a shortage of cruise missiles, one of the US Air Force's most sophisticated and deadly weapons. A batch of missiles that had been ordered was not expected for months, and the stockpiling of adequate supplies would take longer. At the end of December 2001 the inventory of conventional air-launched cruise missiles was reported as fewer than thirty, with hundreds needed for any comprehensive attack on Iraq. Use could be made of the sea-launched Tomahawk cruise missiles, in greater supply, 85 of which had been fired against Afghanistan, but the Tomahawks lacked the range to reach every target in Iraq. At one point in the attack on Afghanistan, the US Navy ran out of the new Joint Direct Attack Munitions (JDAM) system, fitted to 'dumb' bombs to make them 'smart', and had to borrow some from the US Air Force. Boeing's missile production was stepped up in 2002, and the Pentagon had also given the go-ahead for a more sophisticated version of the 'daisy cutter' bomb used in Afghanistan, the BLU118/B device with the explosive power of a tactical nuclear weapon.

In early January 2002 the United States was driven to suspend its funding for the corrupt Iraqi National Congress, because it had failed to account properly for the millions of dollars in US aid granted to strengthen the anti-Saddam groups. At the same time Paul Wolfowitz, uncomfortably aware of the mounting international opposition to a new war against Iraq, was softening his line. In comments to the *New York Times* he suggested that the Bush administration's next priority would be to deny al-Qaʻida sanctuary in countries such as Somalia, the Philippines, Indonesia and Yemen. Saddam was continuing 'to do a bunch of things that concern us', but it now seemed that the planned attack on Iraq would be delayed.

In early February a joint CIA/NSA/Pentagon plan for the overthrow of Saddam Hussein was presented to George Bush. The plan required massive bombing followed by an attempt to turn the Iraqi army against the Saddam regime: 'The argument on whether to act goes on, but the President needed to know what he was up against and how it might be done.' The bombardment would be executed by land and carrier-based aircraft, while US special forces would be active on the ground. With Saddam overthrown, it would be necessary to install a popular new Iraqi leader who must not be seen as an American puppet, though the plan failed to nominate a likely candidate. Now it seemed that Washington, conscious of its international isolation, would be prepared to take unilateral action. Thus Richard Perle said:

> Never has the United States been more unified, never has it been more purposeful, never has it been more willing, if necessary, to act alone. If we have to choose between protecting ourselves against terrorism and a long list of friends and allies, we will protect ourselves against terrorism.

Saddam Hussein, now well aware of US bellicosity, was proposing talks with the UN Secretary-General 'without preconditions' on the matter of weapons inspections.

Colin Powell, abandoning his 'dove' status once and for all and echoing Perle, declared that America was ready to go it alone to achieve 'regime change' in Iraq. Washington was assuming that European support would be given in the event of a US military initiative, with Blair already reportedly offering initial 'moral support' for a new bombing onslaught on Iraq and 'encouraging noises' emanating from France. An official close to the Pentagon declared that the military campaign against Saddam Hussein, while seen as urgent, would not begin until the end of 2002 at the earliest: 'The plan is to run fairly extensive preparations, then give Saddam one last chance. This is in the "urgent but not desperate" class.' Margaret Thatcher was urging Blair to support a Bush war on Iraq, and reports suggested that Washington would grant Russia a NATO role if Putin backed a US military campaign. Where Bush must have been most confident was in support from the American people: a CNN/Gallup poll found that 88 per cent of respondents agreed with the policy of 'regime change'. Said Colin Powell: 'We are looking at a variety of options that would bring that about.'

On 13 February 2002 various diplomatic and US sources told *The Guardian* (London) that the Pentagon and the CIA had begun preparations for an assault on Iraq involving up to 200,000 troops with the aim of removing Saddam from power. President Bush had created a war cabinet, known as the 'Principals Committee', which had held a pivotal meeting in late January on the failure of the policy of containment and the need to take steps to topple the Iraqi leader. Provisional plans for overt and covert actions had already landed on the desk of the US President. Bush declared: 'I will reserve whatever options I have. I'll keep them close to my vest. Saddam Hussein needs to understand that I'm serious about defending our country.'

The Washington war planners were deeply uneasy about Saddam's alleged weapons of mass destruction. If driven into a corner, would he use chemical and biological weapons against American troops and Israel? The US, Israel and Turkey were scheduled to hold joint exercises, Operation Anatolian Eagle, later in the year but in another sign of the escalating situation three such exercises were being planned over a few month period. These were based at the Turkish air force base at Konya, to be upgraded for use alongside Incirlik to facilitate air strikes against northern Iraq.

The US allies in the Middle East had already been informed that a decision to attack Iraq had already been taken, and diplomats in the region were resigned to the inevitability of a war that would threaten the stability of many Arab regimes. One Arab diplomat in Washington spoke of a 'nightmare situation' in which the United States would take 'very drastic action' that would be seen by public opinion in the Arab world as 'American imperialism'. It seemed obvious that Washington would be politically isolated. On 13 February the Iraqi Vice-President, Taha Yassin Ramadan, reiterated his country's rejection of the UN arms inspectors, regarded as 'spies' who collect strategic information for the United States, and he urged all Iraqis to prepare for the US military attack. Bush wanted 'to settle an old score',[32] and 'Saddam's destruction is now a matter of honour'.[33] But none of this could disguise the scale of the mounting opposition to American plans for war:

Turkey will not tolerate unilateral US action against Iraq[34]

Russia steps up criticism of possible US attack on Iraq[35]

Kurdish parties reject US moves to unseat Saddam[36]

US split with allies grows as hawks and doves clash over Iraq[37]

Canada sees no justification for attack on Iraq[38]

Arabs bid to avert US strike on Iraq[39]

Wary Europe cool, even hostile, on US threat to attack Iraq[40]

Germany and France warn Bush on Iraq[41]

President forced to soften war rhetoric in Asia[42]

Stay out of Iraq, Patten [EU Commissioner] tells America[43]

Colin Powell, sensitive to such international opposition, emphasized that the Bush administration would move against Saddam Hussein with 'prudence and patience': 'Chris [Patten] did manage to work himself up a bit, and I shall have to have a word with him . . . The President wasn't speaking in absolutist, simplistic terms. I think he was speaking in very direct, realistic terms.' None the less, there was now a growing expectation that Bush intended to launch a war on Iraq before the end of 2002. Saddam Hussein, as one of his responses to the mounting American clamour for war, authorized the building of a 100,000-seater stadium in Baghdad to enable Iraq to host the 2012 Olympic Games. All materials, it was announced, would have to be tested to American standards, and the toilet facilities would meet British expectations.

On 22 February Washington sources were indicating that Saddam Hussein would be removed from power before President Bush's first term in office ends in January 2005. What had happened to the war campaign scheduled for the end of 2002? The sources indicated also that Colin Powell, long the 'odd man out' because of his occasional flashes of moderation, had decided to fall in line with the hawks, alongside Cheney, Wolfowitz, Perle and others. Tony Blair, eager to play 'a full part' in the fight to stop designated countries from acquiring prohibited weapons, could be relied upon – most of the time. It was announced that Blair would be meeting Bush in April to finalize the details of military action to topple Saddam. On 25 February Kofi Annan, UN Secretary-General, commented after talks with Tony Blair in London: 'I don't think Washington has taken any decision yet as to what to do about Iraq. But I am on record as saying any attack on Iraq at this stage would be unwise.'

Iraq was now confirming that Naji Sabri, Iraqi foreign minister, would lead a team for talks at the United Nations on the topic of weapons inspections. It was suggested that a range of other matters could also be discussed: the lifting of sanctions, preventing aggression against Iraq, and respecting the country's sovereignty, independence and territorial integrity.[*] But such projected talks were not, however, deterring Blair from denouncing Iraq and supporting Bush's 'axis of evil' speech: 'Those who are engaged in spreading weapons of mass destruction are engaged in an evil trade and it is important that we make sure that we take action . . .' On 1 March Geoff Hoon, British defence secretary,

---

[*]   In early April 2002, Iraq requested a postponement of the planned talks because of the mounting Middle East crisis caused by the Israeli invasion of Gaza and the West Bank.

declared that: 'If the right conditions were set out, we would support the United States.' And in the same vein Jack Straw was proclaiming that we could not 'allow Saddam Hussein to hold a gun to the heads of his own people, his neighbours and the world for ever'. If he refused to allow UN inspections 'he will have to live with the consequences . . . let no one – especially Saddam – doubt our resolve'.

The propaganda war was continuing. In early March the United States presented the UN with material purporting to show that Iraq was converting trucks into mobile rocket launchers and military vehicles, a manifest breach of the sanctions system. It was also pointed out that many of the weapons facilities damaged by the United States and Britain in the Operation Desert Fox bombing in 1998 had been repaired. (Such commentary made no reference to the fact that under the UN resolutions Iraq was allowed certain weapons, that only weapons of a certain type were banned.)

The United States was also attempting to pressure Kofi Annan, UN Secretary-General, into taking a strong line on Iraq. Thus John Negroponte, the American Ambassador to the United Nations, visited Annan to 'stiffen his resolve' before the scheduled meeting with the Iraqi delegation. On 7 March 2002 Kofi Annan met Naji Sabri, the Iraqi Foreign Minister, who commented at the end of the two-hour session: 'We started our discussions within a positive and constructive atmosphere and we shall continue in the afternoon.' There was no immediate breakthrough though Annan found the discussion 'frank and useful'. At the same time, ignoring such talks, US Vice-President Dick Cheney was planning a mission to the Middle East to proclaim that the United States was ready to take unilateral action to achieve 'regime change' in Iraq if necessary. Prior to Cheney's preliminary talks in Britain with Blair, Straw and Hoon, a British official said: 'We don't expect there will be any gulf between us. The world in general needs to be prepared for what is about to happen and our European allies need to be prepared for what is going to happen.'

The United States had been building up its forces in the Gulf, and the British armed forces had been taking various measures, including moving Jaguar fighter bombers to Oman, ostensibly for exercises with the Omani air force. Reports also suggested that Saddam had been trying to buy arms on world markets, and working to achieve a rapprochement with Iran (named by Bush as part of the 'axis of evil' with Iraq and North Korea). Some 600 German and Czech specialists in biological, chemical and nuclear warfare were 'on exercise' in Kuwait, and the US Marine Corps had moved most of its Pacific headquarters from Hawaii to Bahrain, already the headquarters of the US Fifth Fleet. It was clear that the build-up of US-led forces was part of the preparation for a new war against Iraq (Figure 1).[44]

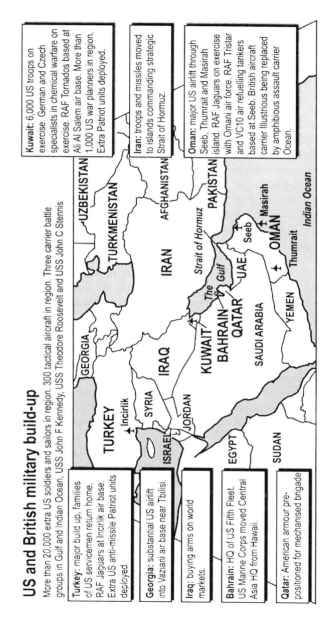

US and British military build-up

More than 20,000 extra US soldiers and sailors in region. Three carrier battle groups in Gulf and Indian Ocean, USS John F Kennedy, USS Theodore Roosevelt and USS John C Stennis

Kuwait: 6,000 US troops on exercise. German and Czech specialists in chemical warfare on exercise. RAF Tornados based at Ali Al Salem air base. More than 1,000 US war planners in region. Extra Patriot units deployed.

Iran: troops and missiles moved to islands commanding strategic Strait of Hormuz.

Oman: major US airlift through Seeb, Thumrait and Masirah island. RAF Jaguars on exercise with Omani air force. RAF Tristar and VC10 air refuelling tankers based at Seeb. British aircraft carrier Illustrious being replaced by amphibious assault carrier Ocean.

Turkey: major build up. families of US servicemen return home, RAF Jaguars at Incirlik air base. Extra US anti-missile Patriot units deployed.

Georgia: substantial US airlift into Vaziani air base near Tbilisi.

Iraq: buying arms on world markets.

Bahrain: HQ of US Fifth Fleet. US Marine Corps moved Central Asia HQ from Hawaii.

Qatar: American armour pre-positioned for mechanised brigade

Figure 1: Regional military activity around Iraq (March 2002)
Source: The Daily Telegraph, 8 March 2002

Tony Blair was moving progressively closer to the Bush policy on the need for *regime change* in Iraq, but he was not carrying his Labour Party with him. On 8 March David Chaytor, a Labour MP, warned that the party could be 'split down the middle' if Blair insisted on backing unilateral US action against the Saddam regime. Chaytor was one of 68 MPs who had signed an anti-war Early-Day Motion, a body of dissent that had swelled to a remarkable 138 signatories by 27 March.[45] By contrast, Bush was keen to describe Blair as a 'good friend', a relationship that inspired the *Daily Mirror* (London) to run the headline 'Howdy, Poodle' in reflection of the fact that, whenever the US President said that 'we' might have to go it alone, it was assumed that Britain would be lining up behind Washington against the rest of the world.

President Bush had decided that the Saddam regime must be ended, and he would be happy if Britain provided 25,000 troops for the task.[46] Cheney was having no success in attempting to coax or intimidate the Arab states into supporting a US-led campaign against Iraq, despite Baghdad's repeated rejection of UN weapons inspectors. Bush, seemingly undeterred by America's growing isolation, recited a speech designed to bolster his imagined allies around the world – concluding, not with the usual 'God bless America', but with 'God bless our coalition'. Was this really a speech-writer's attempt to make Bush's erstwhile political allies feel wanted? The message, delivered on 11 March, was plain: war on Iraq was now inevitable and the rest of the 'civilized world' was being invited to join what Bush had called, with purblind carelessness, the *crusade*.

The speech, given to mark the six-month anniversary of the September 11 attacks, outlined the goals for the second phase of the so-called war against terrorism. The United States, we were told, was determined to deal with the threat posed by weapons of mass destruction: 'Inaction is not an option.' Iraq was not mentioned by name but no one doubted that the virtuous Principal Boy was happily contemplating the expunction of the Demon King:

> Some states that sponsor terror are seeking or already possess weapons of mass destruction. Terrorist groups are hungry for these weapons and would use them without a hint of conscience. We know that these weapons, in the hands of terrorists, would unleash blackmail and genocide and chaos.

But the rhetoric was failing to generate an anti-Iraq coalition. The Europeans, for example, had backed the war on Afghanistan, with the British, the Germans and the French sending forces to the region, but Iraq was another matter. Even in Britain the Blair government was unable to bring its nominal parliamentary supporters into line, despite alarmist propaganda, uttered by Jack Straw and others, that Saddam might have nuclear weapons within five years. Bush, claimed Straw, had adopted a 'cautious and proportionate' approach to Iraq – a judgement that most independent observers found risible.

Vice-President Dick Cheney was finding that his mission to the Middle East had no chance of producing the sort of coalition against Saddam that the first Bush administration had managed in 1990–91. Most Arabs, even the 'moderate' leaders in such countries as Kuwait and Egypt, would have preferred Washington to address the mounting crisis in the Israel–Palestinian conflict, a war of Israeli aggression where the United States, far from being disengaged, was functioning as a pro-Israeli belligerent. At the same time Egypt was bowing to American pressure in agreeing to press Iraq to admit UN inspectors to examine Saddam's alleged weapons programmes.[47]

On 15 March Tony Blair launched a diplomatic offensive to convince the Europeans to back an American war on Iraq, but achieved nothing. German tanks would remain in Kuwait to 'help out' if a chemical or biological attack took place, but there would be no German involvement in a US-led invasion of Iraq. And while the Europeans were signalling their opposition to Blair's transparent war-mongering, Saudi Arabia's Crown Prince Abdullah was appearing on television to say that any American strike against Iraq would be unsuccessful and would simply inflame anti-US sentiment in the region. Asked about the Bush policy of 'regime change', Prince Abdullah replied: 'I do not believe it is in the United State's interests, or the interests of the region, or the world's interest, for the United States to do so. And I don't believe it will achieve the desired result.' Saudi Arabia was making it clear that, unlike the situation in 1990–91, American forces would not be allowed to use Saudi bases to launch an invasion of Iraq. The American isolation was growing, with even one of Saddam's main enemies – Ayatollah Mohammed Baqir al-Hakim, an exiled Shi'ite leader – warning against war: 'We don't agree with an American attack on Iraq. It will cause great damage and suffering to ordinary people.'

On 20 March, at a time when Iraq was suggesting that it might allow specified UN weapons inspections, Geoff Hoon, the British defence secretary, announced that *Britain was prepared to use nuclear weapons against 'states of concern' such as Iraq*. This statement, turning British policy on nuclear weapons upside down, ushered in a new era in which what had been completely unthinkable was now a serious part of military planning. Saddam, declared Hoon, 'can be absolutely confident that in the right conditions we would be willing to use our nuclear weapons', but Hoon could not 'be absolutely confident . . . whether that would be sufficient to deter them from using a weapon of mass destruction in the first place'. Two weeks before, a leaked Pentagon document was suggesting the possibility of using nuclear weapons against certain states.

Alarm was now growing in the Arab world about the likelihood of an American attack on Iraq. Cheney had been rebuffed in the Middle East, with even 40 per cent of polled Kuwaitis hostile to US policies. On 21 March, the Lebanese President Emile Lahoud emphasized that all the Arab countries, even those formerly at odds with Baghdad, were opposed to American military action against Iraq. But this unprecedented degree of support for the Saddam regime was doing little to convince the Iraqi leadership that Washington could be restrained from launching yet another wave of killing and destruction. Security was being stepped up in Iraq, and the families of exiles were appearing on Iraqi television to denounce the anti-Saddam activists abroad. Tribal chiefs were being told to prepare for the imminent American attack, and the Iraqi armed forces were being brought to a state of readiness throughout the country.

On 25 March leaders gathered in Beirut for the Arab League Summit, a meeting that was set to underline yet more graphically the US–UK isolation over Iraq. In an extraordinary rapprochement, Naji Sabri, the Iraqi foreign minister, made a pledge to Kuwait that Baghdad was ready to respect its neighbour's security and sovereignty. A summit communiqué, framed partly in response to the seeds of this new accord, expressed unambiguous solidarity with the Iraqi regime in its escalating confrontation with the United States:

> Leaders . . . affirm they categorically reject a strike against Iraq and any threat against the security and territorial integrity of any Arab country, which would constitute a threat against the national security of all Arab countries.[18]

Many Arab leaders, some formerly hostile to Saddam Hussein, knew that their people were bitterly opposed to the prospect of yet another massive US military onslaught on Iraq. The Iraqi–Kuwaiti rapprochement, still viewed with caution by many Kuwaitis, was sealed with an embrace, broadcast live on television, between Crown Prince Abdullah, Saudi Arabia's *de facto* ruler, and Izzat Ibrahim, Saddam's envoy. In a closed session, Ibrahim shook hands with the head of the Kuwaiti delegation, Sheikh Sabah al-Ahmed al-Sabah, the country's Deputy Prime Minister. Asked about this gesture, the Kuwaiti minister replied: 'What are we? Small children? We were sitting in a closed session of heads of delegations. When someone comes to shake hands with you, what do you do? You won't shake hands?' But everyone knew that such a reconciliation, mediated by Oman and Qatar, would have been unthinkable a short time before. Washington, further frustrated by this demonstration of Arab solidarity, immediately disparaged the reconciliation, with Richard Boucher, a State Department spokesman, commenting: 'If true, that would be good, but Iraq has never evidenced any real intent to respect Kuwaiti sovereignty.'

The US case for war against Iraq – in its various legal and political aspects – was growing weaker by the day. Washington's isolation, the British poodle apart, was complete, and Romano Prodi, President of the European Commission, was citing the mounting catastrophe in Palestine as a further reason why any US strike on Iraq should be opposed:

> If there was an escalation of conflict this would have a terrible reaction everywhere . . . We have no information on Iraq. That is the first thing we need. I worry about enlargement of the conflict to any other country, not only Iraq.

And Prodi urged Britain to abandon its support for a new phase of military action: 'If you are a friend to America, you can warn them of the dangers. That is what a good ally could do.'

The United States was still determined to do whatever it could to hasten 'regime change', and to continue the long sanctions-induced punishment of the ordinary Iraqi people through disease and starvation, and biological weapons of mass destruction. Washington was claiming that the development of 'smart' sanctions (see Chapter 9), whereby the genocidal embargo could be made even more effective, continued to proceed well, with a measure of Russian approval. On 28 March, Washington disclosed that it was collecting data on Saddam's war crimes to facilitate an eventual prosecution. The preparation for war continued. According to Lindsey Graham, a US congressman, the plans had already been laid:

> The United States had completed plans to attack Iraq and to overthrow Saddam Hussein. I don't know when, but I know this President is not going to let Saddam Hussein stay in power . . . I don't know when it's going to be, that's up to the military planners. But I do know that it will be sooner rather than later.

Graham, a member of the House Armed Services Committee, declared: 'We are going after Saddam Hussein, not to contain him, but to replace him.'

Washington, committed to war, faced various problems. More than six months after the September 11 attacks, there was nothing that could even remotely be advertized as an anti-Saddam coalition preparing for military conflict. For once, all the American efforts at bribery and intimidation around the world had failed to deliver. With little publicity, the United States had moved massive military assets into the region and more deployments were under way, though there were still logistic problems that were delaying the onset of hostilities. By May 2002 the US Congress had not been invited to discuss the planned war or to vote on the issue, and there was no prospect of UN authorization for a new military campaign against Iraq, since any draft resolution would face an instant veto by one or more of the Permanent Members of the Security Council.

Moreover, the Blair government, eager to please Washington, was having to contend with a spate of difficulties. Committed to Europe on such issues as monetary policy, Blair and his supporters found themselves bitterly at odds with their European associates on the war issue. Labour MPs in the British parliament had queued to sign the anti-war Early-Day Motion, and there were signs that even the cabinet was irrevocably split on the matter. In addition, just before his planned trip to Texas to discuss war plans with Bush, Blair was forced to abandon plans to release an intelligence dossier on Saddam Hussein. It was felt that the six-page document, prepared by the Cabinet Office intelligence chiefs, would be seen as both inflammatory and weak on information.[49] The US case for war had collapsed and Blair, despite fidelity to Washington, could do little to resurrect it.

A report (March 2002) by the Church of England's Board for Social Responsibility damned the proposed attack on Saddam Hussein as a 'cruel thirst for vengeance' – an action that, far from being a just war, would merely 'reflect the priorities of American foreign policy'. In the same vein, Cardinal Cormac Murphy O'Connor, head of the Catholic Church in England and Wales, was urging Britain and the United States not to worsen the situation in the Middle East by launching yet another military action against Iraq.

In early April 2002, Ariel Sharon launched another massive military onslaught on Gaza and the West Bank. It was not long before witnesses reported massacres, extrajudicial killings, demolished homes, and thousands of Palestinians taken away to unknown destinations. President Bush at first signalled his sympathy with the Israeli action and later made a tardy gesture: 'Enough is enough.' Secretary of State Colin Powell made a delayed visit to the region and met Sharon and Arafat. Nothing was accomplished, Bush had been humiliated, and Washington's co-belligerency support for Israel continued. In its pro-Israel posture and its resolve to wage a new war in the Middle East, the United States continued to demonstrate its contempt for ethics and international law.

Weapons Inspections

Throughout 2002 the United States, despite prodigious effort and continuous propaganda, failed to demonstrate any links between the Iraqi regime and either al-Qa'ida or the 11 September attacks. The hoped-for pretext for a new military onslaught on Iraq could not be used, and so another excuse had to be found. It was soon evident that the issue of weapons inspections would be enlisted to serve the purpose.

Since 1998 Saddam Hussein had refused to allow the withdrawn UN inspectors back into the country, thus violating Security Council Resolution 687(1991) and all the subsequent Council resolutions on the same theme. America was virtually alone in believing that this justified a massive escalation of the war on Iraq, but the Washington strategists needed little excuse.

Hence the persistent refusal of Saddam to allow the inspectors to return would provide an adequate *casus belli* – and even if the inspectors were allowed back, their efforts would inevitably be thwarted by the stubborn Iraqi regime, and so a new war would still be justified. The Bush administration was determined to accomplish 'regime change' in Iraq, and brazen enough to dispense with any hint of legal or ethical justification.

The United States had frequently proclaimed its enthusiasm for destroying Iraq's 'weapons of mass destruction', with no mention of US responsibility for Saddam's weapons potential and no reference to Western weapons development and production. It is useful in this context to remember:

— that the West (and others) supplied Iraq with weapons expertize, equipment, chemicals, biological cultures, etc.;[50]

— that the United States used nuclear weapons in Japan, used biological weapons in Korea,[51] and used chemical weapons in Vietnam;

— that 'American scientists tested humans with mustard gas, other chemical agents, exposed others to radiation tests, and still others to a variety of pathogens without the subjects' knowledge or consent'.[52]

— that America continues to develop weapons of mass destruction: for example, a new generation of nuclear weapons and the Metal Storm cannon that fires a million rounds of heavy artillery a minute (*The Times*, 15 May 2002);

We are not often reminded that in the United States retarded boys have been used in radiation experiments,[33] that US tests on unsuspecting citizens have been conducted over a period of years,[54] that the British Ministry of Defence has admitted 40 years of human radiation tests,[55] that Britain carried out highly secret biological warfare tests off Caribbean islands and told officials to lie,[56] that similar tests were carried out in London,[57] and that the United States and Britain carried out secret mustard gas experiments on about 2000 Australian servicemen.[58]

We now know that American scientists conducted 'at least several hundred tests with human subjects who were not informed of the nature of the experiments, or of the danger to their health'.[59] Thus Sheldon H. Harris, Emeritus Professor of History, California State University, commented in 1994 that human experimentation and the production of biological warfare agents appeared to be flourishing in the United States and elsewhere despite the international agreements prohibiting such activities.[60] In April 1997, the US Senate ratified (74 votes to 26) the Chemical Weapons Convention outlawing the manufacture, storage and use of a long list of chemical weapons; but in February 1998 it emerged that the US, eager even then for an extended war with Iraq, had contrived legislation to allow the American President to refuse admission to international inspectors.*

The new legislation allowed the President to pick and choose inspectors and to deny access to individuals from certain countries – precisely the activities which, when urged by Iraq, were to be used by Washington to justify an expanded military campaign. Senator Joseph Biden admitted that an American 'denial of a duly authorized inspection would violate the Chemical Weapons Convention'; and in the same spirit, Amy Smithson, who had campaigned for US ratification of the Convention, commented:

> We are in violation of the treaty, and it is so ironic that we are about to engage in hostilities against Iraq over the matter of weapons inspections, because Saddam Hussein has registered the same exceptions as we have done.[61]

---

* See also discussion of weapons Conventions on p. 132.

In 1998 two inspectors, a Cuban and an Iranian, had already been struck off the approved list by the US authorities. Thus Clause 307 of the relevant US bill was headed National Security Exception: 'The President may deny a request to inspect any facility in the United States where the President determines that the inspection may pose a threat to the national security interests of the United States.' Put another way, *inspectors would be allowed to inspect the weapons sites except where they were not allowed to do so.* Saddam Hussein could not have said it better. Washington would ignore the UN-linked Conventions on weapons of mass destruction, and there would be no opportunity for a legal challenge.[62]

It was obvious in 1998 and through 2002 that the American pressure for scrutiny of Iraqi weapons sites was contrived as an excuse for war. On 16 December 1998 the United States and Britain launched Operation Desert Fox, the most massive bombing campaign against Iraq since the 1991 Gulf War – with no semblance of UN authorization (see Chapter 8). In 2002 the United States, with predictable British support, was again using the need for weapons inspections as justification for a new military onslaught. But this time the Washington strategists were planning a massive attack to overthrow the Saddam regime.

It was now plain that the UN inspectors had located and destroyed the bulk of the Iraqi military arsenal that had survived the 1991 Gulf War and the subsequent US–UK bombing campaigns. The inspectors had been forced to contend with frequent Iraqi lies and obstructionism, particularly in circumstances where the Iraqis judged that national security was at stake, but it is equally clear that the UN inspectors were offered a high degree of Iraqi cooperation in many of their tasks. The then UN Secretary-General Boutros Boutros-Ghali acknowledged that the weapons inspections in Iraq were 'the most intrusive ever devised in the field of international arms control'.[63] By 1997 the UN inspectors had noted the destruction or removal of:

— an assembled supergun;

— the components for four other such guns and one tonne of propellant;

— 151 Scud missiles, 19 mobile launchers, 76 chemical and 113 conventional warheads for Scud missiles, 9 conventional warheads for Al-Fahd missiles, a substantial amount of rocket fuel and components chemicals, decoy missiles and decoy vehicles, guidance-and-control sets, etc.;

— equipment for the production of missiles and components;

— more than 480,000 litres of chemical warfare agents, including mustard agent and the nerve agents sarin and tabun;

— more than 28,000 filled and nearly 12,000 empty chemical munitions;

— nearly 1,800,000 litres, more than 1,040,000 kilograms and 648 barrels of some 45 different precursor chemicals for the production of chemical warfare agents;

— equipment and facilities for chemical weapons production;

— biological seed stocks used in biological weapons development.[64]

The situation was clear. Before 1998 the UN inspectors had succeeded in removing or destroying the bulk of the Iraqi weapons capability – to the point that Scott Ritter, former head of the inspectors, felt able to declare that Iraq was 'qualitatively disarmed'. At the same time the inspection team had been discredited as a cover for anti-Saddam espionage activities, working with Mossad and other spy networks, designed to achieve the ultimate overthrow of the Iraqi regime.[65]

Iraqi dissidents (for example, Adnan Saeed al-Haideri, a former Iraqi civil engineer) continued to assert that Saddam had a residual weapons capability, while Washington and London worked to stoke the alarmist fires. In April 2002 Prime Minister Tony Blair rushed through an order for 16 million doses of the smallpox vaccine after Dick Cheney, US Vice-President, told him that the planned military attack on Iraq would provoke a biological weapons response against Britain. At the same time, hawks in the Bush administration commissioned a CIA report on Hans Blix, the UN's chief weapons inspector, with the aim of undermining any fresh UN–Iraqi agreement on inspections.[66]

Washington had been forced to admit that the 11 September attacks could not provide a justification for the planned military onslaught on Iraq. A refusal by Saddam Hussein to admit UN weapons inspectors might serve the purpose, but by May 2002 there were growing signs that Iraq was preparing to allow inspectors back into the country, if only to drive a thicker wedge between a belligerent Washington and the rest of the world. However, the US war planners were resolved not to allow any new UN–Iraq accommodation over weapons inspections to disturb Washington's policy of 'regime change' in Iraq. Whatever the Iraqi posture during 2002, the United States would continue to prepare for war.

If Saddam would not permit the return of the inspectors, 'he obviously had something to hide'; and even if he allowed them back into Iraq, any truly penetrative inspection attempts would be stifled by the Iraqi regime. The Catch 22 was clear. There was no policy open to Iraq that could impede the momentum of US military planning. Thus on 5 May 2002 the American Secretary of State, Colin Powell, said that the United States may try to remove Saddam Hussein from power even if there was agreement on weapons inspections:

> US policy is that, *regardless of what the inspectors do*, the people of Iraq and the people of the region would be better off with a different regime in Baghdad. The United States reserves its option to do whatever it believes might be appropriate to see if there can be a regime change (my italics).[67]

Through 2002 it seemed that the launch of a fresh US onslaught on Iraq was only a matter of time, and that the scale of the American attack would be massive. On 13 May 2002 Richard Perle, head of the Pentagon's Commission for Military Policies, said in an interview with the German publication *Spiegel* that *the United States might launch nuclear strikes against Iraq.*

This followed the revelation by United States newspapers on 10 March that the US Department of Defence, under orders from the Bush administration, had prepared a report, 'Re-evaluation of the nuclear situation', preparing contingency plans for the use of nuclear weapons against Iraq and other countries.

Yet again the United States was ignoring international law. General Assembly Resolution 56/25 B (29 November 2001) reaffirms that 'any use of nuclear weapons would be a violation of the Charter of the United Nations and a crime against humanity'. In the same vein the International Court of Justice had already issued an advisory opinion (A/51/218, 8 July 1996) that included the judgement that 'the threat or use of nuclear weapons would generally be contrary to the rules of international law . . . and in particular the principles and rules of humanitarian law'. Such UN and World Court rulings condemn equally the nuclear posture of the United States and the nuclear threats issued by British defence secretary Geoff Hoon (both in public and to a select Committee on Defence) in March 2002.

TWO

1.6 Million Dead and Counting

Launching a Genocide

The comprehensive UN punishment of Iraqi civilians – mainly the old, the sick, pregnant women, infants and babies – began early in August 1990 with the Iraqi invasion of Kuwait. The United States, Europe and other countries immediately imposed an economic embargo on Baghdad, and mandatory UN sanctions followed soon after. Saddam Hussein, a former ally of the CIA in the American war against any hint of leftwing activism, had been provoked into a reckless and illegal adventure.[1] The facts suggested that the Iraqi aggression had grown out of Saddam's earlier firm alliance with the United States, desperate to tame the Iranian ayatollahs and prepared to assist the Iraqi war effort (1980–88) by providing intelligence, military equipment and active belligerent support by bombing Iranian shipping and other Iranian assets in the Gulf.[2] Saddam Hussein had also been supported by vast funding from Kuwait and Saudi Arabia, and by the war materiél supplied by Russia, Britain and France, as well as the United States.[3]

The mounting anti-Iraq rhetoric, following the invasion of Kuwait, owed nothing to inconvenient fact or rational analysis. The human rights record of the Saddam regime was no worse than that of the Saudi monarchy,[4] but Washington was determined to portray Saddam as uniquely evil. Syria's President Assad had killed 15,000 of his own people at Hama, but the 5000 Kurds gassed by the Iraqis during the US-supported Iran–Iraq war was portrayed as an infinitely greater crime.[5] In the same way the appalling human rights records of Israel, Egypt, Kuwait, Morocco and other regional states were ignored by propagandists preparing the ground for a massive onslaught on the Iraqi nation.

The practicalities of a US-led war against Iraq were straightforward. With Iraq accustomed to importing the bulk of its food and medical supplies, a total blockade reinforced by unassailable military power was sure to have a devastating and speedy impact. It was not long before the embargo was striking at the most vulnerable Iraqis in their hundreds and thousands, dying from inadequate nutrition and a lack of medical care, and forced to witness what would become the years-long disintegration of the social and industrial infrastructure of what had been a thriving nation.

The 1991 war helped things on their way. The Coalition, principally US forces, dropped the equivalent of seven Hiroshima atomic bombs on Iraq – in the form of depleted-uranium (DU) ordnance, cluster bombs ('flesh-shredders' designed to turn human beings into mincemeat), massive explosives (that produce fireballs and blast equivalent to those generated by tactical nuclear weapons) and many other unfriendly devices that caused perhaps 200,000 Iraqi casualties at the alarming cost of around 150 American dead (half through 'friendly fire'). Some observers reckoned that the US firing of more than one million DU rounds, later associated with soaring fetal deformity and cancer rates, made the onslaught on Iraq the second nuclear war waged by the United States. And after the US army had bulldozed tens of thousands of Iraqi corpses into desert graves, and encouraged the world to forget them, the blockade remained in place.

Punishing the Innocent

It was not long before reports began to accumulate describing the dreadful and worsening plight of the Iraqi civilian population. Senior UN officials, human rights organizations, academic investigators, journalists, concerned Westerners visiting the country, the desperate Iraqis themselves – all were soon reporting soaring rates of malnutrition and disease, hospitals without drugs and sanitation, wrecked communication systems, devastated schools and colleges, an energy grid in a state of terminal collapse, a poisoned land and a suffering people.[6] All this was evident in the immediate aftermath of the 1991 war, and the sanctions ensured that, through the remainder of the 1990s, Iraq would be denied any realistic opportunities for social and industrial reconstruction.[7] By the late 1990s thousands of Iraqi civilians were dying every month from malnutrition and preventable diseases. Again, thousands of technical and journalistic reports, independent surveys and analyses, and harrowing testimonies from Iraqi victims and traumatized visitors were combining to describe the unrelieved plight of innocent men, women and children. Some independent observers – including Denis Halliday, former senior UN Humanitarian Coordinator in Iraq – were now talking of the *genocide* being perpetrated by the US-dominated UN Security Council against a civilian population.[8] We need only glance at some typical newspaper headlines:

Poisoned Tigris spreads tide of death in Iraq[9]

Death of a Nation[10]

Starvation: the West's weapon of mass destruction against Iraq[11]

Why do Iraqi children have to starve because we want to punish Iraq?[12]

On 26 October 1999, Hans von Sponeck, Halliday's successor as UN Humanitarian Coordinator, described in a press briefing some of the problems confronting the UN-administered scheme designed to alleviate the suffering of the Iraqi people. Food was not available for a substantial proportion of the population, rendering the programme 'inadequate'. Many medical supplies were useless simply because complementary items had not been delivered: for example, a supply of IV fluids could not be distributed because there were no syringes. Iraq had formerly invested on a substantial scale in medical and other social facilities but now, with soaring morbidity and mortality rates, Iraq had been reduced 'to the category of a least developed country'. Moreover, the United States and Britain, acting through the UN Sanctions Committee (see Chapter 3) were blocking the supply of many items:

> The number of items being held back had increased in recent months, making it difficult to implement the humanitarian programme. Some items that could be used for humanitarian purposes had not been released. Complementary items that were on hold were particularly troublesome.[13]

The UN Secretary-General, Kofi Annan, was urging the US and Britain to stop preventing the Iraqi people from receiving necessary humanitarian supplies.

Acknowledging the Genocide

Denis Halliday, appalled at the mounting genocide, had resigned as Humanitarian Coordinator. In February 2000, when he had learned what was happening, Hans von Sponeck followed suit: 'How long should the civilian population of Iraq be exposed to such punishment for something they have never done?' Two days later, on 15 February, Jutta Burghardt, head of the UN-linked World Food Programme in Iraq, resigned from her post, saying that she could no longer tolerate what was being done to the Iraqi people. Thus such senior UN officials were giving unambiguous support to those observers claiming that the United States and Britain were now engaged in what was essentially a criminal conspiracy – violating international humanitarian law by committing a prolonged genocide against a helpless civilian population.

By the end of the 1990s there was mounting opposition to US–UK policy on Iraq. The important Security Council Resolution 1284 had been secured only at the price of abstentions by four Council members, including three Permanent Members (Russia, China and France), and there was a groundswell of hostility to United States policy (echoed as always by London). In November 1999 the National Conference of Catholic Bishops in the United States protested at the 'moral obtuseness' of US policy. Comprehensive economic sanctions were not acceptable: 'We cannot turn a deaf ear to the suffering of the Iraqi people or a blind eye to the moral obtuseness of current US policy.' At the same time US Representatives Tom Campbell and John Conyers were heading a political revolt against Washington's Iraq policy:

> This policy . . . makes the children and families of Iraq into virtual hostages in the political deadlock between the US and the government of Iraq. Morally, it is wrong to hold the Iraqi people responsible for the actions of a brutal and reckless government.[14]

Denis Halliday, in his paper for the Madrid Conference, emphasized 'the terrible impact' of the economic sanctions on the people of Iraq.[15] In January 1999, he had used the word 'genocide' in this context for the first time, noting in November that he was not the first to do so.

> Former US Attorney-General Ramsey Clark, the British author Geoff Simons and a number of British Members of Parliament critical of Labour Government sanctions and military policy, have employed the term to convey their perception of the Iraq Situation. Since the spring of this year [1999], the term has been used frequently by the establishment in the UK and the USA to describe events in Kosovo and East Timor. As far as the US and UK governments were concerned, others 'commit genocide, we do not'.[16]

It had seemed increasingly obvious to Halliday and others that the facts about Iraq tell a different story. Moreover, this situation had come to represent a serious threat to the integrity of the UN organization. Thus Halliday noted:

In conclusion, the *de facto* genocidal impact of the regime of economic sanctions on the people of Iraq, violates the legal instruments that are fundamental to the credible continuation of the United Nations. The Organization urgently needs the protection of an oversight device or devices in regard to the output of the dangerously out-of-control Security Council. In the meantime, men and women of conscience, with moral posture and integrity, will continue to demand the termination of crimes against humanity, indeed genocide, in respect of Iraq.[17]

In December 1999, the British government banned the export of diphtheria, yellow fever and tetanus vaccines to Iraq on the grounds that they could be used as weapons of mass destruction.[18] In January 2000 Human Rights Watch commented on the 'alarming' medical situation throughout the country. The International Committee of the Red Cross had warned of the 'steady deterioration of living conditions' in Iraq as a result of sanctions,[19] and now a prestigious human rights organization was indicating the gravity of the situation: 'The crisis has been particularly acute in the area of public health, putting millions of Iraqis, if not an entire generation, at grave risk.'[20] The conclusion of a UN humanitarian panel, based on the observations of the agencies in the field, was quoted to the effect that 'almost the whole young child population was affected by a shift in their nutritional status towards malnutrition'.[21]

In the United States the Campbell/Conyers campaign was gaining increasing congressional support, protesters were continuing to agitate against American policy, and there was a growing public recognition that the US-sustained campaign of economic sanctions was punishing the ordinary people of Iraq while having no affect on Saddam Hussein and his power base. It was plain that the country's social and industrial infrastructure were continuing to decay, with all that such a process implied for human suffering and the chances of reconstruction in the future. In early 2000 a UN team of experts, after following a detailed itinerary in Iraq, concluded that the 'lamentable state' of the Iraqi oil industry had 'not improved' and that such matters as the oil transportation infrastructure, pollution and safety were not being addressed.[22] The group found that 'all sectors of the industry' were continuing to decline, and that in some areas the decline was 'accelerating'.[23] And the collapse of the oil industry was paralleled by the rapid deterioration of many social facilities. On 23 January 2000, Beat Schweizer, head of the International Committee of the Red Cross in Iraq, warned that the hospital infrastructure was close to collapse: 'We have noticed that, particularly in the hospitals, the situation is such that . . . in only a short time . . . these hospitals will not be functional anymore.'[24]

The Impact of Sanctions

Even human rights advice to Iraq was being blocked under the terms of the sanctions policy. Thus the British government blocked the despatch of two documents to Mosul University in northern Iraq: one containing advice on access to health information, including family planning and AIDS; the other being a UN-generated study of press freedom in democracies. On 17 February a spokeswoman for the Department of Trade and Industry, indicated that a licence would be required for the export of such items to Iraq. In the same spirit the British Library had informed an Iraqi translator that it was prevented by sanctions from sending him books, including a copy of James Joyce's *Ulysses*.[25] Such seemingly trivial prohibitions were matched by bans on countless items essential for the preservation of human life. Many foodstuffs and medicine were in desperately short supply, if allowed at all, and many other areas of public health were in a state of terminal collapse. In Basra and the surrounding area there was reportedly a constant smell 'because the sewage system has virtually collapsed'.[26] Diseases that had been eradicated had returned. Few observers could doubt that the United States and Britain were waging a protracted campaign of biological warfare.

In March 2000 Kofi Annan, UN Secretary-General, issued a report on Iraq to the Security Council.[27] Again he emphasized that the UN programme 'was never intended to meet all the humanitarian needs' of the Iraqi people, with the implication that some humanitarian needs (food, medicines, clean water, housing, etc.) were not being met. Following the report of the UN group of experts, Kofi Annan noted that the deterioration of 'all sectors' of the oil industry would continue unless effective action could be taken (i.e. that the United States and Britain allow Iraq to import the necessary spare parts:

> The suspension of drilling, well work-over and completion activities, and delays in the commissioning of wet-crude treatment plants result directly from a lack of spare parts and equipment. Without prompt action, a continued decline in production is strongly indicated.

There was an 'accelerating deterioration of equipment and ... a decline in the morale and motivation of operating staff', with the situation exacerbated by 'the fact that some applications have been placed on hold [mainly by the US and Britain] for a lengthy period of time'.[28] Kofi Annan had recommended that the Security Council approve extra oil revenues for the purchase of oil spare parts and equipment: 'Regrettably the [US-dominated] Council took no action in this regard.'[29] A further Kofi Annan recommendation, supported by the UN oil experts, was cut in half by the Security Council.[30]

The results of the US–UK policies regarding the Iraqi oil industry were a significant decline in oil exports, 'a massive decline' in the condition and effectiveness of the industry, 'appalling' safety conditions and 'significant environmental damage'. The resulting damage to the oil-bearing structures in Iraq was becoming 'more long-term in nature, resulting in irreversible damage to oil fields and the permanent loss of production and export capacity'.[31] Washington and London seemed intent on securing a permanent crippling of every aspect of social and industrial activity in Iraq. The oil industry was one important example; the port of Umm Qasr, expected to handle the import of bulk foodstuffs, was another. The facilities at the port were suffering a 'serious deterioration', with shipments of cargo frequently 'damaged during discharge due to inadequate equipment' and 'the safety and well-being of port personnel' continually threatened by outdated and damaged equipment. Silt was accumulating in the harbour, often make it impossible for larger vessels to berth,[32] while the United States continued to block the purchase of a harbour dredger. Such matters and many others were contributing to what Kofi Annan emphasized was 'the slow and erratic pace' at which humanitarian supplies were arriving in Iraq.

The UN Secretary-General acknowledged (report, 10 March 2000) the serious predicament of the Iraqi civilian population. The prices of food necessary to supplement the government's inadequate rations were:

> beyond the reach of most Iraqis . . . at 31 January 2000, the total value of holds on applications for food was $5.8 million . . . under the food-handling and food-processing subsector, the total value . . . of applications placed on hold [mainly by the US and Britain] is $185.5 million.[33]

Why should Washington and London be doing what they could to impede the efforts of the Iraqi government to feed its civilian population? And what was true for food was equally true for medicine.

The erratic and uncoordinated arrival of drugs to treat chronic disease had meant that tens of thousands of patients, many of them seriously ill, had not received their regular medication requirements – 'which may have contributed' to the soaring death rates attributable to cardiac, diabetic, renal and liver disease reported by Iraq's Ministry of Health. It was revealed that no more than one child in ten was being correctly treated for pneumonia and other serious illnesses, and that fewer than one in five health workers had received adequate training. Again the medical problems were being compounded by inadequate nutrition. As one example, by 2000, egg production had fallen to less than 10 per cent of the target, representing a per capita production of no more than ten eggs per person per year in the 15 governorates of central and southern Iraq. At 31 January 2000, some 90 agricultural contracts worth $175.3 million had been blocked in the UN Sanctions Committee, mainly by the United States and Britain.

The Iraqi government had also been denied the means to achieve the necessary improvements in the water and sanitation systems (Annan: 'very little improvement over the past two years'). There were delays in the arrival of approved supplies valued at more than $245 million, and contracts worth around $100 million had been blocked in the Sanctions Committee. The erratic electricity industry, also subject to similar contract 'holds', was another major problem in efforts to provide clean water to the civilian population:

> As a result, programme inputs have been able neither to increase the availability of drinking water nor to prevent continued leakage and associated contamination of the network. The water authorities were unable to provide service to some seven million inhabitants, mainly in rural areas.[34]

The evidence was continuing to accumulate: reports, analyses and copious personal testimony were combining to describe the mounting suffering of the Iraqi people. Thus reports in the London-based *Lancet* medical journal (26 May 2000), based on UNICEF fieldwork, indicated that deaths among Iraqi children and babies had more than doubled over the previous ten years because of UN sanctions.[35] In July 2000 Saeed H. Hasan, Iraqi Ambassador to the United Nations, commented to the Secretary-General on Kofi Annan's report (1 June) regarding the implementation of the UN programmes in Iraq. In Hasan's view the report lacked an objective approach to evaluating the humanitarian situation throughout the country:

> The report . . . ignores the cumulative impact of the sanctions on all the economic, social, cultural, educational and even psychological aspects of life for the Iraqi people and their projected impact on future generations even if they were to be lifted now.[36]

Again attention was given to the impact of contract 'holds' imposed mainly by the United States and Britain.

Blocking Supplies: US–UK Policy

The Secretary-General had commented on the continuing telecommunications difficulties in Iraq but had failed to mention why the problems persisted. In fact the Ministry of Health had concluded a contract for modern telecommunications exchanges to link government departments and health facilities, but the United States and Britain had blocked the contract in the UN Sanctions Committee. More difficulties were being caused by the complex procedures demanded by UN administration, by disruptions outside Iraq's control, and by Washington's decision to block contracts for ambulances.[37] In the same way, the US and Britain had chosen to block contracts in the water and sanitation sector, so hampering the reconstruction of a vital humanitarian section of the Iraqi infrastructure. Thus the supply of equipment for four sanitation stations in the Ghazaliyah area had been blocked by the United States, while serious delays had affected the delivery of pipes for the upgrading of water and sanitation networks.

The United States and Britain were also blocking contracts for veterinary drugs, vaccines and related supplies. Iraq had managed to import some necessary agrichemicals, but the US and the UK had placed a block on the agricultural spraying equipment essential for their use. This latter decision was particularly baffling since permission had been granted to import identical equipment during earlier phases of the UN programme. Educational computers and laboratory sets were also being banned by the United States and Britain in the Sanctions Committee, another baffling prohibition. The Committee had demanded that the computers be of a certain class as a condition for US–UK approval. The Iraqis duly complied with this demand, whereupon the United States and Britain imposed a block on the relevant contracts.[38]

It was all part of a pattern. The US and Britain were also blocking or delaying contracts for forklift trucks, meteorological instruments and replacement parts for fire-fighting vehicles. The railways were in an increasingly dilapidated condition, with approval being granted to only four of 47 railway-related contracts in particular phases of the UN-negotiated programme. Rail accidents were becoming more frequent because of US–UK opposition to the speedy replacement of damaged rails.

The Mounting Casualties

In such circumstances the economic sanctions were 'killing Iraq'.[39] Through 2000 the US and British representatives on the Sanctions Committee were preventing countless innocuous items reaching Iraq. It was impossible to obtain books, envelopes and paints for children.[40] One Western photographer, Karen Robinson, took pictures of Iraqi children selling their loved dolls so that their families might eat. Felicity Arbuthnot, indefatigable journalist, described the 'silent Hiroshima' that 'culls a nation's children'.[41] In July 2000 more than 10,000 Iraqis, mainly young children, died because of sanctions: 'Some 7457 Iraqi children under five years of age and 2843 adults died in July of illnesses such as diarrhoea, respiratory problems and malnutrition' (Iraqi Ministry of Health). The infant mortality rate had almost quadrupled over the decade of sanctions, from 24 per thousand in 1990 to 98 per thousand in 2000. Denis Halliday had commented: 'We are in the process of destroying an entire nation . . . It is illegal and immoral'; and Hans von Sponeck, his successor, had spoken of the 'humanitarian tragedy' in Iraq. According to *Arabic News* (8 September 2000), an internet facility, some 1.35 million Iraqi children had been killed by the economic sanctions, while there had been a dramatic increase in the number of women's deaths after delivery. In September, Daw Sweidan, the Arab League's Assistant General-Secretary, reported that the League's executive bureau had urged the lifting of sanctions as the only way to relieve the suffering of the Iraqi people.

It was now being reported that Iraqi families were selling some of their food rations, so increasing the levels of malnutrition, in order to buy clothes and other necessities. Thus Tun Myat, von Sponeck's successor as UN Humanitarian Coordinator, declared: 'The fact is that people have become so poor in some cases that they can't even afford to eat the food that they are given because, for many of them, the food ration represents the major part of their income. They have to sell food in order to buy clothes and shoes or whatever they need.' Now Myat was urging the US–UK-dominated Sanctions Committee to release more than $1 billion-worth of contracts in order to ameliorate the desperate plight of the Iraqi people. He emphasized that the health care services were suffering from a lack of clean water, inadequate sanitation and unreliable electricity supplies. In a special televised report, *Paying the Price – The Killing of the Children of Iraq*, the journalist John Pilger summarized the Iraqi predicament:

What happens when modern civilized life is taken away? Imagine all the things that we take for granted are suddenly not available or severely limited, such as clean water, fresh food, soap, pencils, paper, books, light bulbs and life-saving drugs. Imagine that telephone calls to the outside world are extremely difficult, computers no longer work. When you fall ill, you must sell all your furniture to buy medicine. When you have a tooth out, there's no anaesthetic. No country will trade with yours and your money is almost worthless. Soon children become beggars. It's as if the world has condemned your whole society to a slow death and all because of a dispute over which you have no control. That's what's happened in Iraq, where almost 10 years of extraordinary isolation, imposed by the UN and enforced by the US and Britain, have killed more people than the two atomic bombs dropped on Japan.

On 16 November 2000 the Iraqi Ministry of Health reported that more than 9000 people had died in October as a result of illnesses caused by the sanctions. The total included 6337 children under five who had died of diarrhoea, pneumonia, respiratory- and malnutrition-related illnesses (compared with 272 deaths in the same period in 1989, before sanctions); 3202 people had died of heart problems, diabetes and cancers (compared with 391 deaths caused by these conditions in the same period in 1989). Of course, as we are constantly told, the United States and Britain have 'no quarrel' with the Iraqi people, though it is difficult to imagine what more could be done to them if a real quarrel did exist. It was increasingly being recognized that economic sanctions were being used as a weapon of mass destruction to accomplish a protracted genocide. The word 'quarrel' seemed increasingly trivial in circumstances where millions of Iraqis were being punished all the time and where thousands of Iraqis were now being killed every month: 'Perhaps extermination is a better word.'[42]

In late-2000 it was plain that Kofi Annan, UN Secretary-General, remained deeply concerned about the plight of the Iraqi people. He was prepared to admit that four years into the UN humanitarian programme:

The vast majority of the Iraqi people still faces a situation of decreasing income . . . such patterns as pauperization and growing food insecurity have appeared . . . the programme faces difficulties in addressing the social and economic deterioration in Iraq. . . the humanitarian programme was never intended to meet all the humanitarian needs of the Iraqi population or to be a substitute for normal economic activity . . . the programme is not geared to address the longer-term deterioration of living standards or to remedy declining educational and health standards and infrastructure.[43]

All this seemed a remarkable admission, if only because the *sole* efforts allowed to address Iraq's food, health, education and infrastructure problems were at the behest of the UN Sanctions Committee. If the United Nations was not expected to address some of the fundamental humanitarian problems of the

Iraqi people – as Annan was suggesting – how were the people expected to survive and have even minimal hopes for the future?

The Collapsing Society

Again the UN Secretary-General was cataloguing, seemingly to no avail, the dire predicament of the Iraqi civilian population. The specific points are familiar enough to many observers but it is worth giving a few extracts from a shocking Annan report (29 November 2000):

> I wish to reiterate my serious concern over the lamentable state of the cargo off-loading facilities and equipment at the port of Umm Qasr . . . the deteriorating conditions . . . frequent breakdown of port equipment . . . severe delays . . . Recently, the last remaining functioning forklift was disabled, and consequently cargo is accumulating in the already congested port. (Paragraph 72)

> The mission identified several insufficiencies in the Iraqi food quality testing laboratories, particularly the unavailability of basic items and materials required to carry out laboratory analysis . . . 18 contracts for urgently needed laboratory equipment worth $6.1 million remain on hold. I urge the Committee to consider the early release of these holds to facilitate the provision of safe food to the Iraqi population. (Paragraph 75)

> Much more effort is required . . . to ensure the timely arrival and distribution of the required supplies in sufficient quantities to address the nutritional needs . . . only 24 per cent of estimated malnourished children under five and only 23 per cent of pregnant women and lactating mothers had received at least one high-protein biscuit ration. (Paragraphs 79, 81)

> None of the 15 public health centres or 68 community childcare units assessed in October 2000, had a government vehicle for the distribution of targeted nutrition supplies. (Paragraph 83)

> . . . there was an increase in underweight children from 9.5 per cent to 13.4 per cent, and of acute malnutrition (wasting) from 1.8 per cent to 4.1 per cent. (Paragraph 85)

. . . nearly 90 per cent of raw sewage from the sewage pumping stations in Iraq is currently being discharged directly into rivers and streams. . . many Iraqi people who rely on river water for their daily needs are being compelled to deal with contaminated water, with serious public health implications. (Paragraph 86)

Even Baghdad, given priority in investment options, was 'able to handle only 32 per cent of the city's sewage volume'. Again Annan appealed to the Sanctions Committee to release the holds placed on applications in the water and sanitation sector 'in order to expedite rehabilitation of direly needed facilities'.

By August 2000 large areas of the central and southern governorates were being left without electricity for up to 18 hours per day, though thereafter the reduced seasonal demand allowed significant improvements in many regions. But apart from essential services, the population of Sulaymaniyah was receiving only two hours of electricity per day, while the population of Erbil had no power except that produced by emergency generators.

Nearly 40 per cent of the surveyed schools were unable to provide learning environments that were even 'minimally safe'; and without substantial injections of cash 'the rehabilitation and reconstruction of deteriorated school buildings, the improvement of the learning environment and the promotion of increased enrolment may prove elusive'. Many of the schools remained in a deplorable state, often lacking windows, desks, electricity or basic sanitation; just as other social and industrial sectors were being forced to remain in an appalling condition. Thus the telecommunications services throughout Iraq were in a 'deplorable state' to the point that the entire network was facing 'total breakdown'. And again the familiar Annan appeal to the US and UK representatives on the Sanctions Committee: 'I should like to reiterate my appeal to the Security Council Committee to expedite the release on holds placed on applications for telecommunications equipment.' (Paragraph 110)

The UN Secretary-General concluded his report by noting the failure of the nutritional situation in Iraq to improve, and by indicating the spread of deep-seated poverty. He indicated yet again his 'serious concern over the excessive number of holds placed on applications', many of which were affecting the humanitarian situation:

> Finally, I wish to reiterate what I stated recently, that 'in the case of Iraq, a sanctions regime that enjoyed considerable success in its disarmament mission has also been deemed responsible for the worsening of a humanitarian crisis – as an unintended consequence. I deeply regret the continuing suffering of the Iraqi people and hope that the sanctions imposed

on Iraq can be lifted sooner rather than later . . . I appeal for a renewed and concerted effort by all to reach a solution that would lead to the alleviation of the plight of the Iraqi people.[44]

Kofi Annan was doing no more than acknowledging the increasingly widespread perception in the international community that the US-sustained sanctions were bringing immense suffering to the Iraqi civilian population. Observers noted, for example, that at the Eid al-Fitr feast (27 December 2000) marking the end of the holy month of Ramadan, the Iraqis had little to celebrate. A shopkeeper, Abu Saad, was quoted:

For the poor there is little joy, but the rich celebrate . . . Before 1990 you'd see people singing and dancing in the streets when the Eid came. We are sick of these embargoes. We just wait and wait for them to end . . . I am fed up and I don't follow the news any more.

Colin Powell, the US Secretary of State-designate following the presidential election, was promising to 're-energize' the sanctions.[45]

The Scale of the Genocide

In early 2001, Iraq was claiming that more than one and a half million people, most of them children and the elderly, had been killed by the economic sanctions – sustained by Washington in the teeth of world opinion. An 'entire population' was being destroyed.[46] The UN Department of Humanitarian Affairs had estimated that more than 4 million Iraqis had been forced into extreme poverty. Malnutrition, not a public health problem prior to 1990, had increased massively over the decade and was continuing to spread in 2001, with well over one million children chronically malnourished. The UN Sanctions Committee, dominated by the US and the UK, was dismissive of requests for goods that it judged to be 'non-essential'. Such goods included school blackboards, chalks, pencils, notebooks and paper. It was estimated that the 84 per cent of all schools needing rehabilitation were being denied essential materials and other supplies.[47]

Some estimates were putting the number of Iraqi dead through hunger and disease at more than 2 million.[48] The Chicago-based Islamic Association for Palestine was urging the American people 'to wake up to the realities of the tragedy in Iraq, and to pressure our government to lift the sanctions on this dying nation.'[49] On 17 January 2001 anti-sanctions demonstrators from the US charity Voices in the Wilderness, arrested in New York outside the US Mission to the United Nations, noted the date:

> January 16 marks ten years since the start of the Gulf War. Although the formal Gulf War itself only lasted 42 days, sanctions and bombings in the US- and British-imposed 'No Fly Zones' have killed between 1.5 and 2 million people over the past ten years. UNICEF has stated that one in ten children under the age of one will die before their first birthday as a direct result of the sanctions.[50]

The routine Western denunciations of the Iraqi dictator could no longer disguise the fact that 'UN sanctions have killed far more ordinary Iraqis than Saddam Hussein [has done]'.[51] A Labour Action for Peace meeting in London, organized to condemn the UN sanctions on Iraq, was reported under the heading, 'Ten years suffering – enough is enough'.[52] On 2 March 2001 the UN Secretary-General issued a further report on the humanitarian situation in Iraq:

> The poorer strata of society are often forced to barter what they receive through the food basket in order to procure other basic necessities . . . purchasing power has steadily declined, and while food items are readily available to markets, they are unaffordable to the average Iraqi citizen . . . even though Iraq has a surfeit of vegetables, fruit and animal products,the majority of Iraqis cannot afford to buy them.

It was noted also that medicines were still being rationed to patients: 'One of the serious health risks of this practice is the potential development of resistant bacterial strains during the treatment of infectious diseases where less than the full course of antibacterial agents is provided to patients.' After mentioning the familiar difficulties in various social sectors the Secretary-General again called on 'all parties to take concerted measures to alleviate the plight of the Iraqi people'.[53]

On 15 May 2001 the Iraqi Ministry of Health announced in Baghdad that some 8797 men, women and children had died in the previous month because of various causes arising from the sanctions. It was obvious that the embargo-induced malnutrition and lack of medication were combining to exacerbate the morbidity and mortality rates throughout the civilian population. In April 5696 children under the age of five years had died from diarrhoea, tuberculosis, other diseases and malnutrition compared to 347 children who had died from such causes during the same month in 1989, the last year of a sanctions-free Iraq. The Ministry pointed out also that 3101 elderly people had died in April 2001, compared to the 457 who had died in April 1989. Now it was being estimated that the eleven years of sanctions had killed 1.5 million people, mostly children and others in the most vulnerable sectors of the Iraqi civilian population.

The appalling plight of the Iraqi people was widely known, though given little publicity in the Western media. In particular, the situation was understood by senior UN officials, paradoxically charged with the task of administering the genocidal sanctions regime, while at the same time striving to mitigate the apocalyptic impact of the embargo on ordinary Iraqis. Thus a further report issued by UN Secretary-General Kofi Annan graphically highlighted the catastrophic effects of sanctions and appealed to 'all parties concerned' to implement humanitarian measures 'to alleviate the plight of the Iraqi people, and to refrain from any actions that could exacerbate the already fragile living conditions of the average Iraqi'.[54] Hence in May 2001 the UN Secretary-General was yet again struggling to highlight the scale of Iraqi suffering and, in his characteristically diplomatic terms, urging leading UN members not to make matters worse.

Another Annan Report

It is useful to note some of the observations made by the UN Secretary-General on the state of Iraq almost eleven years after the imposition of sanctions:

> Observation . . . of the railway facilities confirmed the unsafe conditions and insufficient capacity to meet transportation demands for both humanitarian supplies and passengers . . . The state of deterioration of road transport vehicles has been exacerbating demand on the sector . . . Owing to the deteriorating condition of the public buses and the reduction in their number, route coverage has been reduced by 50 per cent.[55]

There were no dredgers for the port of Umm Qasr, essential for the import of humanitarian goods, causing limited draught which, with the presence of wrecks in the port, was reducing the port's operational capacity. The silos used to handle grain imports were being drastically affected by the lack of spare parts, just as the country's food quality-control laboratories, denied essential equipment, could not perform their essential tasks.[56]

All social sectors were continuing to suffer from the accumulating impact of the years-long sanctions regime. There were the inevitable shortages of drugs and medical equipment:

'The results of observations have shown that only 30 per cent of the essential drugs at hospitals' were being received in adequate quantities. Essential medicines were 'still in short supply' and the supply of vaccines 'falls short of annual requirements'.[57]

A number of essential ambulances had been allowed into the country after lengthy delays, but only after the US-dominated Sanctions Committee had insisted that the ambulance radios be removed. In addition, the Committee had prohibited the import of refrigerated trucks, essential for the protection of hospital drugs in transit.[58]

The Secretary-General report noted also that there were still inadequate transportation and storage facilities for foodstuffs and other humanitarian goods, that there were still widespread malnutrition among children, and that the percentage of 'acutely malnourished' children had not changed since November 1997.[59] The contributing factors included inadequate water and sanitation facilities, a substantial volume of unsafe equipment in this sector, and an inadequate agricultural capacity, deliberately constrained by blocks on the import of such items as pesticides, sprayers, veterinary vaccines and equipment for irrigation systems.[60] The inadequate and unreliable supply of electrical power, 'critical' in much of Iraq, was continuing to have an adverse affect on the humanitarian programme.

In mid-2001 there was continuing widespread deterioration in the educational sector:

... throughout the education system, shortages of educational materials and equipment, sub-standard institutional resources and pronounced disincentives to the academic cadres continue to inflict greater structural damage than the [UN] programme can address ... An assessment of 1208 schools confirmed widespread deterioration of school buildings and facilities, a shortage of school textbooks and insufficient classroom space ... 79 per cent of the schools were assessed as being in sub-standard or critical condition ... [61]

Textbooks were found to be in various stages of dilapidation, essential equipment for higher education was in very short supply, and what had been one of the most highly developed educational systems in the region now appeared to be in a state of terminal collapse. Throughout the sector the sanctions-induced 'inadequacies have continued to have a negative effect upon the standard of instruction'.[62] And what was true for transportation, health and education was equally true for such sectors as telecommunications, housing and the levels of employment. Again the UN Secretary-General found it necessary to emphasize the 'constraints and difficulties' of the UN programme and to remind powerful states that they were supposed to be helping the Iraqi civilian population, not making their situation worse: 'I appeal to all parties concerned to preserve the distinct humanitarian identity of the programme . . .' and not to take 'any actions' that could bring yet more suffering to the Iraqi people.[63]

The Genocide Continues

It was highly significant that the UN Secretary-General found it necessary to make such an appeal. In late 2002 it seemed plain that the manifest genocide of a civilian population begun in August 1990 had been maintained through the entire decade of the 1990s and beyond. In April 2001, according to the Iraqi Ministry of Health, a total of 8797 people perished through various causes resulting from the growing malnutrition and lack of medication brought about by the endless embargo on Iraq. Some 5696 children under the age of five years had died – compared with 347 child deaths during the same month in 1989 – from diarrhoea, tuberculosis, other lung diseases and malnutrition. In the same month, 3101 elderly people had died – compared with 457 in April 1989 – because of heart disease, high blood pressure, diabetes and malignant tumours. *The new mortality figures for April 2001 brought the total number of Iraqis who had died as a result of the economic sanctions to 1,489,949.*

In June 2001 the *Jordan Times* commented on the case of Timothy McVeigh, found guilty of planting a bomb at the Federal Building in Oklahoma City that killed 168 people and wounded 500 in April 1995:

He [McVeigh] was trained by the US Army, a decorated Army veteran of the 1991 Gulf War. Americans don't like to be reminded of this . . . Had McVeigh killed 168 Iraqis, he would have been handed the Medal of Honour, because in the court of American justice, it is all right to kill Arabs. It is all right to continue a vicious embargo that has resulted in the deaths of hundreds of thousands of Iraqi babies.

In June more than 9000 Iraqis, 6000 of them children under five, died as a result of sanctions, *bringing the number of Iraqi men, women and children killed by the embargo introduced in August 1990 to 1,508,016.* At the same time, the incidence of many diseases was being exacerbated by the sanctions. In July 2001, delays in the supply of medical provisions were responsible for outbreaks of black fever in the south and centre of the country. In September, nearly 10,000 Iraqis were killed by sanctions (Table 4), a dreadful toll to which Washington and London seemed to be wholly indifferent.

Table 4
Mortality rates of Iraqis, September 1989 and September 2001

Cause of death	September 1989	September 2001
Children under 5 years of age		
Diarrhoea	123	2932
Pneumonia	96	1594
Malnutrition	67	2354
Adults over 50 years of age		
Heart disease, hypertension	106	638
Diabetes	73	557
Malignant neoplasm	260	1701

The embargo was continuing to impact drastically on the lives of most of the Iraqi population. About 40 per cent of Iraq's 22 million people did not have access to clean water, a situation that was encouraging the spread of the water-borne diseases that were the main killers of children. In September 2001, the southern city of Hilla, home to about half a million people, was without drinking water for about 20 days, a typical occurrence in a land that was being denied the ability to purchase spare parts and other equipment in adequate supply. For the same reason, many regions were continuing to suffer acute power shortages and blackouts for periods of up to 20 hours.

Independent observers were acknowledging that the sanctions were killing many hundreds of thousands of children, though some journalists were reluctant to face the fact. Thus the journalist Hala Jaber spoke of the 'highly questionable statistics in a 1999 UNICEF report citing a 500,000 infant-mortality figure.'[64] In response, David Bull, Executive Director of UNICEF UK, emphasized that the surveys were carried out by trained health workers and that their results were reviewed by a panel of experts 'not only from UNICEF but from the World Health Organization and Macro International — which supports demographic household surveys throughout the world'. Also, Bull quoted the UN Security Council Panel on Humanitarian Issues (March 1999): 'Even if not all the suffering in Iraq can be imputed to external factors, especially sanctions, the Iraqi people would not be undergoing such deprivations in the absence of the prolonged measures imposed by the Security Council and the effects of war.'

In November 2001 Hans von Sponeck and Denis Halliday, former senior UN Humanitarian Coordinator in Baghdad (who both resigned in protest at the impact of sanctions), said in a joint article that the West was 'holding the Iraqi people hostage, in order to secure Saddam Hussein's compliance to ever-shifting demands'; and emphasized the UN Secretary-General's statement (October 2001) that *The US and UK governments' blocking of $4 billion of humanitarian supplies was by far the greatest constraint on the humanitarian programme*. In such circumstances, with thousands of Iraqi children dying every month, what justification was there for another military onslaught on the Iraqi people?:

> We are horrified by the prospects of a new US-led war against Iraq. The implications of 'finishing unfinished business' in Iraq are too serious for the global community to ignore. We hope that the warnings of leaders in the Middle East and all of us who care about human rights are not ignored by the US government. What is now most urgently needed is an attack on injustice, not on the Iraqi people.[65]

While Washington was planning a new war against Iraq, the condition of the Iraqi people was continuing to deteriorate. By the end of 2001, major cities were going without electricity for lengthy periods. The supply situation in the northern province of Dahouk was the worst in two years, with residential areas going without power for weeks at a time and experiencing great difficulties in keeping hospitals and other facilities running.[66] One estimate suggested that the national power supply deficit was running at well over 50 per cent, and that the situation would continue until Iraq was allowed to import spare parts and other equipment in adequate quantity and without the usual US–UK-contrived delays (see Chapter 3).

In December 2001 alone, some 15,000 Iraqis died as a result of the sanctions regime; more than 7000 children under the age of five died through (otherwise treatable) diseases such as diarrhoea, pneumonia and malnutrition illnesses. Iraq, having received less than half of the medical supplies it had ordered for the month, accused the United States and Britain of introducing delays into the supply procedure. In January 2002, Baghdad informed the United Nations that '*1.6 million Iraqis had died from diseases that could not be treated because of the embargo.*' The total mortality figure of 1,614,303 included 667,773 children under five who had died as a result of the sanctions.

At the same time, a group of Americans, members of the activist group Voices in the Wilderness, sent a message to President George W. Bush:

We are five Americans writing to you from Baghdad . . . where we have indeed discovered that weapons of mass destruction exist. We see them constantly in use when we visit the children's wards in hospitals across this country . . . hundreds of thousands of little children have died as a direct result of the sanctions the US has maintained against Iraq for over 11 years.

Be bold, Mr President. Let the innocent children of Iraq live. End the economic sanctions at once.

But it seemed unlikely that such an appeal would do anything to shift American policy. In April 2002, Mohammed Aldouri, Iraq's UN representative, sent a letter to the Secretary-General denouncing the US–UK holds placed 'on contracts for drugs and medical equipment for the treatment of the various cancers' caused by the depleted uranium in munitions used against Iraq:

The catastrophic dimensions of the use of depleted uranium against Iraqi civilians are increasing with the passage of time. Their manifestations include a major increase in cancer cases and in exotic diseases and congenital deformities that were previously unknown in Iraq and that will persist for generations . . . The Americans and the British bear responsibility for this human and environmental catastrophe.[67]

In these circumstances the United States and Britain were compounding their action, 'persisting in a policy of mass extermination', by blocking Iraq's access to anti-cancer drugs and medical equipment.[68] But even such indefensible tactics did not satisfy Washington and London, already planning more punitive initiatives: a tightening of sanctions and a new war.

THREE

Blocking Essential Supplies

The British Propaganda

On 6 January 2001 Peter Hain, a Labour Member of Parliament and a minister in the British Foreign Office, declared:

> It is a myth that sanctions cover food and medicines. To export the majority of goods to Iraq – including food, medicines, agricultural, educational and water and sanitation goods – you need simply notify the UN.[1]

This statement was part of an argumentative piece designed to justify the US–UK policy on Iraq, and as such was a blatant item of propaganda. It had *never* been simple, under the terms of the sanctions regime, to export to Iraq, whatever the nature of the goods in question. The Hain statement suggested a straightforward procedure with no impediments and no efforts to frustrate the supposed humanitarian purpose of the UN programme. We may debate whether Hain knew that his comment was deeply misleading or whether he was speaking in ignorance of how the sanctions regime worked. The question is academic. Hain no longer has British responsibility for Iraq, and some of the highest current and former UN officials continue to protest at how the sanctions system is being abused, principally by the United States and Britain.

The Management of Sanctions

The sanctions system, nominally deriving authority from specific UN Security Council Resolutions, has evolved as a highly punitive instrument administered jointly by the official bureaucracies in individual countries and UN-linked bodies in New York,* and policed mainly by US military power. As a response to the growing international outrage at the endless punishment of the Iraqi people – and *to prepare the ground for a new war against Iraq* – Washington has been forced to redouble its propaganda efforts while working hard to sustain a sanctions regime that can be easily abused in practice. The concept of 'smart' sanctions (see Chapter 9) has been developed as a propaganda initiative designed to disguise the continuing efforts of successive US administrations to deny adequate humanitarian relief to the Iraqi people, and to facilitate American war plans.

The procedures for UN control of the supply of goods to Iraq have always been massively bureaucratic, so greatly aiding the American and British representatives in New York who are intent on creating delays and difficulties. It has become plain over a period of years that Washington and London have found the UN sanctions system highly congenial, a welcome device for maintaining Western control over the Iraqi economy, for guaranteeing 'gravy train' payments to approved non-Iraqi claimants, and for denying Iraq the opportunity to rebuild its shattered society.

The UN Office of the Iraq Programme (OIP) described the procedures that governed the supply of goods to Iraq over many years. One specification of the procedures represented an accumulation of decisions taken by the UN Sanctions Committee since 1996.[2] This indicated that a Memorandum of Understanding (MU) must first be established between the UN Secretariat and the Iraqi government, indicating how the oil sales authorized under Security Council Resolution 986(1995) were to be used. The UN Secretary-General was required to approve in principle the agreed MU and the associated distribution plan, whereupon the details were submitted to the members of the Sanctions Committee. This was intended to provide the functional framework within which the individual Committee members were required to assess the thousands of submitted applications.

Once the Memorandum of Understanding was agreed, the Iraqi government or the UN Inter-Agency Humanitarian Programme (for the three northern governorates of Dohuk, Erbil and Sulaymaniyah) approached suppliers with the aim of concluding a range of appropriate contracts for the supply of goods. The specified *Procedures* indicated that contracts could only be agreed under the terms of the Memorandum: 'It is understood that payment of the supplier from the [UN-administered] "Iraq Account" can only take place for items purchased by Iraq that are included in the categorized list referred to in . . . the present Memorandum.'[3] However, all this was only the start of the process. There were

---

* Mainly the UN Iraq Sanctions Committee and the UN Office of the Iraq Programme.

many more procedures to be followed before the agreed goods could be allowed to arrive in Iraq.

When Iraqi officials and intending suppliers had negotiated a contract for the purchase of goods, it was then necessary for the suppliers to apply to their appropriate government department to enable their application to be submitted to the UN Iraq Sanctions Committee in New York for approval. The procedure required to obtain a licence for an application submission to the Committee varied from one country to another – all equally obliged to observe mandatory UN Security Council resolutions – but the bureaucratic elements were broadly the same in all cases. In Britain, for example, applications were to be made to the Sanctions Unit, a department that functions under the Export Control Organization of the Department of Trade and Industry (DTI). Other countries established their own analogous arrangements.

The Office of the Iraq Programme issued a six-page list of Guidelines for the completion of applications to the national sanctions departments.[4] The *Guidelines* included a listing of some twenty reasons why an application may be rejected and returned to the sender ('the application Mission/Organization'). These included submission in the wrong language (only English and French were allowed), failure to indicate a contract number, imprecise quantities specified, wrong prices, failure to list every spare part in a set, and failure to indicate a valid port of entry. It was emphasized that the listed reasons for rejecting an application were 'not exhaustive' and were subject to Committee review 'whenever appropriate'. So new reasons for rejecting an application could be invented at any time at the whim of officials, including the US and UK representatives who were invariably hostile to the Iraqi regime. In fact, the suppliers, generally acting in good faith when they submitted often complicated applications, sometimes omitted minor details – so giving unsympathetic officials ample pretext for throwing out an application. When the rejected application was eventually amended and resubmitted by the supplier, it was returned to the Sanctions Unit queue for attention. Time would then elapse since the DTI department, employing only about a dozen staff, would also be administering sanctions on various other countries. When the application was eventually approved, it was sent to the UN Iraq Sanctions Committee, where fresh obstacles were lying in wait.

For a start, the Office of the Iraq Programme may have reviewed the *Guidelines* in the interval between the submission of the application to the national sanctions department and the arrival of the approved licence in New York – so the Committee may have a reason for rejecting the application before most of the details of the proposed purchase could be considered. The OIP declared itself 'unable to respond to inquiries from companies or their representatives' when they were uncertain about procedures. All such enquiries, often of a technical nature, had to be addressed to the country's Permanent Mission to the United Nations. If the Mission could not answer the enquiry it would contact the OIP for clarification – yet another source of predictable delay.

Copies of the licence applications, once they had satisfied the national sanctions units and the Office of the Iraq Programme, were then circulated to the fifteen members of the UN Iraq Sanctions Committee (so-called 'fast-track' applications were not circulated – see below). The Committee, a reflection of the UN Security Council, comprises representatives of the five Permanent Members (United States, Russia, China, France and Britain) and ten other UN members who happen to be on the Security Council at the time.[5] Any single member of the Sanctions Committee could block an application or delay it indefinitely by asking for more details. Only if no objection or delay was registered by any member was the application then approved. This meant that every Committee member had veto powers, unlike the situation in the Security Council where only Permanent Members can block a proposed resolution. Hence there were more obstacles to approvals in the Committee than there were in the Council – again maximising the likelihood of procrastination and delay.

The meetings of the Sanctions Committee, as today, were always held in closed session and on no regular dates. No record of the discussions were placed in the public domain, and Iraq – whose fate was shaped by detailed consideration of its most important affairs – was not usually allowed to know what had been said. This meant that arguments against particular applications, many of which had vital humanitarian relevance, were kept secret and thus completely immune to any public discussion. An official handout on the operations of the Committee noted that 'with 15 states represented . . . there is plenty of scope for debate on the application of sanctions'; and that debate usually concerns 'whether a particular application is humanitarian or not' and what advice to give to applicants. The 'scope for debate' inevitably meant that decisions were often held over to subsequent meetings, by which time new objections may have surfaced. The quickest decisions ('fast track' apart) that resulted in approval inevitably took months from original contract negotiation to delivery of goods; while the most protracted decisions, if reached at all, took very much longer.

Iraq, as today, was allowed no voice in any of the Committee proceedings. It was not allowed to know the course of the discussions, or why particular applications were blocked or delayed. It was informed of outcomes but given no reasons. Iraq was allowed no appeal against any decision. A Committee member could veto any application – which could have serious consequences for thousands of Iraqi civilians – yet the veto was protected from scrutiny by all the countries not on the Committee, including the one most affected by Committee whim, malice and dispute.

The Sanctions Committee dealt only with governments, required to submit their applications through their Permanent Missions to the United Nations. The Committee could veto (block), hold, modify or approve an application, but for most of the applications there were no time constraints on the decision-making process. There was nothing in the rules of the Committee that obliged it to meet in the event of an urgent humanitarian request, or even to meet at regular intervals. This was all a recipe for *political* delays – important elements in the strategic agenda of the United States shadowed by Britain.*

Targeting the People

The United States had quickly established the framework for a long economic siege of Iraq. In September 1990, Washington objected to a Yemeni proposal that the UN Office of the Legal Counsel should be invited to provide some guidance on the relevance of humanitarian considerations to the plight of the civilian population in Iraq. Washington was determined to retain sole power to decide what was or was not a humanitarian matter, with a view to imposing maximum deprivation on the Iraqi people. This cynical ploy was further exposed when, on 7 September 1990, the United States vetoed a request by Bulgaria for permission to ship baby food to Iraq on the grounds that the food might be consumed by adults. Three days later, Washington blocked an Indian request to send food to its nationals in Iraq and Kuwait. The pattern was established.

In June 1992 the US representative on the Sanctions Committee blocked a request from Denmark to supply heaters to children's hospitals in Iraq on the grounds that the equipment might be used elsewhere. At every stage, with stalwart British support, the United States worked to ensure that Iraq remained in a deeply impoverished state. In 1994 a British company director, involved mainly in exporting medical supplies, described what was involved in trying to trade with Iraq:

---

* The 'smart' sanctions resolutions (SCRs 1284, 1382 and 1409) simplified some of the procedures – for example, by transferring some approval tasks from the Iraq Sanctions Committee to the Office of the Iraq Programme – but still left scope for malicious US–UK delays and still denied Iraq control over its own national economy (Chapter 9).

Before any individual or company can talk to an Iraqi buyer (private or public), they must apply for a licence to negotiate . . . Licences to negotiate could take three or four weeks to issue. Only when the licence is issued can you start talking . . . without fear of breaking the law. Once the buyer and seller agree . . . the seller must then apply for a supply licence, which can take up to 20 weeks to issue. In the meantime, the Iraqi dinar is suffering daily devaluation and inflation beyond control. 20 weeks later the seller receives the supply licence by which time the buyer's situation has changed . . . In nearly 24 weeks, inflation and the continuous devaluation . . . will force the buyer to cancel the order or, at best, reduce the quantity or quality of the goods . . . But any change to the application means that the whole process must start again.[6]

Hence the United States and Britain were working to block the provision of many humanitarian supplies to Iraq where they could, and relying on the massive bureaucracy of the sanctions system to present further difficulties to humanitarian relief. The trader al-Kaisy made a chilling observation: 'UNICEF's expectation that 100,000 Iraqi children would die in 1994 as a direct result of the sanctions has, shamefully, been exceeded.'[7] The Austrian UN Ambassador, Peter Hohenfellner, one-time Chairman of the Sanctions Committee, admitted that 'women and children and other vulnerable groups, like handicapped and old people' had in effect been taken 'hostage', but, because this was a questionable practice, 'I had a very difficult time'.[8] The Washington attitude was shown by its attitude to the Iraqi request for ping-pong balls: they could not be allowed because 'We don't believe that this is an essential civilian need.'[9] And the 'essential civilian needs' could be blocked or delayed in many ways.[10]

The Sanctions Committee rejected various requests for the supply of textiles to Iraq, including thread for weaving children's clothes, on the grounds that such items are an input to industry. At the same time a request from the French CIS company in Paris to supply Iraq with nylon cloth for filtering flour was vetoed by the United States. The supply of glue, used in the manufacture of school textbooks and notebooks, was also vetoed; as was a quantity of wool as an 'unjustified input to industry'. In the same way, US and UK vetoes were put on the supply of polyester and acrylic yarn, polyvinyl chloride (PVC) material for a hospital, cable joints intended for schools and hospitals, concrete additives for housing, and containers of granite for hospitals and healthcare systems.[11]

When Kais al-Kaisy, expecting no difficulties, sought to export shroud cloth to Iraq, he found himself in protracted discussion with the DTI Sanctions Unit. He explained the purpose of the material:

This material can be used for nothing but dressing the dead . . . it could not be used for curtains or clothes – it is shroud material. We do not bury people in smart clothes or shining shoes . . . We wash them, tend them . . . and put them in the ground, wrapped in a shroud.

Some seven months after al-Kaisy lodged his request, he was informed by Peter Mayne of the Sanctions Unit: 'I have to inform you that a licence . . . has not been granted . . . The US representative on the UN Sanctions Committee are [sic] currently blocking the export of cloth to Iraq.'[12]

Attacking a Charity

On 22 January 1996, the Office of Foreign Assets Control (OFAC), US Department of the Treasury, informed Kathy Kelly of Voices in the Wilderness that, if the charity persisted in attempting to collect medical relief supplies with a view to transporting them to Iraq, there would be serious consequences:

Accordingly, you and members of Voices in the Wilderness are hereby *Warned* to refrain from engaging in any unauthorized transactions related to the exportation of medical supplies and travel to Iraq. **Criminal penalties for violating the Regulations range up to 12 years in prison and $1 million in fines. Civil penalties of up to $250,000 per violation may be imposed** . . . [bold type in original].

The letter was signed by David H. Harmon, Acting Supervisor of the Enforcement Division, Office of Foreign Assets Control.[13] In response, Voices in the Wilderness sent a letter to OFAC that by March had been signed by 88 people. It included the words:

We . . . want you to know that we will continue our effort to feed and care for the children and families of Iraq. We will do so by collecting medical relief supplies and then by, openly and publicly, transporting these supplies into Iraq for delivery to people in need. We are governed not by rules that license people to bring aid to people in need, but rather by compassion. We invite you to join us in our effort to lift the current sanctions against Iraq and end the cruel suffering endured by innocent people.[14]

On 17 May 2002 OFAC imposed a $10,000 fine on Bert Sacks, a retired engineer from Seattle, for taking medicines to Iraq without a licence. Sacks responded by saying he would not pay the fine. Instead he, with Voices in the

Wilderness, decided to exploit the publicity and immediately began a campaign to raise $10,000 to purchase and deliver more desperately needed medicines to paediatric wards and clinics in Iraq.

Within seven days of issuing the 'Declaration 2002' appeal, Voices had raised thousands of dollars for medicines. On 30 June it was announced that OFAC had imposed a $10,000 fine on the reverend Randall Mullins, also from Seattle. He too declared that he would work to raise $10,000, not to pay the fine but to deliver more medicines to Iraq.

Blocking Humanitarian Contracts

For the rest of the 1990s and into the new millennium the United States, ever shadowed by Britain, continued to harass 'unauthorized' aid workers, to bomb Iraqi sites, and to frustrate the purpose of the UN humanitarian programme by imposing blocks and delays on supply contracts wherever possible. Thus in August 1999 Kofi Annan, UN Secretary-General, commented on the work of the UN Sanctions Committee: 'There has been a significant increase in the number of holds being placed on applications, with serious implications for the implementation of the humanitarian programme.'[15] Benon Sevan , Under-Secretary-General and Executive Director of the Office of the Iraq Programme, was already complaining that the delays imposed on the shipments of food and medical supplies were undermining efforts to relieve the suffering of the Iraqi people: 'His remarks were targeted at Britain and the United States, which have delayed scores of contracts . . .'[16]

On 23 September 1999, the Iraqi government reported that the United States and Britain had put 328 contracts on hold, valued at $438 million and covering food, medicines, water purification equipment, sewage equipment and spare parts for electric power systems. In addition, the US-dominated Sanctions Committee had failed to approve a further 796 contracts worth $1.3 billion, most of them of direct humanitarian relevance. The Iraqi statement concluded:

> This hostile stand taken by the US and the UK against the people of Iraq is aimed at killing as many Iraqi children, women and elderly people as possible. We call upon the international community to put pressure on the US and the UK to lift the unjust sanctions and to put an end to this genocide.

It should be emphasized that the Iraqi-supplied information, far from mere propaganda, is well supported in official UN reports. In October 1999, Kofi Annan was again expressing his concern at how the Sanctions Committee was treating applications to supply Iraq with essential goods:

> I have expressed concern about delays in the approval of applications . . . I have referred to the growing number of holds . . . and the resultant serious implications for the implementation of the humanitarian programme . . . it is highly desirable to find a prompt solution to this problem.[17]

In an annex to his letter of complaint, Annan noted that 'the number of holds overall continues to increase' and that 'the time required by members of the Committee to review holds is becoming longer'.[18]

The determination of the United States to obstruct the supply of humanitarian goods to Iraq has long been recognized. Thus in January 2000, the human rights organization, Human Rights Watch, drawing attention to Kofi Annan's complaints, declared: 'The ability of a single country representative [i.e. the US on the Sanctions Committee] to place an application on hold . . . continues to be a matter of concern.'[19] In November 1999 Benon Sevan, OIP Executive Director, had noted that 602 contracts worth $1.042 billion were then on hold, and quoted estimates of the UN Food and Agriculture Organization that the $73 million-worth of agricultural contracts on hold had resulted in the loss to Iraq of as much as 20,000 tons of wheat production. Sevan had noted also that holds had been placed on telecommunications equipment, of direct humanitarian relevance, and on contracts for safety equipment in power generation. Human Rights Watch commented that the behaviour of the United States, in deliberately increasing the number of contract holds in various sectors, 'appears to be capricious and unjustified'.[20] It also urged the Security Council to address 'the apparently high degree of politicisation with regard to the decisions of the sanctions committee'.[21]

The sanctions system had evolved over the first decade of its operation, but in 2000 it was still being used by the United States and Britain to guarantee the suffering of the Iraqi people. Holds were being maintained in crucial areas that had direct humanitarian relevance, despite frequent appeals by Kofi Annan and Benon Sevan. Thus on 14 January 2000 Annan noted the 'lamentable state' of the Iraqi oil industry, and drew attention to the contract situation in this sector: '438 applications, with a total value of $217.8 million, have been placed on hold; and 54 applications, valued at $56.2 million, are pending the Committee's decision . . . there remain 416 applications, with a total value of $263 million, which are currently under review prior to circulation' to the Committee members.[22] This meant that essential spare parts and other equipment for the oil industry were being blocked or massively delayed in the Sanctions Committee, which in turn was leading to geological damage in oil-bearing strata, increasingly hazardous working conditions for oil-industry personnel, and a growing threat to future oil production. The Secretary-General concluded his letter with the familiar appeal: 'In the light of the foregoing, I should like to express the hope that the Security Council Committee will proceed as expeditiously as possible in its consideration and approval of applications for oil spare parts and equipment and to review further all applications placed on hold.'[23]

On 1 February 2000 the Office for the Iraq Programme was again indicating the number of contracts on hold for the various phases of the programme: 516, worth $1.26 billion; 22, worth $36.61 million; 177, worth $541 million, and 320, worth $685.3 million. In March Kofi Annan was again complaining about the number of holds being placed on applications: 'There is an urgent need to review further the procedures related to the approval of applications with a view to reducing the excessive number of holds placed on applications, which have been affecting adversely the overall implementation of the programme.'[24] Later in the same report the Secretary-General referred to:

— 'the slow and erratic pace at which humanitarian supplies' were arriving in Iraq;

— improvements in the humanitarian situation 'below expectations';

— food prices 'beyond the reach of most Iraqis';

— food-handling and food-processing contracts to the value of $185.5 million placed on hold;

— the erratic arrival of drugs, 'which may have contributed to the increase in deaths attributable to cardiac, diabetic, renal and liver disease . . . ';

— water and sanitation contracts to the value of $95.6 million placed on hold;

— power generation contracts worth $488 million placed on hold, which 'has had a marked impact in delaying the completion of maintenance work';

— 92.2 per cent and 100 per cent of telecommunications contracts for two phases of the UN programme placed on hold.[25]

After citing these and other holds, Kofi Annan yet again urged the members of the Sanctions Committee to address the situation: 'I should . . . like to reiterate my appeal for a further review and reconsideration of positions taken with regard to applications placed on hold.' It was necessary 'to facilitate the lifting of such holds, which have reached an unacceptably high level'; and to streamline 'the processes by which such holds can be lifted.'[26]

On 20 April 2000 Benon Sevan noted that the total number of holds was 1180 with a total value of $1,726,891,635 (at 14 April):

> As stated by the Secretary-General at the meeting of the Security Council on 24 March, many of the holds on contract applications do have a direct negative impact on the humanitarian programme, and on efforts to rehabilitate Iraq's infrastructure, most of which is in appalling disrepair.[27]

Now, almost ten years after the introduction of the sanctions regime, Benon Sevan was raising the prospect of further deterioration in the Iraqi situation: unless the question of holds was addressed: 'We will continue to sink further into the present untenable quagmire.'[28]

The situation ran on, virtually unchanged, through the rest of 2000 and well into 2001. The United States released some holds and then immediately imposed fresh ones, so that in May 2000, the total value of contracts on hold in the humanitarian and oil sectors was in excess of $1.824 billion. On 20 April, the Security Council had discussed the matter of holds, but to no effect. Benon Sevan had observed that meetings on the subject had produced 'much talk but no result'. It was obvious that holds would remain one of the principal mechanisms used by the United States to continue the genocide. With the sanctions system becoming increasingly complex and bureaucratic, it was easy for Washington to exploit the holds option to maintain the suffering of millions of innocent men, women and children. Already Kofi Annan, urging potential suppliers to use electronic formats, had noted 'the very time-consuming process of manually entering thousands of lines of data'.[29] Excessive bureaucracy was helping all those, principally the United States, who were committed to obstructing the efficient flow of humanitarian goods to the people of Iraq.

In May 2000 Iraq was complaining that the UN Secretariat was ignoring an Iraqi request that $10 million (of Iraq's oil revenues) should be allocated to the purchase of equipment for the printing of the national currency.[30] The Central Bank of Iraq was in urgent need of such equipment so that it could print bank notes for general use, curtail the circulation of counterfeit currency, and satisfy the International Criminal Police Organization (ICPO-Interpol). Moreover, it was important to restore confidence in the Iraqi dinar: ' . . . this would have a positive impact on purchasing power', and so mitigate the plight of the civilian population.

It was inevitable that the Secretariat's indifference to the request would be seen by Iraq as a further hostile attitude: 'Your failure to approve the allocation for the banking sector can only be interpreted by the Government of Iraq as one more obstacle placed in the way of the measures being taken to improve the situation of the Iraqi people, who have been suffering for more than ten years under the unjust embargo . . .'[31] At the same time the United States remained committed to maintaining a wide range of contract holds that were adversely affecting the humanitarian situation.

Sabotaging the Humanitarian Programme

Benon Sevan was now acknowledging that the 'growing tendency [by the United States] to politicize the programme' was having an adverse affect on the implementation on the UN scheme.[32] Yet again he drew attention to the scale of the holds: 'As at 31 January 2000, the total value of holds was approximately $1.5 billion.'[33] A few days later, Mohammed Said Al-Sahaf, Iraq's Minister for Foreign Affairs, was emphasizing how the United States and Britain had 'sought to politicize a purely humanitarian enterprise and to turn it into an instrument of their anti-Iraq foreign policy', with the aim of 'harming the people of Iraq, exacerbating its suffering, making its day-to-day life more difficult and killing more of its children, women and elderly'.[34] Here it was noted that high UN officials – Denis Halliday, Hans von Sponeck and Jutta Burghardt – had felt compelled to resign from their posts in protest at the genocidal impact of the sanctions policy; and that the Secretary-General himself had appealed to the Security Council to carry out an 'urgent' review of the 'excessive number of holds', which were having adverse affects on the humanitarian programme.

In early November 2000 the value of holds was $2.3 billion, of which $2 billion-worth was for humanitarian supplies and $300 million-worth for the oil industry. It was clear that nothing was being done to address the holds issue and the associated plight of the Iraqi people. Some contracts on hold were being released but other applications – including contracts for an irrigation system, fuel tankers, a chemical laboratory, trailers and fibre-optic cable – were being added to the holds list. A report from the World Health Organization indicated that by November some $200 million worth of health-related goods were being blocked, including some childhood vaccines, laboratory supplies and equipment components.[35] At the end of November the UN Secretary-General commented, addressing US policy in the Sanctions Committee: 'I note with concern' that a list of oil spare parts and equipment 'has remained on hold . . . despite repeated reminders by the Executive Director of the Iraq Programme.' Yet again Kofi Annan was complaining at the US policy of sabotaging the flow of humanitarian goods to Iraq:

> I should like to reiterate my continuing concern about the unacceptably high level of the applications placed on hold . . . the volume of holds rose drastically from less than $1.4 billion in mid-August 2000, to $2.31 billion as at 31 October 2000 . . . In a letter dated 27 September 2000 . . . the Executive Director of the Iraq Programme underlined the need for launching yet another campaign in order to contain and reverse the increase in the number of applications placed on hold.[36]

It was plain also that some of the reasons given for blocking contracts were bogus. Thus the United States would sometimes request additional information about an application, but when the further details were provided the contract still remained on hold: 'I must note that in many cases in which the requested clarifications and/or information appeared to have been provided, the applications concerned remained on hold, without any indication of the reasons provided for the continuation of the holds concerned.'[37]

In the final weeks of 2000 the value of contracts placed on hold had continued to rise:

- almost $2.5 billion, including $2.1 billion for humanitarian supplies (OIP weekly update, 25 November –1 December 2000);

- over $2.5 billion, including $2.2 billion for humanitarian supplies (OIP weekly update, 2–8 December 2000);

- over $2.7 billion, including $2.4 billion for humanitarian supplies (OIP weekly update, 9–15 December 2000);

- over $2.9 billion, including $2.6 billion for humanitarian supplies by the end of the year (OIP weekly update, 16–29 December 2000).

In such circumstances it seemed obvious that the United States and Britain, as always acting in concert, were working hard to frustrate the humanitarian content of the current Memorandum of Understanding. Again it was the US and the UK that were exercising their vetoes, sometimes unilaterally and sometimes jointly, to deny the Iraqi people access to crucial humanitarian supplies. The malicious intent behind this joint US–UK policy was plain. Thus contracts were sometimes put on hold on the grounds that they were 'dual-use' items (i.e. items that could be used for both civilian and military purposes), but *every* item can be construed as 'dual-use' where there is malicious intent (basic foodstuffs are essential to both civilians and troops). Moreover, the United States and Britain, acting to a common purpose, were declaring some items 'dual-use' where the OIP chose to make the opposite judgement; and contracts from one source might be blocked, while almost identical contracts from another might be approved. This latter suggests that the United States and Britain were hostile to some of the supplying states, rather than to the items in question – again indicating the politicization of the entire process.

It was also significant that some blocked items, though seemingly minor, were essential to the effectiveness of associated items that had been approved. Thus substantial contracts might win approval, but be sabotaged by such approval being withheld from smaller contributing contracts. Kofi Annan had indicated that some of the holds affect approved contracts, so making the 'only-15-per-cent-of-contracts-are-blocked' argument a misrepresentation of the power of the US–UK sabotage policy. Put simply, equipment denied only 1 per cent of its components may be useless: but to claim that 99 per cent of the items are approved might seem impressive.

Another ploy is for the United States and Britain to give approval for goods destined for the three northern governorates (Erbil, Dohuk and Sulaymaniyah), while withholding approval for identical goods destined for the central and southern governorates of Iraq – so serving the propaganda purpose of proving that the regions administered by the Iraqi government fare less well than those administered by UN personnel.

In March 2001 Kofi Annan was yet again complaining that, in circumstances where most Iraqis could not afford to buy available food and where chronic malnutrition was continuing to increase in rural areas, the United States and Britain were still blocking many contracts for humanitarian supplies: 'I should like to reiterate my grave concern over the unacceptably high level of holds placed on applications. The volume of such holds, with a total value of $3.117 billion, has increased dramatically . . .'[38] Moreover the US-dominated Sanctions Committee was even refusing to discuss the holds issue, as urged by Benon Sevan five months before:

> It is regrettable that it has not yet been possible for the Committee to start a fresh round of technical meetings to review the holds placed on applications in each sector, as has been proposed by the Executive Director

of the Iraq Programme in his letter to the Committee dated 27 September 2000.'[39]

The 'Holds' Continue

There were other problems. Many suppliers, where contract approvals had been given, were either failing to ship the specified goods or were supplying goods of inferior quality. The Office of the Iraq Programme had estimated that items contained in some 1500 to 2000 contracts had become the subject of commercial disputes over the previous year between the Iraqi purchasers and the suppliers. The UN Secretary-General was acknowledging that some suppliers had not been acting in good faith in discharging their contractual obligations.[40] There had been 'poor performance by some suppliers' who had contracted to provide essential foodstuffs: 'The problem of contracted suppliers failing to honour their contractual obligations has persisted and is having negative consequences for the timely delivery of programme commodities.'[41] Again Kofi Annan was drawing attention to the number of holds being imposed on many contracts with obvious humanitarian significance:

> One application worth $42.8 million to procure 30 new locomotives for transporting goods and passengers . . . is on hold. Five applications worth $14.2 million, for the procurement of railway telecommunications and signalling equipment, are still on hold. Without the release of the holds . . . the system cannot operate safely . . .

> United Nations observation reports reveal continuing shortages of some injectable antibiotics, anti-epileptics and drugs used in the treatment of diabetes and heart diseases. Injectable antibiotics . . . had been out of stock for over three months, while cough preparations, simple analgesics and antipyretics had been out of stock for more than six months.

> The number of health items that were short-supplied [partially delivered by the suppliers] and those that did not comply with the specifications of the contract increased during the period under review . . .

> The findings revealed that some machines and equipment in use at the [Samara Drug Industries (SDI)] plants were old and obsolete . . . raw materials, quality control reagents and spare parts are still in short supply . . .

Vaccines for measles, mumps, rubella, pneumonia, tetanus and hepatitis are also in short supply; anti-tuberculosis (BCG) vaccines are not available countrywide . . .

The shortages are due in part to . . . irregular deliveries of orders, holds placed on applications and failures of some of the ordered items to pass quality-control tests . . . two applications, one for tetanus and diphtheria anti-toxins and another for hepatitis-B vaccine, are on hold . . .[42]

And so on and so forth. There had been no deliveries of BCG vaccines since mid-2000, and stocks were exhausted in September. Stocks of DPT (diphtheria, pertussis, tetanus) vaccine were running out. A substantial delivery of therapeutic milk had been certified by the Ministry of Health as contaminated. Only four of 43 water treatment plants had benefited from the installation of spare parts. The government's efforts to mitigate the impact of the 2001 drought were being hampered by contract holds worth $250.7 million on essential irrigation systems. In many parts of Iraq, electricity was unavailable for up to 18 hours a day, with power trippings causing damage to equipment, 'particularly in health facilities, which do not have a steady supply of electricity'.[43]

Again the UN Secretary-General was emphasizing that a simple statement of the number of contract holds in a sector did not necessarily indicate the scale of their impact. Thus a quarter of all electricity contracts had been blocked as at 31 January 2001, but 'because the majority of the components approved cannot be utilized without the use of key complementary parts . . . the consequences of these holds are greater' than the percentage would suggest: *'I therefore reiterate my appeal to the Committee to expedite the release from hold of applications for new power generation systems . . .'*[44]

A quarter of all schools, having had no maintenance over the previous years, were in such a bad state that they could not even provide a safe environment for children and teachers. There were a large number of schools with cracked and humid walls, leaking ceilings, broken doors and windows, an absence of even basic electrical wiring, severe shortages of furniture, and shortages of textbooks and teaching aids. An additional health hazard was caused by the absence of basic sanitation facilities, exacerbated by contract holds on water purification equipment, electrical power spare parts and many other items. The UN Secretary-General noted that the continuing holds on applications for computers in the education sector would have 'serious consequences for the development of human resources and the exposure of Iraqi children to improved technological education'. Similarly, holds had been placed on *all* telecommunications contracts for various phases of the UN programme: '*Any immediate improvement . . . is dependent on the release from hold of these applications . . . I appeal to the Committee to take positive action with regard to the applications submitted and to review further the holds placed on all applications.*'[15]

US–UK Politicizing of Sanctions

The Secretary-General's 'Conclusions and Recommendations' clearly indicate his awareness that the United States and Britain were exploiting the sanctions systems in the interests of agendas that had nothing to do with the humanitarian relief of the Iraqi people. Washington and London had *politicized* the humanitarian programme, were imposing an excessive number of contract holds on applications, and were manifestly indifferent to the prolonged and extreme suffering of innocent men, women and children:

> Although the programme is being implemented within the context of a sanctions regime, it is essential for all parties concerned, now more than ever, to depoliticize and facilitate the implementation of the programme in order to alleviate the continued suffering of the Iraqi people. The Iraqi people must receive all the assistance that they direly need and deserve . . . I very much regret to note . . . the slow pace of implementation of paragraph 13 of Resolution 1330(2000), in which the Security Council urged the Sanctions Committee to review applications in an expeditious manner, to decrease the level of applications on hold and to improve the approval process . . . I should like to appeal to the Committee to review and approve applications in an expeditious manner and to decrease drastically the level of applications placed on hold . . . I appeal to all parties to take concerted measures to alleviate the plight of the Iraqi people.[16]

Kofi Annan, UN Secretary-General, is a highly diplomatic official, keen not to antagonize any UN member state or to raise the decibel level of political debate. In such circumstances, having presided at another time and in another post over the UN fiascos in Somalia, Rwanda and Bosnia, it is perhaps remarkable that he has felt driven to say so much about Iraq. Much of his commentary, though oblique, implies clear criticism of the behaviour of the United States and Britain in the Iraq Sanctions Committee. Kofi Annan has frequently maintained that the needless holds on contracts, mainly the responsibility of Washington and London, are exacerbating the miseries of the civilian population in Iraq. The Annan message could not be clearer – but we may judge that it could be more robust.

The 'Fast-track' Charade

The contract holds remain one of the principal mechanisms for the blocking of humanitarian supplies to Iraq, with the United States and Britain remaining the principal exploiters of the holds option. The international community had become increasingly horrified at the genocidal character of the sanctions regime, with the result that Security Council Resolution 1284 (1999) was drafted to authorize a 'fast-track' provision for the approval of contracts without the need to circulate such applications to the Committee members (see Chapter 4). The aim was to compile approved lists of items in the fields of food, education, medicine, agriculture, oil and water/sanitation. Applications for such items would still have to be made in the usual way but the Office of the Iraq Programme, rather than the Sanctions Committee, would give approval for items on the lists.

The 'fast-track' provision became yet another mechanism for providing a useful propaganda gloss to the genocidal sanctions regime.[47] The US and UK representatives in the Sanctions Committee refused to approve many essential humanitarian items as 'fast-track' products, so destroying the humanitarian thrust of the new provision. Thus most of the 'approved lists' remained small and scarcely affected the expanding volume of holds. For example, the entire food list contains about three dozen items, including such controversial products as soap, biscuits, cups, saucers and breast pumps. It is obvious that thousands of items fall outside the list. By contrast, the education list has well over 100 items, including iron rulers, ball pens, sealing wax, footballs, gymnastic shoes, tape measures, violins, glue, ping-pong balls, sweat suits, copybooks, etc. Is it really necessary for the Office of the Iraq Programme to have to approve the supply of such items to Iraq? Is it on consideration of such things that the peace of the Middle East depends?

The list of approved medical items runs to 103 pages, with about half of the list covering drugs. For the rest, perhaps we are encouraged that such items as pens, food trays and plastic urine collectors no longer require the approval of all 15 members of the Sanctions Committee, but was it really the case that, for year after year, the entire Committee was obliged to deliberate on whether Iraq should be allowed to receive wall-mounted billboards, napkin holders, baby shampoo and ear swabs? Was the provision of wooden toothpicks, cat-gut sutures and surgical stables to Iraq really deemed likely to plunge the region into a fresh war? The very existence of the 'fast-track' lists reveals yet again the vindictive malice with which Washington and London came to regard the ordinary people of Iraq. Was it really necessary to impose delays of months on the supply of stethoscopes, medical gowns and bed sheets?

The 'fast-track' lists were compiled over the period from February 2000 to February 2001, and have had little impact on the overall humanitarian situation in Iraq. Washington and London continue to restrict the size of the lists, and in any case much of the time-consuming application procedure still has to be observed: *'Suppliers should be aware that the signing of contracts and the preparation and submission of applications for goods which may qualify for expedited processing should be carried out in the normal manner.'*[48] So if you want to send a packet of toothpicks to Iraq, there is a detailed six-page list telling you how to fill in the initial contract application for submission to the Office of the Iraq Programme. But do not add a toothbrush to the contract application. If it is not on the approved list the whole contract application will have to be considered – eventually – by the entire Sanctions Committee: 'Applications will continue to be circulated to the Committee for approval if they contain any items not on the lists . . .'[49]

It is easy to see that the 'fast-track' provision has had virtually no affect on the predicament of the Iraqi people. How could such a provision hope to cope with the hundreds of thousands of items that a modern state requires for its humanitarian purposes? How could the sanctions regime, relying on the equivalent of the wholly-discredited concept of central planning, hope to process and control such a volume of manufactured and other items? The 'fast-track' provision was doing nothing to reduce the scale of the contract holds. By April 2001, according to the Office of the Iraq Programme, there had been a further increase in the total value of contracts placed on hold. No less than 1685 contracts, worth almost $3.5 billion, had been blocked, of which some $3 billion-worth were for humanitarian supplies.

The Worsening Situation

On 24 April the Office of the Iraq Programme indicated (for the period 14–20 April 2001) that the contracts placed on hold by the Sanctions Committee had risen to a total of 1703 worth $3.59 billion. Of these, 1158 contracts worth more than $3.15 billion were for humanitarian supplies, while 545 contracts worth $437 million were for oil-industry equipment. For the rest of April there were the usual fluctuations in the number of contracts on hold, but early May saw another significant increase – to $3.7 billion, caused in part by the placing of a hold on a single contract (worth $147.5 million) for the electricity sector. Now

$3.26 billion-worth of humanitarian contracts were still on hold, an obvious demonstration that the Sanctions Committee representatives – principally the US and Britain – remained determined to impede the flow of essential goods to the Iraqi people.

Kofi Annan continued to protest at how the contract holds were damaging the UN humanitarian programme in Iraq. In May 2001 he declared:

> I am gravely concerned that since my previous report in early March [2001], the total value of holds has increased from $3.1 billion to $3.7 billion, as at 14 May 2001.[50]

Later in the report the Secretary-General highlighted the many holds – mostly imposed by the United States and Britain – that were inevitably having a serious impact on the UN humanitarian programme. Thus contract holds had been placed on the import of vital equipment for the electricity sector, dredging and wreck removal equipment for the partly-blocked port of Umm Qasr, equipment for food quality control laboratories, human and animal vaccines, hospital equipment such as autoclaves, protective equipment and forklifts for the water and sanitation sector, agricultural pesticides, equipment for irrigation systems, diagnostic kits for animal diseases, telecommunications equipment, construction machinery for housing, and much else.[51]

Through June and July 2001, according to the UN Office of the Iraq Programme, the total value of contract holds stood at around $3.5 billion.[52] The pattern was well established and the value of the humanitarian contracts blocked in the Sanctions Committee, mainly by the US and UK representatives, was set to grow in the months ahead. By early 2002 it was obvious that the United States and Britain had no intention of relaxing their policy of denying the Iraqi people humanitarian relief in adequate quantity.

In a letter dated 7 January 2002, addressed to the Chairman of the Sanctions Committee, the Executive Director of the Iraq Programme expressed his grave concern at the unprecedented surge in the volume of contract holds placed by the Committee. The total value of blocked contracts then reached $4.956 billion, including blocks on 1265 contracts, worth $4.28 billion, for humanitarian supplies, and 589 contracts, worth $676 million, for oil industry equipment. Some of the holds were placed because of what the Committee claimed was inadequate information; other holds came into effect because Committee members had procrastinated for months, even though the suppliers had provided all the necessary information.[53] Later in January, the total volume of holds passed the $5 billion mark for the first time, standing at $5.038 billion, of which 1333 contracts, worth $4.37 billion, were for humanitarian supplies.

In the week from 12–18 January, four contracts, worth $2.66 million, were released, while holds were placed on 47 new contracts worth $90.3 million.[54] It seemed plain that the pattern would persist.

By the end of January 2002, the contract holds amounted to $5.23 billion, with the bulk of these – on 1410 contracts worth $4.55 billion – relating to badly needed humanitarian supplies. The total value of blocked contracts then dipped slightly, only to rise again – to $5.27 billion by early March and to over $5.3 billion by mid-March. Again, there was a slight decline but, by early April 2002, the total value of blocked contracts still stood at over $5 billion.[55]

The endless Western propaganda constantly suggested that the 'oil-for-food' programme generated enough revenues to meet the needs of the Iraqi people. Even if this were true – and most independent observers denied the claim – the matter was purely academic. The available revenues were always prevented from providing adequate humanitarian supplies in good time, simply because the American and British representatives in the Sanctions Committee were deliberately obstructive in blocking billions of dollars-worth of humanitarian contracts. *This had become one of the main reasons why more than 1.6 million men, women and children had died unnecessarily through the 12-year economic siege on an entire national population.*

On 7 May 2002 the Office of the Iraq Programme reported that the total value of contract holds stood at over $5.2 billion, covering 2123 contracts for the purchase of various humanitarian supplies and equipment items. At the same time the Iraqi authorities were claiming that the situation was worse than was being admitted. Thus Iraqi trade minister, Mohammed Mehdi Saleh, quoted by the official Iraqi News Agency (INA), declared that the United States and Britain were blocking 2590 contracts worth $7,983 billion. Whatever the precise value of blocked contracts, it was obvious that Washington and London were doing nothing to expedite the flow of humanitarian goods to the Iraqi people.

In this context the adoption by the Security Council of Resolution 1409, the so-called 'smart sanctions' resolution, on 14 May 2002 was no more than obvious window dressing, a transparently cynical exercise designed by Washington to give a further cosmetic gloss to the continuing sanctions regime (Chapter 9). Security Council Resolution 1409 was a propaganda device intended to cloak the US preparations for war.

FOUR

Crucial UN Resolutions

US Reasons for War

The long US-led war on Iraq – which arguably began in early 1990, before Iraq's invasion of Kuwait – continued to hold many attractions for Washington. Elsewhere, considering Iraq as a case study, I indicated reasons why the 1991 phase of the war (Operations Desert Storm and Desert Sabre) was particularly appealing to the United States:

– US military hegemony could be demonstrated.

– The arms factories could be kept running.

– Profits to corporate America could be boosted.

– The US grip on Middle East oil could be strengthened.

– Increased oil prices could benefit US producers (and such Texas oil-men as George Bush and James Baker), Saudi Arabia and Kuwait.

– A new range of hi-tech weapons could be tested 'in the field'.

– Useful data could be collected in such areas as electronic surveillance and computer gaming.

– The vast US budgetary allocation to 'defence' could be justified.

– George Bush could dispel his 'wimp' image in an election year.

– The Vietnam Syndrome could be exorcized once and for all.[1]

Most of this still applies, more than a decade later. The United States continues to punish the Iraqi people through bombing, sanctions and other means, so most of the points remain relevant. The global oil situation can be discussed in the light of Iraq's varying output through industry deterioration and political strategy. The Vietnam Syndrome has *not* been exorcized 'once and for all' (Washington still trembles at the thought of body bags).

When Washington strategists try to explain why the United States is continuing its war against Iraq, they rarely mention the need to boost the profits of American corporations or how useful it is to refine their data on aerial bombing procedures. Instead they urge the need to stop Saddam Hussein again becoming a 'threat to his neighbours' (the neighbours, Israel apart, do not seem unduly concerned at the alleged Iraqi threat), and suggest that, if only Saddam Hussein would observe the relevant UN resolutions, then the US-sustained bombing and sanctions would at last be ended. Since the entire publicly-declared US justification for the long war on war rests on Security Council resolutions, it is essential to understand their significance in the context of the Iraq Question.

The most important resolution that Saddam is currently supposed to observe is Security Council Resolution 1284, adopted by the Security Council on 17 December 1999 as a vital successor to earlier Council resolutions. In early April 2001, Hans Blix, chief (would-be) weapons inspector,[2] commented: 'The message I understood from US officials was that sanctions are in place until Resolution 1284 is implemented.'[3]

In fact Washington had publicly-declared objectives that went far beyond the demands incorporated in SCR 1284. One of these was the intention of using the sanctions and military force to overthrow Saddam – the stated goal of 'regime change'. Here it is useful to consider the explicit terms of SCR 1284, rather than any covert elements in its drafting. It is helpful also to glance first at UN resolutions in general and some of 1284's important precursors.

The Nature of UN Resolutions

Resolutions can be adopted by both the UN Security Council and the UN General Assembly. Security Council resolutions may or may not be mandatory, according to the chapter of the UN Charter under which they are adopted. General Assembly resolutions are never mandatory, though it is arguable that in certain circumstances they have legal weight. Council resolutions ('decisions') are adopted by an affirmative vote of nine members out of fifteen, with any one of the five Permanent Members being able to veto a proposed resolution. In fact, the veto is a complex matter. For example, if a drafted resolution is sure to be vetoed, it may never reach the Council.[4] When a mandatory Council resolution is adopted it has substantial legal weight, demanding universal observance and even having the power to supplant existing treaty obligations. Such considerations are very important since a superpower Permanent Member that can bribe or intimidate the Council into adopting resolutions, or into abandoning others, is in a unique position to shape the character of international law. This has proved to be a crucial factor in the US control over the UN resolutions on Iraq from 1990 to the present.

It should also be noted that Security Council resolutions, whilst demanding universal observance, are often not tightly drafted as legal statements. There is room for interpretation – which often means that the spirit of a resolution can be ignored by powerful states. Moreover, the spirit of a resolution can be exploited to provide a spurious justification for unilateral actions that are not authorized by any of the wording in the resolution. In summary, the resolutions are advertized as authoritative products of the Security Council designed to promote peace and justice, whereas in fact the resolutions are often devised to strengthen the foreign policies of powerful states. In this fashion the United States has frequently suborned the Security Council to serve American interests. This was never more true than in the case of Iraq.

UN Resolution 678

On 29 November 1990, the Security Council adopted Resolution 678 by a vote of 12 in favour, two (Cuba and Yemen) against, and one (China) abstaining. This was the resolution that allegedly authorized the use of force to expel Iraq from Kuwait, but the reporting of the Council decision generally gave little attention to how the United States had secured the vote. Council members had been variously bribed and intimidated to support US policy, a well-documented detail[5] that had immense legal significance. The Vienna Convention on the Law of Treaties stipulates (Articles 51 and 52) that a treaty that has been obtained through coercion is 'without any legal effect' and 'void'. A UN resolution is not a treaty but, as a legal instrument, it is subject to similar protocols. If the resolution widely interpreted as authorizing a US-led war against Iraq was 'without any legal effect' and 'void', the entire legal case for the war and all the ensuing actions against Iraq can be seen to collapse. This would mean that Iraq was under no obligation to observe the sanctions resolutions or any other Security Council decisions that rely on the legitimacy of Resolution 678. The first sanctions Resolution was 661 (6 August 1990), adopted long before 678 (29

November 1990), but the most important sanctions resolution – SCR 687 – authorizing the massive intervention in Iraqi affairs, relies on the authority of all the earlier resolutions, including SCR 678.

Resolution 678 faced another significant problem, in addition to its legal shakiness. The vast majority of Western politicians, pundits and commentators have taken authorization for 'all necessary means' (678, Paragraph 2) to remove Iraqi forces from Kuwait to include the use of military force. This interpretation relies on the impression that 'all' logically entails *every* conceivable option, without giving due attention to the adjective 'necessary'. Who was to say what was *necessary*? The resolution itself made no stipulation as to how the 'necessary means' would be determined at the expiry of the 16 January (1991) deadline. Was every UN member state expected to make a unilateral estimation? This cannot have been what was intended. The United Nations itself could not decide since no relevant protocols had been articulated in the resolution. Moreover, the Military Staff Committee (UN Charter, Article 47), designed to maintain UN control over approved military action, had not been established – a manifest violation of the Charter. Resolution 678, an essential piece of window-dressing for the US-orchestrated war against Iraq, destined to last for more than a decade, was secured through bribery, threat and a deliberately incomplete draft. It violates both the UN Charter and the Vienna Convention on the Law of Treaties. And it set the scene for many of the US-contrived illegalities and injustices yet to come.

UN Resolution 687

One of the principal enabling mechanisms for the sanctions war on Iraq (i.e. for the protracted genocide) was Security Council Resolution 687, adopted on 3 April 1991 by 12 votes to one against (Cuba) with two abstentions (Ecuador and Yemen). SCR 687 is a vast instrument, by UN standards, comprising an unusually long preamble and 34 paragraphs running through nine sections (A to I). This highly significant resolution, like most sacred texts, contains a plethora of principles and demands that interested parties could select and quote according to their whim. It is interesting that the second sentence of the preamble affirms not only the assumed sovereignty of Kuwait but also the sovereignty of Iraq, this latter a meaningless provision in the context of a residual foreign occupation, a denial of the right of Iraq to market its own oil, a denial of its right to enforce law and order in its own territory, and a denial of its right to control its own airspace. Sovereignty, in the context of 687, was to be defined at the whim of Washington.

Resolution 687 also recalls 'the objective of the establishment of a nuclear-weapons-free zone in the region of the Middle East' – which clearly indicated that Israel too (never mind Saudi Arabia, Syria, Egypt, etc.) was under obligation to abandon any interest in possessing or hosting nuclear weapons. What of US forces in the Gulf? Were any of the American ships carrying nuclear weapons? And was anyone going to say?

There is reference also to 'the use by Iraq of ballistic missiles in unprovoked attacks' which can be referring only to the Iraqi missile attacks on Iran in the Iran–Iraq War (1980–88), and to the missile attacks on Israel and Saudi Arabia in the 1991 war. Washington was an ally of Iraq against Iran, and at the time made no complaint against Saddam's use of missiles. Israel had bombed Iraq in the early 1980s, and Saudi Arabia had facilitated the massive onslaught against Iraq in 1991. 'Unprovoked'?

The Security Council also notes 'with grave concern' earlier UN reports on the situation in Iraq, and expresses 'the necessity to meet urgently the humanitarian needs in Kuwait and Iraq'. This latter is an absurdity in view of the main aim of Resolution 687, namely to secure a permanent sanctions regime against the Iraqi people, which would clearly do nothing to alleviate the appalling humanitarian situation throughout the country. The purpose and context of 687 are plainly conveyed in the lengthy preamble, and thereafter all the principal matters to be settled are specified: delineation of boundaries, elimination of Iraq's weapons of mass destruction, abolition of all capacity to develop such weapons, payment of reparations, and ending Iraqi support for terrorism. The important Paragraph 22 signals that once Iraq had satisfied the Security Council on all matters, the economic sanctions would be lifted. And who would decide that the Council was satisfied? – the United States as the bullying Council member in an unassailable position to impose its will.

Resolution 687 had given the approval of the 'international community' to the US stranglehold over the Iraqi economy and in particular to the ultimate American control over Iraqi oil. This outcome, no accident, was highly congenial to Washington strategists. The sanctions war, using economic blockade as a 'weapon of mass destruction' against the Iraqi people, was set to run for more than a decade.

UN Resolution 688

Resolution 688 (5 April 1991), adopted by ten votes to three (Cuba, Yemen and Zimbabwe) with two abstentions (China and India), enshrined the Security Council condemnation of 'the repression of the Iraqi civilian population in many parts of Iraq, including most recently in Kurdish populated areas'. It demanded that Iraq 'immediately end this repression' and insisted that Iraq 'allow immediate access by international humanitarian organizations to all those in need of assistance in all parts of Iraq'. Washington was determined to exploit this resolution to maximum effect: both to justify the continuation of the sanctions regime and to provide a basis for the so-called 'no-fly' zones, allowing Western planes to range over wide areas of Iraq and denying Iraq the right to use its own air space. Resolution 688 has important limitations, which are rarely emphasized in the Western press.

The resolution was not a mandatory resolution, and therefore carried moral rather than legal weight. It was adopted *after* Resolution 687, so cannot be interpreted as relevant to sanctions matters (688 does not mention sanctions). Resolution 688 does not specify what action should follow in the event of non-compliance by Iraq. In isolation, 688 cannot be used to justify the US–UK bombing in the 'no-fly' zones, just as SCR 660 (demanding Iraq's withdrawal from Kuwait) did not authorize military action in the event of Iraqi non-compliance, which is why SCR 678 (supposedly authorising force) was needed. Moreover, Article 2(7) of the UN Charter stipulates that the United Nations is not authorized 'to intervene in matters which are essentially within the domestic jurisdiction of any state . . .' It is acknowledged that 'enforcement measures under Chapter VII may be necessary, but the clear implication is that these are only justified when, for example, there is an act of aggression. Thus 'enforcement measures', which may have domestic consequences, may be justified – but not to achieve a domestic objective. Finally, it should be noted that 688 reaffirms 'the sovereignty, territorial integrity and political independence of Iraq'. How can such a resolution be used to violate that very *sovereignty* and *territorial integrity*?

UN Resolutions 706, 712 and 986

The idea of allowing Iraq to sell some oil to buy food and medicines was first considered in 1991, following the accumulating reports that exposed the dire humanitarian plight of the Iraqi people. Washington faced a dilemma: how not to appear vindictively cruel while maintaining the merciless sanctions war against a civilian population. The answer was Resolutions 706, 712 and 986, designed to give the appearance of US concern while the genocide continued. Resolution 706 (15 August 1991) and the two subsequent resolutions were introduced at crucial moments in the public relations agenda. Sometimes US spokesmen let the cat out of the bag. Thus a Bush administration official told

The New York Times that Resolution 706 was 'a good way to maintain the bulk of sanctions and not be on the wrong side of a potentially emotional issue' – the *potentially emotional issue* being the US-induced starvation of the Iraqi people. Resolution 706 allowed Iraq to sell 'up to $1.6 billion-worth of oil to buy food and medicines', but the offer was rejected, whereupon the West denounced Saddam yet again for being willing 'to watch his people starve'. In fact it was only Iraq's rationing system that prevented mass starvation under the pressure of sanctions. It should be remembered that 706 (and 712 and 986) were designed also to fund compensation payments to US-friendly claimants, to fund UN costs in carrying out 687 tasks, and to fund 'the full costs' of various other UN activities. This meant that only a proportion of the realized oil revenues could be used to buy food, medicines and other humanitarian supplies – and anyway the contracts could be blocked in the Sanctions Committee (see Chapter 3). Compensation payments to a host of claimants countries and organizations would *not* be blocked (see Chapter 10).

Resolution 712 (19 September 1991) never got off the ground, though the plain 706/712 propaganda exercise had been exploited to the full by Washington. It was left to Resolution 986 (14 April 1995), eventually agreed by Iraq in a state of mounting desperation, to pull off the trick. Resolution 986 nominally increased the amount of money involved, altered the distributing monitoring mechanisms, and changed the revenue proportions that would be allocated to the various purposes. The '*sovereignty and territorial integrity of Iraq*' was again reaffirmed – which was no less a nonsense this time – and it was soon plain that Iraq would be excluded from all the relevant decision-making tasks that concerned the management of its own national economy and the survival of its own civilian population. A growing number of states (Russia, France, China, Indonesia, etc.) were now declaring that it was time to lift sanctions altogether, with Russia and France commenting that there was no point in adopting a resolution merely as a 'public relations tool enabling the US and Britain to continue blaming Iraq for hardships caused by sanctions.'[6]

The picture is now grimly familiar. Iraq agreed to Resolution 986, but only in circumstances of mounting humanitarian despair as the Iraqi dead through hunger and disease were not being counted in the hundreds of thousands. There then followed a long and punishing charade of inadequate funds, blocked contracts, black anti-Iraq propaganda, vast compensation paid to Kuwaiti and other claimants, and deepening misery for the Iraqi civilian population. Resolution 986, still being used today, has evolved as a cynical tool to allow the continuation of sanctions in perpetuity, to protect US control of Iraqi oil revenues, to deny Iraq control of its own economy, and to provide an endlessly useful propaganda device for Western strategists. Today the propaganda weight of SCR 986 is supplemented by that of Security Council Resolution 1284, yet another contrivance invented by a suborned Security Council to deploy against the Saddam regime and to prolong the punishment of innocent men, women and children.

UN Resolution 1284

Resolution 1284 was adopted by the Security Council on 17 December 1999 by a vote of 11 in favour, none against and four abstentions. The vote looks to be impressive, and the resolution is frequently hyped by the United States and Britain as demonstrating the determination of the 'international community' to ensure that Saddam Hussein complies with all relevant UN resolutions. In fact, the resolution does not represent the moral victory that is claimed. Washington and London struggled for months to secure the Council decision, in order to bolster the crumbling case for genocidal sanctions, and in the event were forced to accept abstentions from three Permanent Members of the Security Council (Russia, China and France) and Malaysia. The US and the UK had been forced onto the defensive. The horrors of the sanctions regime were plain to the world, and Washington and London were desperate to create the impression that they were not as callous and vindictive as their behaviour showed them to be. However, even after months of arm-twisting, corridor lobbying and blandishments the United States and Britain had to acknowledge that a majority of the Permanent Members were not prepared to support the new cosmetic resolution. The reality was that Resolution 1284 did *not* provide a route to the abolition of sanctions, as the US–UK propagandists claimed, and in some ways it was more hostile to the hopes of the Iraqi people than were earlier Security Council decisions.

The 1284 preamble, like that of Resolution 687, recalls 'the goal of establishing in the Middle East a zone free from weapons of mass destruction' – which would logically include the abolition of Israel's 'weapons of mass destruction', about which Washington and London clearly refused to take any action. It is also interesting that an objective specified in 687 – that of establishing 'a nuclear-weapons-free zone' in the Middle East – is mysteriously absent in Resolution 1284. Could this be because of all Israel's weapons of mass destruction, its nuclear weapons have received the most publicity?[7] It has been estimated that Israel possesses 100 to 200 nuclear warheads, an obvious deterrent to any concerted Arab attempts to address the Israeli genocide of the Palestinians. Hence nuclear weapons were condemned in a 1991 UN Resolution

(SCR 687), but were unaccountably absent in a 1999 Resolution (SCR 1284) hyped by the United States and Britain through 2000 and in subsequent years.

One sop to Iraq, albeit meaningless, survives in the 1284 preamble. Again, in accord with Resolutions 687 and 688, the Security Council reiterates 'the commitment of all Member States to the sovereignty, territorial integrity and political independence of Kuwait, Iraq and the neighbouring States'. Again we can ask what the 'sovereignty' of Iraq means in this context? Iraq had lost control of its principal natural resource, there was massive foreign interference in its economy and social provisions, it was not allowed to administer substantial areas of the country, it had lost control of much of its air space and territorial waters, and it was allowed no voice in crucial decisions that affected every aspect of its social, industrial and political existence. Some sovereignty! Some commitment!

Resolution 1284 replaced the UN Special Commission (UNSCOM), massively discredited as a US-serving spy unit, with the UN Monitoring, Verification and Inspection Commission (UNMOVIC). What is in a name? UNMOVIC and the International Atomic Energy Agency (IAEA) were then assigned various responsibilities – again a largely meaningless specification (it was unlikely that UNMOVIC staff would be allowed back into Iraq and the IAEA had virtually completed its work in the country[8]). The resolution reiterated Paragraph 30 of 687, requiring Iraq to cooperate with the International Committee of the Red Cross to facilitate the repatriation of 'all Kuwaiti and third country nationals'; removed the limitation on the quantity of oil exports; established the 'fast-track' provision for contract approvals; addressed how the sanctions regime could be suspended; and requested the Secretary-General to appoint a group of experts to report on the state of Iraq's oil industry, on how petroleum production might be increased, '*and on the options for involving foreign oil companies in Iraq's oil sector, including investments . . .*' (my italics). All these provisions invite careful consideration.

The reference to Kuwaiti and other nationals necessarily implied that Iraq was lying when it claimed that there were no such people in the country – a claim that remains difficult to judge. The removal of the cap on oil exports, seemingly useful, had to be set against the appalling deterioration of the Iraqi oil industry, as reported by the group of UN experts.[9] The group also noted that the collapse of the oil industry was being caused in part by the extent of the holds placed by the United States and Britain on contracts for spare parts. It was found that a number of factors were contributing to the decrease in oil production: the failure to replenish depleted wells, delays in implementing projects, the failure to carry out major overhauls, delays in carrying out repairs, the continuing decline of the national power system, and the limitations of the oil storage and transportation systems. Thus the expert UN group identified a number of 'problem areas', including:

— The long delays in obtaining approval of individual contracts, in some cases exceeding a year, after which contracted suppliers may not wish to perform as contracted, either on price or delivery, which has an adverse effect on the planning and scheduling of repairs and maintenance.[10]

— Large contracts placed on hold because one, or a few, items are considered unacceptable . . .

— The lack of specificity in reasons given for holds. Non-specific reasons, such as 'dual usage concern' and 'not directly related to the repair of the Iraqi oil infrastructure for the purposes of increasing exports', effectively result in holds that cannot be removed and allocated funds cannot be utilized for other essential needs.

— The lack of time limits. Delays for [contract] evaluation for 'mission clarification' and holds 'pending further clarification' remain in place seeming indefinitely.

— The lack of consistency regarding holds between phases. Spare parts and equipment approved, contracted and delivered in phase 4 are placed on hold in phases 5 and 6.[11]

Of the total of 145 holds placed on contracts for the oil industry, 128 were placed by the United States and eight by the United Kingdom (the remainder were listed as pending or were unspecified). Hence one unintended consequence of UN Resolution 1284 was to provide abundant additional evidence of the extent to which the United States, backed by Britain, was deliberately sabotaging the Iraqi oil industry.

Another 1284 provision, the 'fast-track' approval of contracts (discussed in Chapter 3), was soon seen to be a nonsense. The massive bureaucracy of contract applications was preserved intact, there were inevitable OIP delays, many items were deliberately excluded from the 'fast-track' lists, and even with US–UK goodwill – which was lacking – there was no way that the cosmetic shortlists (each with no more than a few dozen items) could address the hundreds of thousands of humanitarian items legitimately required by Iraq's 22 million people.

Resolution 1284 specified also that, if the UNMOVIC and IAEA teams (the former not allowed into Iraq, the latter already largely satisfied) reported that Iraq had cooperated 'in all respects' with the inspections, then 120 days after the Security Council had received the favourable reports and the 'reinforced system of ongoing monitoring and verification' was seen to be fully operational, the sanctions on 'the sale, supply and delivery to Iraq of civilian commodities and products' would be suspended. There was no doubt that UNMOVIC would have its quota of anti-Iraq personnel, probably communicating with Mossad and the CIA (as some UNSCOM staff had done), so favourable UNMOVIC reports on Iraq were highly unlikely. Moreover, even with favourable reports the sanctions were to be only 'suspended', not given 'no further force or effect' following Iraqi compliance (as specified in Paragraph 22 of Resolution 687). Hence Resolution 1284, with many of the same limitations as SCR 687, was in some respects much harsher. Sanctions could only be suspended, not abolished, with the US option of reintroducing them 120 days later, whenever Washington had the whim (see SCR 1284, Paragraph 33). In short, there was less chance that sanctions would be removed in 2001 than there had been in 1991. Resolution 1284 was represented by Washington and London as a 'new chance for Iraq' to rejoin the community of nations or whatever. In fact, it was a recipe for continuing comprehensive economic sanctions and an endless genocide.

The US–UK efforts to secure Resolution 1284 had occupied nine months and produced a range of predictable responses. Kuwait thought that 1284 was wonderful and again blamed Iraq for all the troubles of the Iraqi people. Russia castigated those members of the Security Council who had been intent on pursuing their own unilateral goals, and again emphasized that the Council had given no authorization to the US–UK-maintained 'no-fly' zones or to subversion against the Iraqi government: 'Such illegal unilateral actions must be halted.' Russia was also concerned that Resolution 1284 might be used as an excuse for further military action against Iraq: 'The fact that the Russian Federation was not blocking the imperfect resolution should not be taken to mean that it was obliged to go along with a forceful implementation of it.' Sergey Lavrov, for Russia, emphasized that 'no concrete proof' had been submitted to the Security Council to show that Iraq was now a threat.' The Council must behave in 'an unprejudiced and unbiased way . . . must be seen to be objective', and must 'not let its work become politicized'.

Hasmy Agam (Malaysia) suggested that if it had not been for the behaviour of the erstwhile UNSCOM head, Richard Butler, the UN weapons inspectors would still have been active in Iraq. Agam suggested that 1284 was unclear about triggering the suspension of sanctions, and that it provided no timeframe for the final lifting of sanctions. Danis Dangue Rewaka (Gabon) regretted that the effort of the past months had not led to a resolution that broadly took into account the observations of most members of the Security Council. Ana Maria Ramirez (Argentina) suggested that the opinions of Iraq should be allowed some role in the process, but was broadly optimistic about the new resolution. By contrast, Qin Huasin (China) expressed dissatisfaction with the draft as a whole: 'If Iraq could not see light at the end of the tunnel, why would it comply and cooperate?' Moreover, there were broader issues to consider:

> The Iraqi and Kosovo crises had demonstrated that the wilful use of force, especially unilateral actions without Council authorization, severely damaged the Council's status and authority and further complicated the situation. The role of the Council in maintaining international peace and security could not be substituted by force. The no-fly zone in Iraq had never been authorized or approved by the Council. Members concerned should cease immediately such actions that flouted international law, and the Council's authority. Those members must show real sincerity if they wished to address the Iraq issue.

The criticism was clearly levelled at the United States and Britain.

Gelson Fonseca (Brazil), Alain Dejammet (France), Jassim Mohammed Bu Ali (Bahrain), Robert Fowler (Canada), Martin Anjaba (Namibia) and Peter Van Walsum (Netherlands) all recognized the difficulties in the current situation and acknowledged that the resolution was far from perfect. Dejammet, like other observers, noted the ambiguity and lack of clarity in the text. Peter Burleigh, for the United States, unsurprisingly applauded the resolution and chose to highlight Iraq's alleged history of 'cheat and retreat'. Washington expected *all* members of the Security Council, whether they had voted for the resolution or not, to press for its implementation.

It was not long before further detailed criticisms of Resolution 1284 were emerging in the public domain. The Campaign Against Sanctions on Iraq (CASI), based at Cambridge University, England, offered a detailed analysis, and judged:

> The resolution has deliberately obscured what is required of the Government of Iraq and what benefits the Government of Iraq can expect . . . It is therefore unlikely that the humanitarian benefits contingent upon Iraqi cooperation will be realized. The resolution's deliberate obscurantism is unlikely to reduce tensions between the Iraqi, American and British governments.[12]

Tariq Aziz, the Deputy Prime Minister of Iraq, declared on 18 December 1999 that the purpose of America and Britain in supporting the resolution was to deceive world opinion. The illegal 'no-fly' zones would be maintained and the US–UK aggression would continue. In the same vein, Voices in the Wilderness judged that SCR 1284 'has more to do with public relations than with solving the ongoing humanitarian crisis' of the Iraqi people.

Further criticisms of Resolution 1284 were published through 2000 and into 2001. The Surrey (England) organization Friendship Across Frontiers suggested that 1284 had done no more than to widen the diplomatic chasm between Iraq and the US–UK axis. It seemed that the 'deliberate degradation of an entire nation' (i.e. Iraq) would continue. Voices in the Wilderness was again stressing the clear immorality of the economic sanctions:

> Our campaign has never suggested that lifting economic sanctions against Iraq should be contingent on the actions of the Iraqi government. We believe the sanctions should be lifted because they have in the past cost many, many lives and will, in the future, continue to cause unfair deprivation. This is immoral and should be stopped unconditionally. Eye witness accounts . . . have all likened the effects of economic sanctions to a form of warfare far more lethal and destructive than even the worst of the bombardments Iraqis have endured since 1991 . . . economic sanctions are contrary to the UN Charter and constitute crimes against humanity because they target innocent civilians.[13]

In May 2000, CASI noted: 'It seems extremely unlikely' that the humanitarian situation would improve 'as SCR 1284 requires that the Government of Iraq trust that the US will interpret generously its vague terms.[14]

The United States remained strongly committed to the genocidal system of economic sanctions. Analysis of Resolution 1284 had clearly demonstrated that there was no US–UK intention to improve the miserable plight of the Iraqi population, and that the new resolution had been conceived as no more than a necessary ploy in the propaganda war. The contract holds continued to mount (Chapter 3), many thousands of Iraqis, mainly children, were dying of hunger and disease every month (Chapter 2), and Robert Zoellick, an advisor to George W. Bush, was urging the dismemberment of Iraq into several different states.[15] This last detail well illustrates the US contempt for inconvenient clauses in UN resolutions: consider, for example, the preamble of Security Council Resolution 1284 ('Reiterating the commitment of all Member States to the sovereignty, *territorial integrity* and political independence of . . . Iraq') (my italics).

It was obvious that SCR 1284 was a totally ineffectual Security Council decision. There was no reason for Iraq to believe that the resolution embodied a genuine humanitarian intent or signalled a route to the ending of punitive sanctions. In early 2001 CASI noted, reflecting the general international opinion, that thirteen months after the adoption of SCR 1284 there had been 'no movement forward in the endeavours to have it accepted by Iraq'.[16] In fact Washington and London had never judged it likely that an amended version of SCRs 687 and 986, in some ways tougher than them, would ever be accepted by Iraq. Again the Western aim had been to put a propaganda shine on the US–UK determination to perpetrate a seemingly endless genocide against the Iraqi civilian population.

Other UN Resolutions

Various Security Council resolutions on Iraq followed the adoption of SCR 1284: for example, 1302 (2000), 1330 (2000) and 1360 (2000). These Council decisions, though significant, were relatively unimportant and need not be considered here. Three further Security Council resolutions *were* important in the context of Washington's cynical manipulation of the sanctions regime: SCR 1352 (2001), adopted on 1 June 2001; Security Council Resolution 1382 (2001), adopted on 29 November 2001; and SCR 1409 (2002), adopted on 14 May 2002. These last three resolutions are discussed in the context of 'smart' sanctions (see Chapter 9).

In summary, the general US approach to Security Council resolutions is clear. They are not seen by Washington as internationally-approved tools to support human rights, to liberate subject peoples or to protect world peace. They are perceived as mechanisms for the support of American foreign policy, as devices for the cynical consolidation and expansion of US hegemony. The specific Council resolutions on Iraq, and the manner of their implementation (while ignoring resolutions on Israel), amply justify this interpretation. Washington characteristically manipulates the United Nations in pursuit of what in the 21st century has come to be called 'full spectrum dominance' – the American use of propaganda, economic and military means to pursue the objective of global hegemony.

FIVE

Subverting the United Nations

Superpower Ploys

There are many perquisites to being a *superpower*, not least the freedom of action on the international stage that such status confers. History and current affairs teach us that a regional or global superpower is less constrained than are other states by such burdensome matters as morality and law. Superpowers have always been tempted to have super ambitions, and these are often not best realized when pedantic attention is given to ethical norms or to legalistic protocols. The inevitable corollary is that superpowers, of whatever epoch or political orientation, often behave as bullies or tyrants, largely indifferent to ethical appeals and cynically interpreting the law as they go along. The superpower, while not omnipotent, enjoys a freedom of manoeuvre that is denied to weaker states. And it is particularly enjoyable to be a superpower if you are the only one.

The United States, the world's only global superpower, rejoices in being the most powerful operator in the international arena. There are constraints on US behaviour but many more on lesser nations. There are times when other states, by no means always powerless, are able to counter superpower whim, caprice and ambition. Acting alone or in concert they can often erect obstacles to American imperialism, but there is no single state or organization that can invariably do the job. In particular, the United Nations Organization, with Washington securely ensconced in all its centres of power, cannot serve the purpose. In fact the very reverse is true. The United Nations has been thoroughly suborned by the United States to underwrite a host of American ambitions – from prising open vulnerable national economies for US capital penetration, through the creation of illicit political courts for the punishment of 'pariah' states, to 'legitimizing' the endless punitive war against Iraq.

Some purblind American observers – Jesse Helms and his ilk,[1] keen to rail against their mistaken view of UN activities – do not grasp the reality that the

United Nations has become an immensely useful tool of American foreign policy, at negligible financial cost to Washington and with no requirement that the United States observe the UN Charter, to which Washington is a signatory, or any other UN-linked laws and protocols that may be judged unhelpful to American ambitions.[2]

Abusing the UN Charter

Washington's contempt for the United Nations is shown in many ways, not least by its total disregard for many Articles of the Charter – an attitude that has fuelled its behaviour to Iraq over more than a decade. Consider Article 2(4) of the UN Charter: 'All Members shall refrain in their international relations from the threat or use of force against the territorial integrity or political independence of any state . . . ' Yet the United States has repeatedly threatened to use force against Iraq, well beyond the provisions of any mandatory Security Council resolution; and force has been used on hundreds of occasions, causing thousands of civilian casualties, in the total absence of any UN authorization. And even in circumstances (e.g. SCR 678) where the United Nations has given authorization, however questionable, for the use of force the United States has never been willing to observe Articles 45–47 of the UN Charter, designed to establish a Military Staff Committee (comprising the Chiefs of Staff of the permanent members of the Security Council) as a means of ensuring UN control of any military operations. This latter meant, in the case of Iraq, that as soon as Washington had accomplished the specious justification for war (through SCR 678), the United Nations was thereafter excluded from all involvement in the conflict – in direct violation of the spirit and letter of the UN Charter.

Korea, Vietnam, Israel, Indonesia

There are many other examples of US violations of the UN Charter and international law, some of which predate the Iraq crisis of 1990–91 and helped to shape the American treatment of Iraq through the 1990s and beyond. For example, US action in the Korean War (best dated 1949–53) began before the adoption of an enabling resolution in the Security Council, so establishing the precedent for a *decision to go to war* predating a useful UN authorization.[3] The US invasion of Vietnam and the subsequent war (1963–75) violated the UN Charter, the SEATO Treaty, the US Constitution and the Geneva Conventions, so providing yet another set of precedents for the comprehensive violation of international and domestic law. In 1968 President Lyndon Johnson ordered CIA chief Richard Helms to allow Israel to keep contraband uranium, so violating the Nuclear Non-Proliferation Treaty (1968). In 1975 the United States supported the Indonesian invasion of East Timor, in violation of the UN Charter; and subsequently provided military and diplomatic support to the Suharto dictatorship that was determined to ignore the Security Council resolutions condemning the invasion and demanding immediate withdrawal.[4]

Grenada and Nicaragua

In 1983 President Ronald Reagan launched the invasion of Grenada, violating that country's national sovereignty, protected by the UN Charter (Article 2(1)), and violating also Article 2(4) of the Charter. On 27 June 1986, the International Court of Justice at The Hague (the World Court), having rejected US claims that it lacked jurisdiction, delivered a multipart verdict that the United States was in violation of international law in committing a terrorist campaign against the sovereign state of Nicaragua. Washington refused to acknowledge the verdict of the Court and refused to pay the specified compensation, so again violating the UN Charter (Article 94(10)): '*Each Member . . . undertakes to comply with the decision of the International Court of Justice in any case to which it is a party.*'

Panama, Russia and North Korea

The US invasion of Panama in 1989 was a violation of the UN Charter, the Charter of the Organization of American States, the Rio Treaty (Inter-American treaty of Reciprocal Assistance) of 1947, the Declaration of Montevideo (1933), and the Panama Canal Treaties (1977–78). Again it was obvious that the United States was totally indifferent to treaty obligations if it judged that American interests were best served by military aggression. Many other violations of the UN Charter and international law have not involved resort to force. Thus the United States violated the UN Charter when it promoted the placing of the Russian Federation in the former-Soviet permanent seat in the Security Council, *without the necessary two-thirds majority vote in the General Assembly* (specified in Article 108 of the Charter). Similarly, during the nuclear dispute with North Korea in 1991 the United States threatened military action, so violating the UN Charter; and refused to refer the dispute to the World Court, so violating Article 17 of the UN-linked International Atomic Energy Agency (IAEA) Statute (1956, amended 1973).

Libya and Cuba – Sanctions Again

The US treatment of Libya in connection with the Lockerbie bombing represented a compound violation of international law (in particular, an abuse of the 1971 Montreal Convention), various violations of the UN Charter, and further humiliation for the United Nations.[5] In enacting domestic anti-Cuban legislation (for example, the Cuban Democracy Act of 1992 and the Cuban Liberty and Democratic Solidarity Act, the so-called 'Helms-Burton' Act of 1996), the United States violated international laws governing freedom of trade between nations, and condemning the targeting of civilians ('*Starvation of civilians as a method of warfare is prohibited,*' Protocol 1, Article 54, 1977 Addition to the 1949 Geneva Convention). In 1995, the United States provided military aid to factions in Bosnia, via Military Professional Resources Inc., so violating SCR 713 (25 September 1991) and the UN Charter.

It was all part of a pattern. Ethics and law could be ignored when a superpower wanted to pursue its ambitions – in the Balkans, Iraq and elsewhere.

The War Against Serbia

The US attitude to the United Nations was well illustrated by NATO's 1999 war against Serbia. Here a principal American aim was the further dismemberment of a socialist Yugoslavia – an objective aided by the illegal Kosovo Liberation Army (branded as terrorist in UN Resolutions 1160 and 1199); by such KLA figures as Akim Cecu, the ethnic-cleanser of thousands of Serbs in Krajina; and by a massive and wholly illegal bombing campaign. The pretext for the bombing of Serbia was a document that became known as the *Rambouillet Accords: Interim Agreement for Peace and Self-Government in Kosovo*, a Hitlerian diktat designed to hive off Kosovo from Yugoslavia, to ensure that the economy of Kosovo 'shall function in accordance with free market principles', and to guarantee – by the sheer extremism of its demands – that war would be inevitable.

The blatant extremism of the Rambouillet document is made explicit in its *Appendix B: Status of Multi-National Military Implementation Force*. This specifies that NATO personnel shall be allowed to enter any part of Yugoslavia; shall be immune from all Yugoslavian laws; shall be assisted by Yugoslavia in the movement of all NATO military equipment through Yugoslavian airspace, ports, airports and roads; and shall be given, 'free of cost', electricity, water, gas and other resources that NATO forces might require. In short, the government of a sovereign state was being asked to hand over its territory, its roads, its ports, its airports, its airspace, its territorial waters, its utilities and its telecommunications facilities to a Western military alliance that was to be recognized as above all the laws of the country. No government in the world could have accepted such outrageous demands – but the predictable Yugoslavian response gave the pretext for war.

The United States 'invited' the Security Council to adopt a resolution that would authorize a military response to the Yugoslavian rejection of Rambouillet. The Council, facing the prospect of a Russian veto, never adopted an enabling resolution, forcing Washington to launch an illegal war without UN authorization and in contravention of the purely defensive North Atlantic Treaty itself:

> The parties undertake . . . to settle any international dispute by peaceful means . . . and to refrain . . . from the threat or use of force . . .' (Article 1)

The authority of the UN Charter is acknowledged in Articles 1 and 5 (of the 14-Article NATO treaty); the authority of the UN Security Council is acknowledged in Article 5; the 'primary responsibility of the Security Council for the maintenance of international peace and security' is acknowledged in Article 7; and the authority of the UN Charter is again acknowledged in Article 12 – all this when the US-led NATO alliance unambiguously violated the UN Charter and sought no authorization for war from the UN Security Council.

The US war against Serbia again demonstrated Washington's approach to the United States: exploit it where you can and ignore it where you cannot. The United States knows that it will suffer no effective criticism from a US-managed Security Council or a US-approved Secretary-General. It is easy to trace the US approach through the 11-year war on Iraq. First impose sanctions and then gain UN authorization; then agitate for a 'force' resolution (Security Council Resolution 678), and use bribery and threat to secure it.[6] Next, push the Security Council into adopting a procession of resolutions that further punish the Iraqi people, tighten the US grip on the Iraqi economy, expand US hegemony, and do nothing to constrain the pro-US regional hegemony of Israel (Chapter 6).

Abuse of the United Nations

The United Nations has been consistently exploited by Washington in this way, but that is only part of the story regarding Iraq. In addition, the United States has ignored Iranian and Turkish aggressions against Iraq (this latter relying on US-supplied arms to attack the 'safe haven' of northern Iraq), has enacted domestic legislation (Iraq Liberation Act, 1998) to fund an anti-Iraq terrorist campaign, and has imposed illegal 'no-fly' zones to facilitate surveillance and continued bombing. Aggressions, coup attempts, terrorism and bombing campaigns (e.g. Operation Desert Fox, December 1998) – none of this has UN authorization but represents a multifaceted violation of the UN Charter and a continuing humiliation of the UN institution.[7] Boutros Boutros-Ghali, former UN Secretary-General, recorded how the United States had tried to suppress a report on the deliberate Israeli shelling of a refugee camp,[8] and noted the illegality of the US–UK-maintained 'no-fly' zones over Iraq.[9] Today, with a highly diffident Secretary-General, Kofi Annan, in post, the United States frequently issues public statements as if it is speaking for the United Nations, and yet there is no suggestion that such commentary derives either from Security Council debates or discussions with appropriate UN officials.

The Iraq issue is constantly represented in the Western media as a UN matter, rooted in Security Council resolutions (see Chapter 4), but the United Nations seems powerless to influence the course of events. The sanctions regime and the continuous US–UK bombing campaign are opposed by the majority of General Assembly members and by three of the five Permanent Members of the Security Council. Yet the United States is still able to persist with its genocidal onslaught on the Iraqi people. Washington's continual reference to UN resolutions in this context is an abuse and a humiliation.

The US Refusal to Talk

The United States has frequently declared that it has no interest 'in any dialogue with Iraq', despite the UN Charter provision (Article 2(3)) that all international disputes shall be settled by peaceful means. On 18 April 2000, Taha Yassin Ramadan, Iraq's Vice-President, declared that Baghdad would welcome talks with the United States, provided that such dialogue was 'with mutual bilateral interests and not a dialogue between master and slave'. A US State Department official, dismissing the idea, commented that compliance with UN resolutions was not a matter to discuss, adding that as long as President Saddam Hussein was in power it was unlikely that Iraq would 'be able to return to the international community as a responsible member'. Was this the same Saddam who, on 12 April 1990, was courted by five US senators,[10] who was praised by US Ambassador April Glaspie, who had welcomed business contracts with clients of (Henry) Kissinger Associates, and who in the 1980s had been protected by President George Bush from the imposition of sanctions?

In September 2000 Tariq Aziz, Iraq's Deputy Prime Minister, was again suggesting that there should be talks between Washington and Baghdad: 'The golden rule in solving a crisis between nations is to talk. The Americans have talked to their adversaries, even shaken hands . . . ' (for example, President Clinton had shaken hands with Cuba's Fidel Castro) '. . . but with Iraq they refuse to do that.'[11] Aziz then observed that Security Council Resolution 687 had stated the need to free the region of weapons of mass destruction, but nothing had been done to address Israel's possession of such weapons ('The region includes Israel'). As always, the United States refused to talk to Iraq, but perhaps talks between Iraq and the United Nations would be useful.

UN–Iraq Talks

It was announced in November 2000 that the Iraqi government and the United Nations had agreed to hold talks with the aim of ending the two-year deadlock over weapons inspections and addressing the matter of the 10-year-old sanctions, now having a terrible impact on the lives of Iraqi civilians. A UN official, insisting on remaining anonymous, judged that the talks would begin after the end of the holy month of Ramadan, at the beginning of 2001. American officials were keen to downplay the prospect of UN–Iraq talks, at the same time expressing their displeasure at Kofi Annan's appointment of Rolf Knutsson of Sweden, thought to be too sympathetic to Iraq, to replace Jean-Claude Aimé as head of the UN Compensation Commission.

On 3 January 2001 a UN spokesman announced that the planned talks between Iraq and the United Nations might be delayed until February. Already, at the end of December, Kofi Annan had met with Izzat Ibrahim, Vice-Chairman of Iraq's Revolutionary Council, at Qatar during an Islamic summit. Now there were suggestions that Iraq was prepared to discuss, 'without preconditions', the return of the weapons inspectors. It remained to be seen how Washington would react to such talks, and whether *any* useful progress could be made without US approval.

On 9 January President Clinton signed, and transmitted to Congress, a report on the provision of various forms of assistance to the Iraqi National Congress (INC), the main Iraqi opposition group.[12] The report[13] outlines plans for supplying some humanitarian assistance, and for supporting INC radio, television and publications.[14] This was all essentially about propaganda. Only a proportion of a measly $4 million was being made available for the planning of 'humanitarian relief operations inside Iraq', while broadcasting was seen as one of the INC's 'most important operations . . . to promote a transition to democracy in Iraq'.[15]

Apart from a brief reference to the 'UN program in northern Iraq', there is no suggestion that the Iraq issue might be mainly a matter for the United Nations. Here it is plain that the United States is intent on pursuing a campaign for 'regime change', despite the fact that no such objective appears in any UN resolution, and notwithstanding the INC's fragmented character. Again it is clear that the US perception of its foreign-policy needs is the major concern. The United Nations must not be allowed to intrude in any way on the American pursuit of its own interests.

The planned UN–Iraq talks were encountering further delays, for reasons that were not being made clear. On 20 February Kofi Annan declared that despite the 'awkward' timing of the fresh US–UK bombing attacks on Iraq (see Chapter 8) the talks scheduled for later in the month would aim to break the deadlock: 'Obviously the timing is a bit awkward for the talks I am going to have on the 26th, but the Iraqis have confirmed that they are coming so we will be able to pursue our attempts to break the impasse and pull them in to cooperate with the UN.' Annan, UN Secretary-General, confirmed that he had not been consulted before Washington and London had launched the new bombing campaign. On 20 February a senior UN official, insisting on anonymity, charged that the United States was imposing unnecessary suffering on the Iraqi people:

> The Americans are, I am afraid, the real villains in all this. Sanctions are ineffective because certain very clear and obvious weaknesses are allowed to exist and have been allowed to exist from day one. Some are easy to explain: Turkey is allowed to take in all the oil it can smuggle because it provides the Incirlik base from which British and American planes patrol the northern no-fly zone over Iraq. The programme is full of loopholes the Americans choose to turn a blind eye to . . . You have to ask . . . what it is about the status quo that the Americans like . . . Saddam is in his box . . . he is . . . certainly not threatening their No. 1 ally, Israel.[16]

On 27 February 2001, Iraq and the United Nations confirmed that talks were being conducted with a view to ending the deadlock over sanctions and weapons inspections. Kofi Annan declared himself cautious but optimistic, warning against a miracle but emphasizing that Baghdad was keen to make progress: 'We had good discussions in a good atmosphere, and we are going to continue.' He was not surprised by Washington's new talk of 'smart' sanctions (see Chapter 9), and he noted US Secretary of State Colin Powell's aim of 'strengthening the disarmament regime and giving relief to the Iraqi people'. And again, the Annan caution and diffidence were on display: 'I would not want to prejudge or pre-empt what the Council members may do . . . I hope that out of all this will come something constructive.' Washington, with shameless malice, was committing genocide, but the UN Secretary-General, guardian of the world's humanitarian conscience, did not want to prejudge the matter.

On 1 March Mohammed Said al-Sahaf, Iraq's foreign minister, expressed satisfaction with the two days of talks, which had allowed Baghdad to outline the complete range of Iraqi grievances over 10 years of punitive sanctions: 'We have gone through many details in regard to very, very sensitive and complex issues in regard to the relationship between Iraq and the Security Council . . . my assessment is that it went smoothly during the four sessions of this round of dialogue.' At the same time, al-Sahaf was keen to criticize Resolution 1284, which had authorized the creation of the new inspection mission: Hans Blix, appointed to head UNMOVIC, was 'a detail from a bad resolution'. The adoption of SCR 1284, under pressure from the United States and Britain, was unhelpful: 'We think this resolution is complicating the whole issue. It is intended . . . only to block the way for a real lifting of sanctions. It is a bad rewriting of the basic Resolution 687. It is a classic example of moving goalposts.'

Already US and British diplomats at the United Nations were disparaging the UN–Iraq talks, offering no support and expressing doubts that they would lead to any breakthrough. On 28 March 2001, Kofi Annan, attending a two-day Arab summit conference, expressed the hope that talks scheduled for May would produce results. Jordan's King Abdullah declared to the conference: 'As for our brethren in Iraq, its inconceivable suffering has gone on for far too long'[17] But, little had changed. The genocidal sanctions remained in place, constantly bolstered by a malign and unyielding superpower. The United States would continue to abuse the UN, suborning its institutions, 'cherry-picking' from the UN Charter and UN resolutions, and contemptuously dismissing those resolutions that it found inconvenient.

US Abuse of Human Rights

In May 2001 the United States failed to gain re-election to the Geneva-based Commission on Human Rights, a major UN body working under the auspices of the Economic and Social Council (ECOSOC). Fred Eckhard, US spokesman, noted that this was the first time since the Commission's inception in 1947 that the United States would not serve on the Commission – an obvious humiliation that the US would seek to reverse as quickly as possible. In March 2002 the United States resorted to vote-rigging to regain its seat: Italy and Spain, at one time intending to stand, were pressured to drop out of the running so that the US would stand uncontested in the May elections. Washington's desire to regain its seat on the Human Rights Commission was ironic in view of the poor US human-rights record around the world. The UN, the main international protector of human rights, has been repeatedly humiliated by a United States prepared to ignore all the United Nations human-rights instruments in the interest of perceived American strategic and commercial advantage.

There is mention of human rights in various Articles of the UN Charter; for example:

> The Purposes of the United Nations are . . . to develop friendly relations among nations based on respect for the principle of equal rights . . . (Article 1(2));

> With a view to the creation of conditions of stability and well-being which are necessary for peaceful and friendly relations among nations based on respect for the principle of equal rights . . . the UN shall promote . . . universal respect for, and observance of, human rights and fundamental freedoms for all without distinction as to race, sex, language, or religion (Article 55, preamble and (c));

> The basic objectives of the trusteeship system . . . shall be . . . to encourage respect for human rights . . . (Article 76(c)).

In addition, the UN Charter is buttressed by a range of other instruments that are designed to protect human rights. Here we need mention only the Office of the UN High Commissioner for Human Rights; the Universal Declaration of Human Rights; The International Covenant on Economic, Social and Cultural Rights; the International Covenant on Civil and Political Rights; and the two Optional Protocols to the latter Covenant. The Universal Declaration laid the groundwork for more than eighty UN Conventions and Declarations on human rights.

Much of this comprehensive human rights machinery is ignored by the United States, both in its domestic practice and in its protection of derelict states around the world. Domestic abuses of human rights in America include:

- widespread torture in jails (humiliation, beatings, burnings, use of electric shocks, denial of medical attention, near suffocation, etc.);

- shootings (often fatal) of unarmed suspects;

- excessive use of electroshock stun guns;

- inadequate or totally absent legal representation of defendants (even those facing possible execution);

- execution of innocent defendants;

- execution of juveniles;

- execution of the mentally retarded (under review);

- brutal execution methods (one man in the electric chair caught fire while he was conscious; another was electrocuted over a period of 45 minutes before being pronounced dead);

- the complicity of medical professionals in torture and brutal executions;

- discriminatory sentencing on the basis of race, class and religion.[18]

Such domestic abuses are characteristic, not only of the United States, but of many other countries, some of which are firm American allies. For example, Saudi Arabia is marked by endemic corruption, religious persecution, torture, public mutilation, the absence of any civilized legal process, sexual suppression, an incidence of slavery that has both *de facto* and *de jure* support, and, in one account, the plucking of children off the street to steal their bodily organs.[19]

The United States, in violation of many UN human-rights instruments, directly aids Saudi repression by supplying weapons, surveillance support and training for security personnel. When an American citizen was tortured during a 39-day detention he tried to seek compensation by suing the Saudi government in the US courts, but all his efforts were blocked by the Foreign Sovereign Immunities Act.

Turkey, another strategic US ally, practises institutionalized torture, oppresses organized labour, and frequently resorts to aggression against other sovereign states. Thus Ilhan Karatepe, a left-wing journalist, was one example of serious abuse among thousands. Sentenced to 18 years in jail on a trumped-up charge, he was tortured at the headquarters of the Turkish secret police in Ankara. He was blindfolded, hung on a cross, and electrocuted via his penis and one of his toes, with water thrown over his body to heighten the agony. 'Paula', a 26-year-old Kurdish woman, was stripped, her hands then tied behind her back, hoisted off the floor, doused with water, given electric shocks, and sexually abused. She was tortured for seven hours on the first night and periodically for days afterwards. In the same spirit, Israel has abused many victims by subjecting them to strippings, beatings, incarceration in tiny cells, hooding, sleep deprivation, violent shaking, and deprivation of food and drink for long periods. Israel, while denying the use of systematic torture, has admitted using harsh interrogation methods.[20]

The United States, politically committed to such states as Saudi Arabia, Turkey and Israel, humiliates the United Nations by encouraging gross violations of its many human rights provisions. In addition, the United States has committed many war crimes against humanity around the world, not least against the people of Iraq.[21] Moreover, in violation of both the spirit and letter of many UN resolutions, declarations and statements, the United States has perpetrated many acts of which Washington claims Iraq to be culpable. Some of these relate specifically to weapons of mass destruction.*

US and Weapons of Mass Destruction

In September 2001 it was reported that the Pentagon had built a germ factory equipped to make enough lethal microbes to wipe out entire cities. The factory, purportedly a defensive measure, was constructed without any congressional knowledge or reference to the UN Biological Weapons Convention, and thus the entire enterprise was a violation of international law. It was revealed also that the United States was planning to test warheads containing live microbes at the US Army's Edgewood Chemical Biological Centre in Maryland.[22] Experts commented that the scale of the experiments suggested that new biological weapons were being developed. Moreover, the US government had refused to destroy its stocks of smallpox, and was continuing to develop new and more lethal forms of anthrax, allegedly for defensive purposes. The Federation of American Scientists warned that the new research was 'dual use', just as relevant to attack as to defence.

In December 2001 the US negotiators effectively sabotaged the UN Biological Weapons Convention by rejecting the 'verification protocol' that was

---

*   See also earlier discussion of the Chemical Weapons Convention on p. 58.

essential for the banning of bioweapons. One European delegate, incensed at the American obstructionist tactics, declared (of the US negotiators): 'They are liars. In decades of multilateral negotiations, we've never experienced this kind of insulting behaviour.'[23] Under the Bush presidency, even routine verification of biological weapons capability had been blocked, since US officials rejected some inspectors and would only allow visits to agreed parts of the designated sites – specifically the inspection restrictions of which the United States had long accused Saddam Hussein. The US protection of its own chemical and biological weapons capabilities shows contempt for the responsible controls and prohibitions that concerned UN officials are striving to establish.

This American attitude has never been more clearly demonstrated than by the US manipulation of the Organization for the Prohibition of Chemical Weapons (OPCW), the body responsible for enforcing the Chemical Weapons Convention. In April 2002 the United States, already in violation of the Convention (see Chapter 1), took further steps to ensure that the OPCW behaved only in ways that met with US approval.

The OPCW director-general, Jose Bustani, had worked for several years as a very successful head of the Organization. His inspectors had overseen the destruction of two million chemical weapons and two-thirds of the world's chemical weapons facilities, and he had raised the number of signatories to the Convention from 87 states to 145. In May 2000, as a tribute to his remarkable record, Bustani was re-elected unanimously by the member-states for a second five-year term, even though he had yet to complete his first one. US Secretary of State Colin Powell later wrote to him to thank him for his 'very impressive' work, but then Washington performed a spectacular U-turn. In January 2002 the US State Department asked the Brazilian government to recall Bustani on the ground that it did not like his 'management style' – a demand that directly contravenes the Chemical Weapons Convention ('the director-general . . . shall not seek or receive instructions from any government'). Brazil refused whereupon, in March, the US demanded Bustani's resignation.

The ultimate sin of Jose Bustani was his attempt to make the United States subject, like other countries, to the terms of the Convention. The OPCW, true to its mandate, had sought to examine facilities in the United States with the same rigour that it examined facilities anywhere else, causing Washington to denounce Bustani's 'ill-considered initiatives'. In denying the right of the OPCW to inspect American facilities, the United States was behaving in exactly the same way as Saddam Hussein – and Bustani would have to pay the price for exposing the fact.

On 21 April 2002 an emergency meeting opened in The Hague to hear an unprecedented American demand in international law – that the sitting head of a United Nations organization be ousted. Bustani declared: 'If one member state or even a few can dictate the departure of the director-general today, then who will do it tomorrow, and for what reason?' Washington remained bitterly resentful that Jose Bustani had tried to bring the United States within the law, and that he was working to bring Iraq within the terms of the Chemical Weapons Convention – which would have made it harder for the US to launch a new war over the weapons-inspection issue.

In the event, the United States secured Bustani's dismissal on 22 April – by the usual US method of coercing enough states to vote in support of American policy: 48 states voted for dismissal, 43 abstained, and only seven – courting US reprisals – were brave enough to support Bustani. As part of its coercive campaign, Washington had paid only half its annual dues to the OPCW, already in debt, making plain the choice facing the Organization's member states: support the Washington line or see the collapse of the OPCW. A senior OPCW member said, of American arm-twisting: 'This was clearly horrendous. We are now living in a completely different world.'

US War with the UN

At the same time and in a similar way the United States succeeded in removing Dr Robert Watson from his job as chairman of the UN-sponsored Intergovernmental Panel on Climate Change – since he had criticized America's energy policy. Here it emerged that the US oil company ExxonMobil – a big contributor to the Bush election campaign – had asked the White House to unseat Dr Watson, who the company said had an 'aggressive agenda'. Kate Hampton, for Friends of the Earth, commented: 'The Bush administration and its friends would rather shoot the messenger than listen to the message.'

Such examples show that the United States has no intention of observing either the letter or the spirit of the organizations and legal instruments developed by the UN to safeguard human rights and to protect peace, where such organizations and instruments are perceived as unhelpful to American policies. In particular, the implementation of US foreign policy suggests strongly that Washington is guilty of war crimes, crimes against humanity and – in the case of Iraq (and other states) – genocide ('1.6 Million Dead and Counting').

These crimes are specifically identified in Articles 6 to 8 of the Rome Statute of the International Criminal Court, adopted on 17 July 1998. In these circumstances, even though the Court cannot act retrospectively, the United States has shown bitter opposition to its creation – even to the point that in May 2002, when the Court was due to become effective, the Bush administration withdrew the American signature (prior to Congressional ratification) given by President Clinton. The Court, having secured enough state ratifications, was established – and Washington pledged to ignore it.

Dr Anthony Grayling, a senior lecturer at Birkbeck College, University of London, commented on the US attitude to the International Criminal Court:

> The Rome Treaty is one of the more hopeful things to have happened in recent years. America's bid to wreck it, or at least to stand aside from it, is not just unworthy but unacceptable. It is up to the rest of the world community to insist that the US should live by the same civilized rules that its own wisest counsel sees as desirable for everyone else.[24]

On June 30 the United States acted in support of its campaign to win legal immunity for all US military personnel overseas. Washington cast its veto in the UN Security Council to block the routine 6-month renewal of the UN's police-training operation in Bosnia. This was a way of forcing an American withdrawal from peacekeeping in the Balkans and of undermining the International Criminal Court. Kofi Annan, UN Secretary General, commented that the American move 'may have implications for all UN peace operations'. Again the United States had demonstrated its determination to ignore international law in pursuit of American foreign policy.

This accurately characterizes the American attitude, not only to the Court but to many other UN contributions in ethics and law. Through 2002 the American derelictions continued to accumulate. On 22 July the United States announced that it would not pay the $24 million that Washington owed to the United Nations for birth control programmes run by the UN Population Fund to assist poorer countries with family planning. On 24 July the Bush administration announced that it would not support a United Nations protocol designed to strengthen the international laws against torture. In August the United States was reportedly assuming powers to board any foreign ships on the high seas – a manifest abuse of international maritime law.

In such a fashion the United States variously ignores, exploits or abuses the UN machinery and legal instruments – in particular, suborning the Security Council, through bribery and intimidation, to serve American foreign policy. Washington's cynicism and contempt with regard to the United Nations are never more graphically illustrated than by the decades-long American support for Israeli ethical and legal derelictions.

SIX

The Israel Factor

The Relevance of Israel

The status of Israel is highly relevant to the US treatment of Iraq. In one interpretation the United States provoked the 1990 crisis and launched the 1991 Gulf War to prevent a destabilizing Israeli attack on Iraq's expanding military capacity. On 7 June 1981 Israeli aircraft had bombed an Iraqi nuclear reactor near Baghdad, an action that was condemned by the UN Security Council as a 'clear violation of the Charter of the United Nations and the norms of international conduct.' SCR 487 (1981)

– Condemned the military attack by Israel . . .

– Expressed deep concern about the danger to international peace and security caused by the premeditated Israeli air attack . . .

– Called upon Israel to refrain in the future from any such acts or threats. . .

– Considered that the Israeli attack constituted a serious threat to the entire IAEA safeguards regime . . .

– Recognized the inalienable sovereign right of Iraq . . . to establish programmes of technological and nuclear development . . .

– Considered that Iraq was entitled to appropriate redress for the destruction it has suffered, responsibility for which had been acknowledged by Israel.

However, despite the unambiguous words of Resolution 487, it was possible almost a decade later that Israel was planning further military strikes.

Iraq was, and remains, deeply hostile to what it rightly perceives as the Jewish theft of Arab land, and Israeli security could not be guaranteed if Iraq were allowed to become a powerful military state in the region. In this context it is not surprising that Washington remains keen to ensure a permanently emasculated Iraq while pumping arms and finance into Israel, ignoring its weapons of mass destruction, and underwriting its many ethical and legal derelictions.

From Holocaust to Sovereign State

For centuries, indeed millennia, the Jews had struggled for land and human rights.[1] The long agony of a dispossessed and persecuted people reached its climax in the 20th century when a Christian nation set about committing unspeakable outrages against humanity.[2] It is one of the supreme ironies of history that the obsessively anti-Semitic Adolf Hitler was one of the main forces behind the creation of the modern state of Israel. At the end of the First World War, Britain had assumed the Palestine mandate on behalf of the League of Nations, but in 1947, with no appetite for its mandated responsibilities, referred the Palestine question to the infant United Nations In the event, the UN Special Commission on Palestine (UNSCOP) recommended that the British mandate should be ended, that by September 1949 Palestine should be partitioned into sovereign Jewish and Arab states, and that Jerusalem should be inter-nationalized.

On 29 November 1947, the Arabs in Palestine and elsewhere watched with dismay as the UN General Assembly voted, by 33 to 13 (with 10 abstaining), for the creation of a Jewish state on Arab land. The Arabs, rightly seeing no justice in an imposed theft of Arab land, pledged that they would reject partition. The scene was set for all the turmoil of future decades.

The United States, a principal player in this situation, had vacillated throughout the period in which the Jews were creating their nation state on someone else's territory. What finally determined the US position was the need for campaign funds in a presidential election. President Harry Truman was facing re-election in 1948 and he desperately needed both the Jewish vote in New York, California and elsewhere, and Jewish financial support. Abe Feinberg, an ardent Zionist, organized a fund-raising drive for Truman that netted $100,000 (big money in 1948) within two days of a presidential appeal for cash. Other well-placed Jews, such as the jewellery store magnate Ed Kaufman, made substantial financial contributions, and such matters helped to concentrate the presidential mind. Stephen Smith, brother-in-law of John F. Kennedy, declared: 'Two million dollars went aboard the Truman train in a paper bag, and that's what paid for the state of Israel.'³ Truman had earned his money. He had not only swung the US vote but also, under Zionist pressure, ordered that quasi-colonies of the United States, such as the Philippines, Haiti and Liberia, vote for partition. The French were told that, if they did not vote for the creation of a Jewish state, they would lose American aid, whereupon they capitulated. Most of the authoritarian Latin American republics, firmly in the US camp, were happy to do as they were told (though some officials held out for hefty bribes).⁴ Jewish money had bought the vote that authorized the theft of Arab land.

The Palestinian Catastrophe (al-Nakba)

On 11 May 1949, Israel was admitted to the United Nations as a sovereign state. Israel, having become a signatory to the UN Charter, then set about violating its spirit and letter in the decades that followed. The Arabs, bitterly resenting the theft of land on which Arab families had lived for generations, were initially committed to the early destruction of what some Arab states chose to call the 'Zionist entity', but the Israeli response to legitimate Arab grievance has always been brutal and disproportionate, a US-supported abuse of Arab rights that has always inflamed a volatile situation.

The Palestinian Arabs, those not forced to become refugees, have always felt under political pressure and military siege, fearing fresh Israeli encroachments on residual Arab land. In August 1971 alone, Ariel Sharon's Israel Defence Force destroyed some 2000 Palestinian homes, making at least 16,000 people homeless. At that time thousands of Arabs were arrested, deported and murdered as Sharon sought to expand and consolidate the Israeli occupation of Arab land. The growing Jewish lobby in the United States guaranteed that such outrages would never provoke an effective response in the United Nations. The Security Council would pass frequent resolutions condemning Israeli behaviour and demanding remedial action, but Washington would only tolerate such resolutions on the assumption that no action would be taken by the international community in the event of Israeli non-compliance. In fact Israel chose to ignore all the UN resolutions designed to protect Arab rights.

The behaviour of Israel, reinforced by US diplomatic protection and massive shipments of arms and technology, has represented a decades-long humiliation for the United Nations. Israel has consistently flouted UN resolutions, Conventions and Statements, violating the UN Charter and many elements of international humanitarian law, but Washington has never permitted the international community to respond with sanctions or other measures. Israel is a nation apart, above the law, a continuing rebuke to those people working to strengthen international law and respect for human rights. When, by contrast, Iraq is perceived as ignoring UN resolutions, a years-long genocide is visited on its people. When Israel does the same, it is rewarded with billion-dollar arms shipments, trade agreements and overt political approval.

Some Abused UN Resolutions

One of the main Security Council resolutions on Israel, which it has successfully resisted for more than three decades, is Resolution 242 (22 November 1967), which urges the 'withdrawal of Israeli armed forces' from what was then recently-occupied territory. After further Arab/Israeli conflict, SCR 242 became transmogrified into Resolution 338 (22 October 1973), which demanded the implementation of Resolution 242 'in all of its parts'. Israel, citing the need for national security and confident of US support, ignored SCR 338 just as it had long ignored 242. These were not the only Security Council products that Israel chose to ignore over the years. Thus, with tacit approval from Washington, Israel has made no attempt to observe the demands and conditions laid out in:

— *Resolution 465* (1 March 1980), which condemns Israel's restrictions on Arab freedom of travel, its illegal changes to the status of occupied Arab territories, and its 'flagrant violation' of the Geneva Convention relative to the Protection of Civilian Persons in Time of War.

— *Resolution 476* (30 June 1980), which condemns the prolonged occupation of Arab lands, illegal changes to the status of Jerusalem, and Israel's 'flagrant violation' of the Geneva Convention.

— *Resolution 478* (20 August 1980), which condemns a violation of international law over Jerusalem, the continued violation of the Geneva Convention, and the consequent 'serious obstruction to achieving a comprehensive, just and lasting peace in the Middle East'.

— *Resolution 672* (13 October 1990), which condemns the killing in Jerusalem of more than 20 Palestinians and the injuring of more than 150 people, 'including Palestinian civilians and innocent worshippers', and demands that Israel observe its obligations under the Fourth Geneva Convention.

The Israel Factor

– *Resolution 673* (24 October 1990), which notes 'the continued deterioration of the situation in the occupied territories', and deplores the refusal of Israel 'to receive the mission of the Secretary-General to the region'.

Resolutions 672 and 673 are particularly significant since the Security Council adopted them unanimously a few weeks after the 1990 Iraqi invasion of Kuwait and during the run-up to the 1991 Gulf War. Here was a situation in which Israel's flouting of international law, its ignoring of UN resolutions, and its denial of human rights – as expressly recorded in the relevant resolutions – were met by no more than a reprimand; whereas Iraq's derelictions were to bring a massive military response, leading to the total devastation of a country, several hundred thousand immediate Iraqi fatalities, and millions of casualties over subsequent years.

The United States had been in a dilemma. Its support for Israel was not affected by the further slaughter of Palestinians on 8 October 1990, but it seemed that the anti-Iraq Coalition, usefully containing some Arab states, might be damaged. With Egypt, Kuwait and Saudi Arabia then horrified at the scale of the Palestinian casualties, it was plain that Washington would have to make some gesture. When Iraqi troops had fired on protesting Kuwaitis, killing one woman, the Americans had immediately called the act 'murder'. Now President George Bush brought himself to declare that the Israeli killing of 20 Palestinians and the wounding of more than 150 was 'saddening'. In addition, Bush managed to persuade President Mitterrand to moderate a draft resolution condemning the Israeli action. Palestinian leaders had made a desperate appeal to the Security Council: 'We do not understand how the Security Council can ignore our plea for protection when it is prepared to send troops to fight a war in the Gulf region. Once again we issue a plea to the civilized world . . . Protect us against Israeli soldiers, settlers and armed religious zealots.' No such protection was forthcoming.

War Crimes in Lebanon

The Israeli mindset was already well understood by the Arabs of the region. In June 1982 Israeli forces, using the latest and most sophisticated American weapons, had invaded Lebanon causing huge human casualties and massive material damage. An estimated 20,000 people, mostly civilians, were killed and more than 100,000 were made homeless. More than 6000 children, Lebanese and Palestinian, were orphaned. The damage to buildings and other civic installations amounted to billions of dollars.

141

In August 1982 a prestigious body of international jurists convened to examine Israel's legal status in the light of the invasion of Lebanon. This International Commission of Enquiry addressed a number of questions:

1. Has the Government of Israel committed acts of aggression contrary to international law?

2. Have the Israeli armed forces made use of weapons or methods of warfare forbidden by international law, including the laws of war?

3. Have . . . prisoners been subjected to treatment forbidden by international law, including inhuman or degrading treatment?

4. Has there been deliberate or indiscriminate or reckless bombardment of . . . hospitals, schools or other non-military targets?

5. Has there been systematic bombardment or other destruction of towns, cities, villages or refugee camps?

6. Have the acts of the Israeli armed forces caused the dispersal, deportation, or ill-treatment of populations, in violation of international law?

7. Has the Government of Israel valid reasons under international law for its invasion . . . for the manner in which it conducted hostilities, or for its actions as an occupying force?

8. To what extent . . . were the Israeli authorities or forces involved . . . in the massacres . . . in the refugee camps of Sabra and Chatila in the Beirut area between the dates of 16 and 18 September?[6]

The Commission, having considered the evidence and the relevant rules of law, concluded that Israel had committed many violations of international law. These included: aggression, the use of forbidden weapons, the inhuman and degrading treatment of prisoners, the bombing of civilian targets, the deportation of populations, and involvement in the Sabra and Chatila massacres.[7] The majority of the Commission concluded that Israel had committed acts that constituted 'a form of genocide'.[8] Graphic details were included concerning many of the Israeli violations, including the Sabra and Chatila massacres, perpetrated by the Lebanese militiamen with Israeli assistance:

. . . piles of bodies were found . . . people had been executed against walls and other patterns of the slaughter included families being butchered en masse in their homes and victims who had been tied up with rope and subjected to other forms of torture before being executed . . . militiamen killing five women and children . . . a Palestinian doctor . . . was shot dead while carrying a white flag . . . a Palestinian nurse, Intisar Ismail, aged 19 . . . had been repeatedly raped and murdered . . . Two nurses were taken. One was raped ten times and then killed . . . gunmen start entering the houses, killing men, women and children . . . the screaming of women and children . . .[9]

The total number of dead has never been determined with certainty. The International Committee of the Red Cross initially counted 1500 corpses, many of them slashed, mutilated and blown apart. By 22 September 1982 the count had risen to 2400, and on the following day a further 350 bodies were found: 'The precise number of deaths is impossible to ascertain. Many bodies were removed from the scene; others were placed in huge mass graves.' The Commission, noting the terrible events at Sabra and Chatila, recorded also 'the extent to which *Israeli participation in prior massacres directed against the Palestinian people creates a most disturbing pattern of political struggle carried on by means of mass terror directed at the civilians, including women, children and the aged*' (my italics).[10]

More Illegal Expulsions

The Israeli abuse of the Palestinian civilian population continued through the 1980s and beyond. On 14 December 1992, after further actions by Hamas, an extremist Palestinian organization, the Israeli authorities sealed off the West Bank and Gaza. Three days later, Israel dumped more than 400 Palestinians, without food or water, in a desolate area of southern Lebanon. Washington voiced 'strong objections' to this gross abuse of human rights, whereupon the Security Council adopted Resolution 799 denouncing the outrage. SCR 799 noted Israel's new violation of the Fourth Geneva Convention, reaffirmed the sovereignty of Lebanon, and demanded that Israel 'ensure the safe and immediate return to the occupied territories of all those deported'. US President-elect Bill Clinton announced that he was 'concerned'. No serious effort was made to force Israeli compliance with Security Council Resolution 799. The UN Secretary-General, Boutros Boutros-Ghali, indicated that he might urge sanctions on Israel but no one imagined that Washington would support such a course. Again Israel had violated international law and ignored the resulting Security Council resolution.

Eventually, after many international expressions of outrage, the Israeli government offered a compromise. Perhaps a quarter of the deportees – some of them sick and deported in error – might be allowed to return. SCR 799 had demanded the return of '*all* those deported' (my italics), and Israel was offering to take back perhaps 100 out of the 400. US Secretary of State Warren Christopher declared: 'The US believes that this process is consistent with UN resolutions . . . further action by the Security Council is unnecessary and could even undercut the process under way . . .'[11] Israel had demonstrated yet again that it could act with impunity in violating international law, enjoying American support whatever the ethical or legal dereliction.

Israel was now pursuing the dual-track policy of consolidating its grip on occupied Arab land and pushing for yet more territory. The Palestinians were being denied permits to build on their own land, while the Israeli government was encouraging the expansion of Jewish settlements into Arab territory. On 29 August 2000 some two hundred heavily armoured Israeli troops, supported by army helicopters buzzing overhead, sealed off the Shofat refugee camp near Jerusalem and destroyed three Palestinian houses that had been built without Israeli permission. Palestinians argued with the troops as bulldozers moved in to destroy the Arab homes, while construction work could be seen nearby at the Jewish settlement of Pisgat Zeev. A Palestinian statement complained about the new Israeli aggression, 'another sign that while Israel talks of peace at the negotiation table, its actions on the ground reflect a war mentality'. Eric Asherman, a member of Rabbis for Human Rights, denounced the Israeli action as an attempt to deprive the Palestinians of the basic right to housing.

'Excessive Use of Force'

It had become apparent also that Israeli snipers were using hollow-nosed bullets, the 'dumdum' bullets banned in international law, against stone-throwing Arab youths.[12] Such bullets opened like an umbrella on impact, and then spun about to mangle internal organs. Dr Hosni Atari, having treated seven wounded Palestinians, commented that the bullets were 'intended to cause the maximum amount of damage to a person'.[13] On 7 October, in response to escalating Israeli attacks on the Palestinians, the UN Security Council adopted Resolution 1322 condemning the Israeli action. This resolution, despite serious American misgivings, recorded that the Security Council:

1. *Deplores* the provocation carried out by the Israelis at Al-Haram Al-Sharif in Jerusalem on 28 September 2000, and the subsequent violence there and at other Holy Places, as well as in other areas throughout the territories occupied by Israel since 1967, resulting in over 80 Palestinian deaths and many other casualties;

2. *Condemns* acts of violence, especially the excessive use of force against Palestinians, resulting in injury and loss of human life;

3. *Calls upon* Israel, the occupying Power, to abide scrupulously by its legal obligations and its responsibilities under the Fourth Geneva Convention relative to the Protection of Civilian Persons in Time of War of 12 August 1949.

Other paragraphs urged an end to violence, the need for an enquiry into 'the tragic events of the last few days', and an 'immediate resumption' of negotiations to achieve an early settlement between the two sides. The UN condemnation of the Israeli actions, signalling the gravity of what had been perpetrated, was truly remarkable, bearing in mind the US veto powers in the Security Council. However, SCR 1322 remained mere words: Washington would prevent the international community from taking any punitive action against its delinquent ally.

Israel was now blockading the Palestinian areas, one of its many chosen methods of imposing 'collective punishment'. Mr Roed-Larsen, a respected Norwegian negotiator, observed: 'Palestinian living conditions are falling fast, and safety nets are wearing thin.' He had witnessed a 'stark increase' in poverty among the Palestinians, now being denied many basic commodities. Palestinian unemployment had reached 40 per cent; 9000 Palestinians were wounded; massive tax revenues had been lost; and the al-Mazen Centre for Human Rights in Gaza claimed that Israeli heavy weapons had destroyed 431 houses, 13 public buildings, 10 factories and 14 religious buildings in a six-week period. The Israeli forces had also attacked Palestinian agriculture, destroying more than 44,000 trees, mainly grapevines and other agricultural trees. Some Israelis were pressing for even harsher measures, tighter economic isolation and a cutting off of power supplies. Roed-Larsen commented:

> This policy is fuelling anger and is the major instrument for the radicalisation of the population. The risk here is that one produces through these policies a new generation of Palestinians whose hatred, anger and resentment will

stay for decades. This, in the longer and shorter term, is the greatest threat to the security situation.[14]

There were no signs that the Israelis were about to alter their harshly vindictive policies. The bulldozers had driven scores of Palestinians from their homes in the Gaza Strip, crushed livestock, and destroyed hundreds of acres of citrus and palm groves. Qasem Ali, an expert on militant Islamic movements and with a doctorate from St Anthony's College, Oxford, said that the Israelis were 'driving the most moderate of academics into the camp of extremists', and seemed 'incapable of understanding' the vicious circle that they were creating. Mrs al-Bayouq, a Palestinian, commented on what she had witnessed: 'They gave us no warning. We had watched them bulldozing the orchards for days and we never thought they would come to our houses. Then they just drove up and started to crush our homes. We ran out with what we could carry, but the animals were all buried. When we tried to sit on our land, they shot over our heads and so we fled.'[15]

At the same time Israel was continuing to demonstrate its contempt for the United Nations. In early December 2000 Israeli soldiers pushed, kicked and detained Palestinians escorting Terje-Rod Larsen, a UN envoy, as he tried to inspect a former girls' school seized by Israeli forces and converted into a military base. The incident was reported to UN Secretary-General Kofi Annan. On 12 January 2001 Israel was claiming that it could not give UN peacekeepers maps of minefields in south Lebanon since such maps did not exist. In violation of normal military convention no minefield charts had been kept, putting the peacekeepers at risk as they tried to clear the deadly residue of the Israeli occupation. Three Lebanese soldiers were wounded as they struggled to defuse a mine near the town of Marjayoun. On 10 February, Israel was making it clear that it would not cooperate with a UN mission due to start gathering human rights information in the Middle East. The team, set to investigate the sweeping 'collective punishment' imposed by Israel on 1.2 million Palestinian civilians in Gaza, intended to 'investigate humanitarian rights violations and breaches of international humanitarian law'. Israel, whose troops had killed hundreds of young Palestinians and wounded thousands, called the enquiry 'vile and one-sided'. Mary Robinson, UN Human Rights Commissioner, had declared herself 'shocked, dismayed and even devastated' at what she had witnessed in the region.

On 14 February, in response to the killing of eight Israelis, Israel sealed off more Palestinian areas as an expansion of the 'collective punishment' campaign. Tens of thousands of Palestinians had already been banned from travelling to work, and now the situation was continuing to deteriorate. Palestinian leader

Yasser Arafat commented: 'What is happening is an Israeli military escalation that has direct consequences on the feelings of the Palestinian people. If the military escalation and the use of internationally-banned weapons continues, no doubt it will be a difficult position for everyone.' Now Israel was also attracting international criticism for its admitted policy of assassinating leading Palestinians, with even Britain expressing shock at the 'murder' of Massoud Ayad, a bodyguard of Yasser Arafat. At least a dozen Palestinians had been assassinated in this way.[16] On 21 February, Amnesty International condemned Israel's use of death squads as 'a policy of state assassination' and declared: 'The acceptance by Israel of unlawful killings and the failure to investigate each killing at the hands of the security services is leading to a culture of impunity among Israeli soldiers and it is fuelling a cycle of violence and revenge in the region.' Now, witnessing an escalation of Israeli attacks, Palestinian officials were pleading for UN protection – an option that Washington would be sure to block. Israel and the United States, keen to demonstrate their solidarity, were currently carrying out joint missile tests in the Israeli desert.

It was now emerging that thousands of Palestinian boys and young men would be permanently disabled following the escalation of Israeli violence.* Some 11,000 Palestinians had been wounded, many by the fragmentation bullets fired by Israeli M-16 weapons. Such ammunition was known to break into tiny pieces after penetration, much like illegal dumdum bullets, causing multiple internal injuries but not always death. Hospitals in the West Bank and Jordan were accumulating X-rays that showed what the forensic specialists were calling a 'lead snowstorm', the clear fragmentation of high-velocity ammunition often fired at close range. Thus, at the Eretz checkpoint dividing Gaza from Israel, troops fired at 18 Palestinian stone-throwers from a distance of 25 metres. The 18-year-old Fadi Mohamed was hit by a single bullet that shattered two vertebrae, damaged his kidney and paralysed both legs. The 15-year-old Mahmoud al-Medhoun was shot three times by Israeli soldiers firing from a tank. Doctors removed part of his colon, and his right leg was paralysed.

The Israeli forces have used a wide range of high-calibre munitions, including concrete-busting machine-gun bullets, grenade launchers, 120-mm tank shells and Hellfire rockets fired from US-supplied Apache attack helicopters. Rubber-coated steel balls ('rubber bullets') have been used at close

---

* John Mahoney, Executive Director of Americans for Middle East Understanding (AMEU) has described in detail the Israeli tactics: deliberately crippling Arab youths to keep mortality statistics down; use of 'dumdum' bullets, poisoning of Palestinian wells with typhus and dysentery bacteria, use of tear gas in confined spaces (causing deaths), firing of toxin-bearing needles, use of depleted-uranium munitions, etc. (see Mahoney, *The Link*, AMEU, January–March 2001).

range to kill and cause permanent injuries. There was evidence that the Israelis were deliberately wounding large numbers of Palestinian youths. Dr Robert Kirschner of the Nobel-Prize-winning Physicians for Human Rights commented: 'I consider it a form of torture. There's no question in my mind' that Israeli troops intended 'to wound people as a form of intimidation of the population . . . probably several thousand young Palestinian men will end up with permanent disabilities.'[17] More than 95 per cent of the dead and wounded have been Palestinians or Israeli Arabs, with the Israel Defence Force admitting that, in the vast majority of clashes, there was no Palestinian gunfire. One IDF sniper said that Palestinians could be fired upon if they seemed to be over the age of 12: 'Twelve and up is allowed'; and a senior IDF officer commented: 'Nobody can convince me that we didn't needlessly kill dozens of children.'[18]

Laying Siege to Civilians

In early March, the Ariel Sharon government was urging Israel's parliament to approve a law that would allow the security services to torture Arab prisoners. Shin Bet officers, commenting on their interrogations of 'hundreds of Palestinians every day', complained that it had taken them a long time to obtain a confession from a Palestinian girl: 'If we had been allowed to apply physical pressure she would have confessed after a couple of hours.' Palestinian prisoners were known to have died under Shin Bet torture, and in fact 'moderate physical pressure' was allowed until September 1999. Now it seemed likely that the Israeli security services would again be resorting to torture, prohibited by international law.[19] In the West Bank the Israeli forces, sealing off more Palestinian communities, were effectively creating detention camps for much of the Arab population. Palestinian protesters against this policy were being attacked by Israeli troops using a new type of weapon, 'flechette' ammunition, an anti-personnel cluster bomb or rifle grenade that sprays a target with dozens of needle-like projectiles.

The Israeli forces had sealed off much of the West Bank and Gaza, effectively making more than 100,000 Palestinian workers unemployed. Many Palestinian towns and cities were under siege, roads were blocked with concrete blocks and mounds of bulldozed earth, armoured personnel carriers were positioned at the entrances to Palestinian communities, and hundreds of thousands of men, women and children were struggling to survive in circumstances of growing deprivation. Even Washington was now warning Israel that it would be unhelpful to force the collapse of the tottering Palestinian Authority, and the European Union was considering action against Israel to protest its abuse of human rights.[20] Chris Patten, the EU Commissioner for External Relations, commented: 'It does not seem to us that everything that is being done in the West Bank and Gaza can be justified in security terms.'[21] Patten then observed that the Israeli-imposed siege, which had cost the Palestinian economy well over $1 billion, would only exacerbate the security problems of the region.

On 15 March 2001 Israeli troops threw a stun grenade into the courtyard of a school in the West Bank city of Hebron, seriously injuring six children aged from 10 to 13. The children were carried screaming from the school into ambulances. One child, being treated for burns to his hand and back, said that the Israelis had thrown the grenade 'while we were sitting there'. A few days later, the Israeli authorities in Jerusalem were approving the building of 3000 more homes at Har Homa, one of the most controversial Zionist settlements on the edge of the city. Prime Minister Ehud Barak had pushed ahead with plans to build 6400 homes at the site, and few observers doubted that the newly-elected Ariel Sharon had every intention of encouraging further encroachments on Palestinian territory. There were now some 150 Jewish settlements in the West Bank and Gaza, effectively fragmenting the Palestinian regions and providing a pretext for repeated Israeli troop incursions. Ariel Sharon, once famously described by US Secretary of State James Baker as 'an obstacle to peace', had now visited Washington and 'astutely pressed all the Bush buttons'.[22] Continued US protection for Israel, whatever the crimes against humanity, was guaranteed.

The Israeli authorities were now hampering the work of charities struggling to help beleaguered Palestinian families. On 23 March Walter Stocker, Head of the International Committee of the Red Cross (ICRC) office in Jerusalem, complained that Israel was hindering the charity's efforts to supply aid. The aim was to help 120 Palestinian families in the Gaza Strip whose homes had been demolished by the Israeli forces, and 35,000 people in 60 West Bank villages where joblessness had soared because of the Israeli siege. Stocker declared that Israel's closure of towns and villages breached international humanitarian law enshrined in the 1949 Fourth Geneva Convention, and that Israeli troops were firing on clearly-marked ambulances. The members of the Arab League, having ended a two-day summit in Jordan, pledged financial aid to the Palestinians, edged towards an economic boycott of Israel, and expressed 'dismay and rejection' of the US veto in the UN Security Council of a move to send an official observer force to Gaza and the West Bank. James Cunningham, US representative in the UN, declared that the proposed resolution was 'unbalanced and unworkable and hence unwise'. If Israel were to persist with its crimes against humanitarian law, it was inappropriate that there should be any international witnesses.

The Bush Posture

President Bush was soon making his position very clear: the Palestinians should stop the violence, and he hoped that Yasser Arafat would hear the message 'loud and clear'.[23] No matter that the vast majority of the casualties were Arab; no matter that more Palestinian land was being stolen; no matter that Palestinian homes were being bulldozed, that Palestinian towns and villages were under siege, that Israeli policies – in violation of the Geneva Convention – were striking at Palestinian civilian communities.[24] Bush was now signalling an American attitude that was enraging much of the Arab world. The *al-Bayan* newspaper, United Arab Emirates, commented: 'The blatant US bias towards Israel and its repressive practices against the Palestinian people . . . reveals the contempt of the United States towards Arab feelings and human rights.' In Saudi Arabia the *al-Madina* newspaper declared that the US veto of the proposed Security Council resolution was a blatant attempt to prevent anybody from arresting Israeli violence: 'This honest [peace] broker does not want anybody to intervene in the right of death to ensure that the result was in favour of the stronger party.' Hanan Ashrawi, a member of the Palestinian Legislative Council, judged that Israel would not have dared to escalate the violence 'without American approval, and without American consent on the use of its weapons, including the Apache helicopters'.[25]

The Palestinian casualties were continuing to mount. The Western media gave much prominence to the tragic death of a Jewish baby in March, but in recent months some five Palestinian girls, aged between 24 days and ten years, had been killed by the Israelis. For example, the 22-month-old Baru Abu Samra died of a brain aneurysm caused when a bomb hit her home. Sama Uweidah, general coordinator of the Arab Women's Forum in Ramallah, spoke of the death of Palestinian girls and women: 'Some of them died on detours they take to go to work, to university, to do the shopping or to get medical treatment for themselves or a member of their families.'[26] Women in need of urgent medical attention had died en route to hospital after Israeli soldiers had knowingly delayed their ambulances. Some women had been shot dead in front of their houses, and the Israeli use of gas attacks in residential areas had caused miscarriages and infant deaths. In one estimate the Israeli troops had wounded 21,900 Palestinian civilians.[27]

Building Illegal Settlements

Israel was continuing to expand the illegal settlements, bringing Western criticism, including US condemnation of the scheme. The sieges were being maintained and Palestinian property was being destroyed. On 11 April 2001 Israeli tanks and bulldozers razed 32 homes, leaving 400 more Palestinians homeless and two more dead. Peter Hansen, head of the UN Relief and Works Agency for Palestine and the Middle East (UNRWA), commented: 'If Mr Ariel Sharon wants to increase anger and hatred and deepen the vicious circle we're in, then this is probably the way to do it. It is difficult to imagine a peace process being built on the ruins of the homes here.'[28] Every element of the Khan Younis homes had been destroyed – furniture, clothes, cookers, carpets and mattresses – bulldozed into the rubble of the Palestinian houses. The resulting firefight left two Palestinians dead and 40 more wounded: 'Like the nightly shelling of Beit Jalla village, the Israeli onslaught on Khan Younis was more than disproportionate; it was a deliberate attack on civilians . . . Needless to say, Mr Bush was silent.'[29]

It had become increasingly obvious that the Iraq and Palestinian situations were intimately linked. In April 2001 Jawad al-Hamad, President of the Amman-based Middle East Studies Centre, expressed a common perception in the region:

> The sanctions are part of the US plan to weaken the Arab stand against Israel. The Americans believe Iraq is playing a key role in building up Arab solidarity against the interests of the US and Israel in the region. Iraq has always served as the strategic centre of the Arab world against any foreign military aggression.

He observed that, in this context, the US-led war in 1991 had three main targets, besides liberating Kuwait. These objectives were:

1. weakening Arab solidarity against Israel;

2. undermining any developing ties between Iraq and the Arab Gulf states, and

3. controlling the oil resources of the Gulf.

'Iraq's strategic importance irritated the US and Israel and was an obstacle to flexing their political and military muscles against the Arab world.'[30] Here it was acknowledged that the United States was being driven to formulate a new policy in the region, if only because of the mounting international opposition to the economic embargo: 'It is true that the US is formulating a new policy towards Iraq, but it will not last for long as its allies in the Arab region are more aware of its intentions' (Jawad al-Hamad).[31]

The bulk of the Western media continued to represent the Israeli–Palestinian conflict in terms that suggested parity between the two sides, where compromises should be made by Jews and Arabs alike. In reality, the parties to the dispute remained totally mismatched, with the Palestinians completely out-gunned and under comprehensive siege in shrinking communities that were being denied the very essentials of life.

On 14 May 2001 there was a fresh spate of unprecedented violence against the impoverished Palestinian areas of Gaza and the West Bank. Elements of the US-armed Israeli Army, Navy and Air Force launched heavy assaults on residential and other targets, with the densely-populated Gaza rocketed from Navy gunboats, Air Force helicopters and surface-to-surface Army missiles. Dozens of Palestinians were killed and hundreds injured. When Yasser Arafat, President of the Palestinian Authority, denounced the Israeli onslaught against defenceless communities, US Secretary of State Colin Powell commented: 'That kind of language I don't think is very helpful, especially during the time Israel is celebrating its anniversary.'[*]

There was fresh international criticism of the new Israeli aggression, though no suggestion that the United States would halt the flow of weapons to Israel. On 18 May, UN Secretary-General Kofi Annan declared that he was deeply disturbed 'by the disproportionate Israeli response' to Palestinian actions.

Such strictures did nothing to discourage Israeli attacks on Palestinian communities. Through June and July, the Israelis continued their policy of bulldozing Palestinian homes, tightening the siege of Palestinian areas, destroying agricultural plantations, and assassinating Palestinian leaders. On 11 July, Israel responded to international criticism by pledging to continue its policy of demolishing Palestinian homes.[32] The Arab casualties, vastly greater than those on the Israeli side, continued to mount. One newly-born Palestinian baby died when the mother and baby were delayed at an Israeli checkpoint. On 17 July Israel sent fresh tank and infantry units into the West Bank, while missiles were launched at a Palestinian farm south of Bethlehem. As tanks and hundreds of Israeli troops moved to the edge of Palestinian towns, the Israeli spokesman Avi Pazner commented: 'This is a stop sign. This concentration of troops is a message to Arafat: Stop violence, stop terrorism.' But however, where the Israeli casualties were numbered in the dozens, the Palestinian casualties amounted to

---

[*] 15 May was the 53rd anniversary of Israel's declaration of 'independence'. To the Palestinians it is commemorated as Al-Nakba ('the Catastrophe').

tens of thousands. In the six years of the first *intifada* (Palestinian uprising, 1987–93) the Israelis wounded some 18,000 Palestinians; in the first months alone of the new *intifada* (October 2000), the Israelis shot and injured more than 7000 Palestinians.[33]

Israel was refusing to accept international monitors in the region;[34] on 20 July 2001, Jewish gunmen fired dozens of bullets into a Palestinian car carrying eight people home from a pre-wedding party, killing or wounding seven adults and killing also the three-month-old Diza Tmaizeh;[35] Ariel Sharon, the Israeli Prime Minister, was being forced to hire a lawyer in response to Belgian charges that he was implicated in the 1982 Sabra and Chatila massacres;[36] and Israel was continuing its policies of laying military siege to Palestinian communities, destroying Arab homes and agriculture, using weapons banned in international law, and expanding Israeli settlements onto fresh Arab land in Gaza and the West Bank.

The Aggression Continues

In August 2001 the United States, as an obvious co-belligerent of Israel in its war against the Palestinians, signalled that it would not object to the use of US-supplied helicopters in targeted assassinations. The US Arms Export Control Act requires that US weapons supplied to other countries be used only for defensive purposes, but Washington was quite ready to agree with Prime Minister Sharon when he claimed to acting in 'self-defence'. In the same spirit of military cooperation, the US and Israel were continuing to work together on missile research. Thus the Arrow missile system developed jointly by American and Israeli technicians, was tested successfully at the Palmachim test site in Israel and was scheduled to be tested again in 2003 at the White Sands US Army testing site in New Mexico. Washington was funding the full-scale deployment of the system, estimated to cost the US taxpayer an extra $2–$7 billion over the next few years. In addition, the United States was funding two further programmes to complement the Arrow system: the Boost Phase Intercept Programme ($53 million) and the Tactical High Energy Laser ($139 million). In one estimate, Washington was contributing $10 billion a year to Israel to maintain its military dominance in the region.[37]

The Israeli government was continuing to authorize the building of settlements – condemned as illegal by SCR 452 – on occupied Arab land. Some two dozen settlements were built in the West Bank during 2001, expanding the number of Israelis illegally occupying Arab land to more than 200,000. Moreover, the rate of settlement building was accelerated under Sharon.

Between February 2001, when Sharon came to power, and March 2002, some three dozen new settlements were built, compounding both the tensions in the region and Israel's violations of international law.[38] The building of illegal Israeli settlements has been widely condemned as one of the principal obstacles to peace, not least in the Mitchell Report (April 2001): 'The Government of Israel should freeze all settlement activity, including the "natural growth" of existing settlements.'[39]

By 2002 the situation had deteriorated yet further. Some 114 signatories of the Geneva Convention, gathering in Switzerland on 5 December 2001, together reprimanded Israel for its 'indiscriminate and disproportionate violence' against Palestinian civilians in the occupied territories. A joint declaration expressed deep concern about a 'deterioration of the humanitarian situation' in Palestinian areas, condemned the Jewish settlements as 'illegal' and urged Israel to refrain from 'grave breaches' such as 'unlawful deportation', 'wilful killing' and 'torture'. The Palestinians, responding in desperation to their endless humiliation and abuse, sent suicide bombers into Israel and caused dozens of Jewish casualties – which in turn provoked a massively disproportionate military invasion of the West Bank and Gaza by the Israeli armed forces.

Two Security Council resolutions, 1402 (30 March 2002) and 1403 (4 April 2002), and then President Bush and Secretary of State Colin Powell, called for a withdrawal of Israeli troops from Palestinian cities 'without delay'. Sharon, true to form, ignored the UN resolutions and – to the public humiliation of Bush – his US ally. The new Israeli aggression, begun on 29 March 2002, had caused thousands of civilian casualties, wrecked the administrative machinery of the Palestinian Authority, and plunged the Palestinian people into even deeper destitution and despair.

The Israeli armed forces, under the cover of its own alleged 'war against the terrorist infrastructure', had targeted homes, office buildings, civil computer records, water supplies, electricity systems, hospitals, ambulances, churches, highways, refugee camps and civilians. Israel itself claimed to have killed hundreds, and then retracted the claim, with independent observers saying that 'extrajudicial killings' and 'massacres' had taken place. Israel ignored SCRs 1402 and 1403, the unambiguous UN demand for an Israeli withdrawal from the new occupied Palestinian towns and cities, and it was about to ignore yet another Security Council resolution.

On 16 April 2002 the UN Human Rights Commission denounced Israel for what it called 'mass killings' of Palestinians, and demanded the withdrawal of Israeli troops from the Palestinian territories. A commission resolution condemned Israel for 'gross violations' of human rights, including arbitrary detentions, shelling of Palestinian residential areas and the killing of Palestinian civilians in refugee camps, including Jenin.[40] The Palestinians were claiming that hundreds of bodies had been buried in mass graves in Jenin, with many more bodies transported out of the area by the Israelis to disguise the scale of the massacre. On 19 April 2002 the UN Security Council adopted Resolution 1405 – noting 'the dire humanitarian situation of the Palestinian civilian population' in Jenin; calling for a lifting of the Israeli restrictions 'on the operation of humanitarian organizations'; and stressing the need of all concerned 'to respect the universally accepted norms of international humanitarian law'.

The new Security Council resolution welcomed the initiative of Kofi Annan to send a high-level fact-finding team to the Jenin refugee camp to ascertain the scale of death and destruction. Israel, inviting further worldwide criticism, decided to argue about the character of the team and its operational terms of reference. By the end of April 2002 the team, authorized by Resolution 1405, had still not been allowed to begin its mission – whereupon a pliant Kofi Annan, unwilling to contest the Israeli intransigence backed by Washington, aborted his fact-finding initiative.[41]

The character of the Sharon regime, claiming to be acting against terrorism just as the United States was acting in Afghanistan, was plain for the world to see. Now the Bush–Blair axis, with the approval of the Sharon government, was planning a new war on another Arab nation.

SEVEN

Towards an Arab Consensus?

Arab Heterogeneity

The Arab Nation, though rooted in Islam, is not a homogenous entity but a deeply fragmented mix of beliefs, attitudes and politics. Secular monarchists, religious monarchists, would-be democrats, Ba'thist authoritarians, secular dictators – all jostle together in the Arab world. A common element, apart from multifaceted Islam, is the colonial past suffered by all the regional states, variously dominated, abused and exploited in recent history by European imperialism: Italian, French, British. Today the United States – lured in the traditional way by prospects of commercial hegemony, oil resources and strategic advantage – imposes a dominant imperialism. The differences and similarities between the Arab states, all clouded by the shadow of American ambition, have shaped the responses of the Arab Nation to Iraq in recent years.

A Route to Consensus?

Towards the end of the 1990s there were growing signs that various Arab states, increasingly responsive to national outrage at the sufferings of the Iraqi civilian population, were prepared to contemplate the possibility of challenging US policy in the region. Washington's support for the Israeli abuse of the Palestinians was doing nothing to buttress America's anti-Iraq policies, and soon it was clear that the gradual rehabilitation of Saddam Hussein into the Arab world had begun. For example, Jordan, still prepared to prosecute an Italian pilot, Nicolas Trifani, for flying through Jordanian airspace to Baghdad, was considering sending its own relief aircraft to Iraq. On 20 April 2000 the United Arab Emirates became the fourth country from the six-nation Gulf Cooperation Council (GCC) – after Bahrain, Oman and Qatar – to renew its diplomatic representation in Baghdad. The UAE diplomat Sheikh Ahmad bin Abdullah reopened the embassy at a simple ceremony at the Rashid Hotel, chosen to temporarily house the mission. Sheikh Ahmad declared to reporters that the reopening was 'a reactivation of cooperation between two brotherly countries and aims to help charity associations deliver aid to the Iraqi people and help their mission in Iraq'. At the same time the UAE role 'will consist of helping Emirati businessmen and tourists travel to Iraq and also help Iraqis, including businessmen, travel to the UAE'. Bahrain had announced that it would open its Baghdad embassy on 'humanitarian grounds' after the ten-year break.

In early June the Qatari foreign minister, Sheikh Hamad bin Jassim, presented a proposal to the Gulf Cooperation Council that the GCC members, including Kuwait and Saudi Arabia, should begin a regional initiative to lift the economic sanctions on Iraq. A subsequent GCC statement declared: 'The ministers listened to an explanation by the Qatari Foreign Minister on ideas to end the humanitarian suffering of the Iraq people.' However, the Arab states were still anguishing over the extent to which they could flout the will of the United States. The Iraqi parliament, well aware of this sensitivity, had appealed to Jordan 'to allow civil air traffic between Iraq and the rest of the world as this does not contravene UN resolutions'. What would Washington say? When Sheikh Ahmad raised the UAE flag at the Rashid Hotel he gave no overt support to an anti-sanctions campaign, but there were obvious signs of a growing Arab desire for solidarity in the face of Israeli and American threats.

On 7 August 2000 Saeed H. Hasan, Iraq's Permanent Representative to the United Nations, lodged a letter with the President of the Security Council, noting the 'increasing calls' in the Arab world and elsewhere 'for the lifting of the inhuman sanctions that have been maintained against Iraq for more than 10 years and for a halt to all forms of aggression against the country . . .' Thus the Council for Arab Economic Unity – whose membership includes Syria, Jordan, Yemen, Libya, Iraq, Sudan and Palestine – had adopted Resolution 1123 (7 June 2000) condemning the embargo and the 'no-fly' zones, and urging increased Arab trade with Iraq. Thus in Resolution 1123 the Council:

1. Reaffirms its previous resolutions and urges the international community to lift the embargo . . . this would have the positive effect of mitigating the suffering of the fraternal Iraqi people . . . and of enhancing the Arab economic integration . . .

2. Demands the immediate implementation of paragraph 22 of Security Council Resolution 687(1991) and, with the country having met all of its obligations, the lifting of the total embargo imposed on Iraq.

3. Urges the countries of the world to adopt a resolute stance against all measures . . . aimed at perpetuating the unjust embargo . . .

4. Reaffirms its call to the Arab States to take appropriate measures to expand their trade with Iraq so as to help mitigate the effects of the embargo.

5. Calls upon Arab and non-Arab States to give effect to Article 50 of the Charter of the United Nations.[*]

6. Affirms the maintenance of the unity, sovereignty and territorial integrity of Iraq and rejects interference in its internal affairs.

7. Rejects the no-flight zones . . . as being in breach of the norms of international law and given their negative and dangerous repercussions for the economic and social conditions of the fraternal Iraqi people.

8. Calls upon Arab and non-Arab countries to resume their flights to Iraq and to facilitate the movement of goods and persons by land, sea and air.

9. Condemns the recurring Turkish military incursions into . . . Iraq, which constitute wanton aggression against Iraq, and affirms respect for Iraq's sovereignty and territorial integrity.

10. Requests the Secretary-General of the Council to monitor the implementation of this resolution by member States and to submit a report thereon to the Council at its next session.'

Saeed Hasan noted that resolution gave clear expression to the truth that the embargo did not only affect Iraq but also had a direct impact on Arab economic integration. Iraq was 'a basic element in joint Arab action for development and progress', and the embargo was:

---

*   Article 50 (UN Charter): *If preventive or enforcement measures against any state are taken by the Security Council, any other state . . . which finds itself confronted with special economic problems arising from . . . those measures shall have the right to consult the . . . Council with regard to a solution of those problems.*

blatantly incompatible with all the relevant international Conventions and Covenants and with the goals of the United Nations . . . the Council also affirms Arab rejection of the bellicose conduct of the United States and the United Kingdom . . . a violation of the Charter of the United Nations.[1]

Attitudes to Iraq

The Council for Arab Economic Unity, in producing Resolution 1123, had made a highly significant gesture of solidarity with Iraq, but this did not represent a consensus among Arab states. The monarchies of Kuwait and Saudi Arabia, though not necessarily their people, were maintaining their support for the punitive sanctions regime and for the illegal 'no-fly' zones. Both these states, courted and protected by Washington because of oil, had appalling human rights records characterized by torture, mutilations, executions, shameful court practices, the abuse of women, censorship, slavery, etc. – but such matters are routinely ignored by the United States and Britain. Kuwait continues to claim that missing Kuwaiti and third-party nationals have not been accounted for by the Iraqis, and that such missing persons justify the continued genocide of Iraq's civilian population. In fact the International Committee of the Red Cross (ICRC) has stated that 7023 prisoners-of-war (POWs) and civilians have been repatriated by the Iraqis, with the Iraqis claiming that it remains impossible to settle the issue of 627 files on missing persons:

> For investigating the fate of these persons it would of course have been necessary for the Iraqi authorities to search the records of the relevant services of the Governorates in the south and centre of the country. Everyone knows . . . that all the official establishments of those Governorates were raided by saboteurs who burned, destroyed or looted all the records . . . large numbers fled the Iraqi detention centres . . . after the outbreak of the riots in the first week of March 1991 . . .

Salem al-Sabah, chairman of the Kuwaiti committee on missing persons and POWs acknowledged on 3 May 1995 that 5772 POWs out of more than 6000 were freed as a result of the 'revolution' in southern Iraq: 'Some of them made their way back on foot to Kuwait, while the rest took refuge with the ICRC and returned to Kuwait.' The Iraqis have claimed that such circumstances have made it impossible to check a number of individual cases. The point is important, not least because in June 2000 there were 1150 Iraqi missing persons, about whom the Kuwaitis had provided either 'scanty and contradictory information' or none at all. And what is to be said about the tens of thousands of unidentified Iraqi corpses bulldozed into mass graves in southern Iraq by the US army?

The dispute over the issue of missing persons was one of various matters that Kuwait was exploiting to keep alive the sanctions regime and the illegal bombing of Iraq, so directly fuelling political tensions between Arab states. Other disputes concerned the allegation that Iraq had failed to return Kuwaiti property (see Chapter 9), and an expanding Kuwaiti access to disputed oil deposits. Kuwait had few wells in the shared Rumailah and Zubair oilfields but, after the boundary was redrawn in Kuwait's favour following the 1991 Gulf War, many Iraqi oil wells fell into Kuwait's newly acquired territory. Kuwait then invited American and British companies to sign long-term contracts for the exploitation of its newly acquired oil resources.

This meant that the sinking of wells no more than 50 metres from the boundary line facilitated an effective transfer of oil in the Rumailah and Zubair fields from Iraq to Kuwait. Because of the sanctions and the associated holds on oil contracts, Iraq has been unable to initiate countervailing technological developments to halt the transfer of oil. The Iraq version of events claims that Kuwait is 'stealing and plundering' Iraqi oil:

> The statements made by Kuwaiti officials and their endeavour to incite others against Iraq are . . . an attempt to cover up the thefts they are perpetrating. They claim that the drilling is taking place in Kuwaiti territory, but the modern drilling techniques in use and the confirmed information available to Iraq indicate that Kuwait is engaging in lateral drilling that extends for several kilometres into the Iraqi reservoirs beneath the surface of the earth. This would explain the high production levels achieved . . . when prior to 1990 the Kuwaiti wells had been almost dry and had ceased production because of the high levels of reservoir water they contained.[2]

It is an easy matter to find independent sources, not least the UN itself, that give weight to the Iraqi case. The boundary was indeed redrawn, under UN auspices, to give Kuwait territorial and oil-resource advantages; Kuwaiti oil production in the two cited fields has indeed vastly increased; and Iraq, because of the harsh sanctions, is forced to watch the progressive deterioration of its own oil industry.[3] Such matters, serving Kuwaiti and US interests, add to the tensions in the Arab world and so preserve the US-friendly disunity in the Arab Nation.

On 29 October 2000 an aircraft carrying eight Palestinians, wounded in clashes with Israeli troops, flew to Iraq for medical treatment, despite Iraq's parlous hospital conditions, and to demonstrate their opposition to the sanctions. At Gaza International Airport director Sulaiman Abu Haleeb commented: 'We are thankful to Iraq for receiving eight of our wounded . . . Palestine is joining other countries of the world in the initiative to break the siege on Iraq.' Now a growing number of countries, including France and Russia, were arguing – against the US view – that flights carrying humanitarian supplies to Iraq need only give the Sanctions Committee notification, without any need to obtain permission. Now Iraq and Syria were agreeing to open the oil pipeline, closed since 1982, between the two countries – so that Baghdad could export 200,000 barrels per day of low-priced crude to Syria's domestic refineries. At the same time, Ali Abu al-Ragheb, Jordan's Prime Minister, was arriving in Baghdad to agree an Iraq–Jordan oil deal under which Baghdad would supply Amman with five million tonnes of crude and by-products over the coming months.

All such developments were irritating Washington, keen to prolong the privations of the Iraqi civilian population. On 6 November, the US State Department registered its concerns for the safety of civilian aircraft flying humanitarian missions to Baghdad. Spokesman Richard Boucher commented:

> We are particularly concerned because of aggressive Iraqi activities south of 33 degrees north latitude and north of 36 degrees north latitude. It is important that any foreign aircraft that do fly to or from Iraq avoid these areas . . . Foreign aircraft operators . . . should comply fully with Security Council resolutions and all applicable . . . Sanctions Committee procedures.[4]

Other observers judged that it was unlikely that the Iraqis would want to shoot down aircraft bringing humanitarian relief.

On 14 November, Baghdad announced that talks would begin with Kofi Annan, the UN Secretary-General, with a view to ending the stalemate over sanctions and Iraqi disarmament. Saddam Hussein was now urging Arab leaders to cut their ties with Israel, but to keep their borders open to allow the transit of Arabs committed to the liberation of Palestinian: 'If you do not want to fight, at least let others pass through to the battlefield.' In seven weeks of conflict between the Israelis and the Palestinians about 250 people, most of them Arabs, had been killed and thousands wounded. Now it was obvious that Saddam's robust anti-Israel posture was winning him friends throughout the Arab world. On 16 November, Sheikh Hamad bin Ali bin Al-Thani, a member of the Qatar royal family, presented Saddam Hussein with the gift of a Boeing 747 aircraft in Baghdad, calling the gesture an expression of solidarity with Saddam and the

Iraqi people. Washington immediately branded the gift illegal and urged countries to impose sanctions on Qatar:

> The government of any country involved in this prohibited transfer of an aircraft to Saddam has an obligation to seek the return of the aircraft and to take all possible steps under national law both to prevent future transfers and to punish those involved in this transfer. We urge other states in the region to conduct their own investigations and impose whatever sanctions are appropriate, including the possibility of prohibiting the operation in their territory or any person or company involved in this illegal transfer . . . we will consider our own action against those involved.[5]

Breaching the Sanctions

On 21 November, a Syrian official announced that Iraqi oil had begun to flow to Syria: 'Iraq started pumping on November 16 and the flow is now up to about 150,000 barrels per day of Basra Light.' There still seemed to be ambiguities as to whether these new arrangements fell under the terms of UN resolutions. Four days later the fourth Jordanian aircraft to fly to Baghdad, in seeming defiance of the sanctions, departed from Marka airport carrying more than 150 Jordanian, Yemeni, Tunisian and Palestinian dentists. The plane, a Jordan Aviation Boeing 737, had been leased by the Jordan Dentists Association to fly the dentists to the 22nd Annual Iraqi Dentists Association's Scientific Conference in Baghdad. Ahmad Qadiri, President of the Association, commented: 'This flight is an embodiment of the defiance of the unjust air embargo on the Iraqi people that is not even part of the UN resolutions imposed on Iraq.' Jordan had been the first Arab country to send a humanitarian aircraft to Iraq. Another flight, following the September groundbreaker, carried writers and cultural figures representing the Jordan Writers Association.

Now there was confusion about whether Iraq was pumping oil to Syria. Benon Sevan, head of the UN Iraq Programme, had received assurances from the Iraqi and Syrian missions that the oil was not being pumped for export but purely to test the repaired pipeline. Moreover, the United Nations had authorized Iraq to sell oil at two ports: Ceyhan, the Turkish Mediterranean port, and Mina al-Bakr, Iraq's offshore platform in the Gulf. Use of the new pipeline could be represented as a compound violation of the sanctions regime. On 25 November Tariq Aziz, Iraq's Deputy Prime Minister, flew to Damascus aboard the first direct Iraqi flight to Syria in nearly two decades. After talks with Farouq al-Shara, Syrian foreign minister, Aziz again declared that the UN sanctions did not ban air travel. Already more than two dozen countries had flown to Baghdad in what many observers were saying were clear violations of the sanctions regime.

The Royal Jordanian Airlines was now planning to resume its regular commercial flights to Baghdad within a matter of weeks, making Jordan the first Arab country to run regular flights to Baghdad since the start of the embargo in August 1990. Musa Keilani, writing in the *Jordan Times*, urged the need for a campaign to achieve the lifting of sanctions: 'It is a disgrace for the international community to maintain the sanctions on civilian Iraq citizens. We need to launch an all-out effort to convince the UN political powers that we Jordanians do not believe that the sanctions are justified and we would not respect those curbs on Iraq.'[6] Here it was acknowledged that the isolation of Iraq was 'slowly being eliminated . . . now is the time for us Jordanians to add our loud and clear voice to the demand to end the sanctions on Iraq'.[7] On 27 November, a Boeing 737 carrying 160 passengers left for Baghdad, the eighth Jordanian flight in two months. This plane was carrying people representing various political parties, professional associations, sports clubs and the National Jordanian Committee for the Defence of Iraq. Fawaz Zreiqat, Committee Member, noted that many people had wanted to participate, but the plane could not accommodate everyone 'and so we had to apologize to a large number of people'. Jordan's King Abdullah, in his Speech from the Throne to the Jordanian parliament, had declared that the government was working to end the suffering of the Iraqi people: 'We reiterate our commitment to the unity and territorial integrity of Iraq.'

On 30 November Saudi Arabia claimed that the kingdom had no relation with the US and British aircraft that were bombing Iraq: Saudi territory was not being used to launch air strikes. Fawzi bin Abdel Majeed Shobokashi, the Saudi Ambassador to the UN, asserted also that the United States had not used depleted-uranium (DU) munitions in the 1991 Gulf War – a clear absurdity since Washington had long admitted the use of such weapons, claiming that they posed no hazards to coalition forces. In early December Jordan and Tunisia agreed to hand back Iraqi aircraft impounded during the Gulf War, with Saeed al-Sahaf, Iraq's foreign minister noting that work to make the planes airworthy had already begun. Again the gesture was an indication that Iraq's relations with other Arab states were slowly getting back to normal.[8]

If some Arab states were keen to encourage a gradual erosion of the economic sanctions, Kuwait seemed desperately committed to their protection. During 2000 the Emirate had seized some 25 vessels for trying to smuggle oil and other products out of Iraq – including, in early December, a shipment of

520 goats, 402 sheep, 872 tonnes of Iraqi dates, and various other goods. These were being transported on five wooden ships manned by 51 sailors of various nationalities, who had reportedly brought the vessels into Kuwaiti territorial waters. Again it seemed plain that Kuwait was Iraq's principal Arab opponent, a permanent obstacle to the normalisation of relations within the Arab Nation.

On 6 December the trade ministers of the Arab League's 10-member Council for Economic Unity (see also above)[9] decided to meet in Baghdad from 6–7 June 2001, for trade and other talks. Iraq had already persuaded Egypt and Libya to agree in principle to announce a free-trade zone between the three countries, as part of a wider move towards the abolition of tariffs in the Arab world. There were suggestions that the various Arab states, Kuwait apart, were considering the creation of a region-wide free-trade zone, in which Iraq would be a leading member, by 2007. Egyptian ministers had announced that Egypt had dramatically expanded its exports to Iraq, under the terms of the sanctions regime, from $400 million-worth in 1999 to $1.2 billion-worth in 2000. Fouad Sanyoura, Lebanese finance minister, declared in Beirut upon arrival from Baghdad that Iraq and Lebanon had agreed to revive the work of a joint committee created to remove obstacles to bilateral trade and economic cooperation, and that Lebanon would welcome the pumping of Iraqi oil from the Syrian–Iraqi pipeline to Lebanon's northern port city of Tripoli. The Lebanese plane, the fourth to fly from Beirut to Baghdad since October, had carried a cargo of ten tonnes of food and medicines for the Iraqi people.

Iraq and the Palestinians

Saddam Hussein was continuing to garner support in the Arab world by sending funds to the Palestinians, increasingly oppressed in the Occupied Territories. At the end of 2000 he was giving $10,000 to the family of every Palestinian 'martyr' and $1000 to anyone wounded in clashes with the Israelis. Such largesse compared with the $2000 being provided by Yasser Arafat's Palestinian National Authority to compensate families of the dead. On 12 December Saddam asked the United Nations to divert to the Palestinians $800 million of oil revenues, with about $300 million set aside for 'martyrs' and the rest to be paid to the Palestinian Authority. Hence, despite the miseries in Iraq, Saddam Hussein was trying to match the $1 billion pledge by Saudi Arabia and other Gulf states. Muhammad al-Shahaf, Iraq's Foreign Minister, said: 'Aid for a people fighting for their independence and freedom figures at the top of the list of priorities of the UN Charter.'[10]

On 12 December Rakad Salem, head of a pro-Iraqi delegation handing out cheques in the West Bank, acknowledged that many Palestinians were rejecting the charity, telling him that 'people in Iraq deserve it more'. Salem commented: 'The Ba'th Party has come on behalf of Saddam Hussein to pay our condolences. Ramzi [the son of Adnan Bayatneh, to whom a cheque was being given] is a martyr of Palestine and he will join the rest of the martyrs in Paradise. Our people will continue the struggle until we achieve our goals and our own state. Iraq has always stood behind us and Iraq's President, Saddam Hussein, considers the issue of Palestine central to the Arab world.'[11] Bayatneh, bereaved and embarrassed, mumbled his thanks.

There was no prospect that the Sanctions Committee would allow the diversion of Iraqi oil revenues to the Palestinians, and the Israelis were using 'deliberate delaying tactics' to hamper the entry of urgent humanitarian aid to the Occupied Territories. Thus Atallah Khairi, the Palestinian Chargé d'Affaires, complained:

> This time the Israeli authorities are using a different strategy to prevent new emergency aid and food from reaching the Palestinians. They have refused the entry of new aid on claims that the custom's warehouse at the King Hussein Bridge is filled with a flour shipment from Iraq. Israeli security authorities claim that the stock of flour was being held back due to the border closures, but how can they justify this knowing that all trucks undergo thorough security checks before being permitted access into the Palestinian territories.[12]

Four trucks laden with emergency aid had been turned away and denied access to the Occupied Territories.

Obstacles to Consensus

On 19 December 2000 the Gulf Cooperation Council (GCC) reiterated its position on Iraq, urging Baghdad to fully implement the relevant UN resolutions. A statement indicated that the GCC states had always helped the Iraqi people, and they would continue to do so in line with UN resolutions. The Iranian occupation of three GCC islands and the barbaric Israeli treatment of the Palestinians were condemned, though no practical remedies were proposed. Iran, frequently hostile to Iraq, was now prepared to tolerate Iraqi passenger planes crossing Iranian airspace. Thus Yadollah Adibi, Director General of the Public Relations Office of the Civil Aviation Organization in Iran, suggested that Iraqi aircraft using Iran's airspace would be obliged to pay a tax, but humanitarian flights would be exempt.[13] The United Nations had apparently raised no objection to such overflights.

Kuwait and Saudi Arabia had prepared a joint paper on Iraq for presentation to the GCC summit, scheduled to be held in Bahrain on 30 December. Here it was said that relations with Iraq were conditional on Baghdad's implementation of the UN resolutions, especially those dealing with the non-violation of the fresh Iraqi–Kuwaiti borders, the release of Kuwaiti prisoners-of-war, and the return of stolen Kuwaiti possessions. The joint paper suggested that Kuwait and Saudi Arabia were 'not against the lifting of the embargo on Iraq or its continuation': the embargo was an international decision that Iraq should observe. Neither country would have direct contacts with Iraq until there was full compliance with UN resolutions.[14]

Kuwait continued to assert that Iraq was holding Kuwaiti POWs, and Robin Cook, British foreign secretary, had confirmed: 'Sanctions cannot be lifted until this issue is resolved.' Captain Khalid Sachit Aziz al-Janabi, a defector from Iraqi intelligence, asserted that Kuwaiti POWs had been tortured and were being held in special houses under the direct charge of Qusay, Saddam's younger son.[15] Janabi had left Iraq in 1998, but remained convinced that hundreds of Kuwaitis were still being held in Iraq. Baghdad continued to dismiss such charges, and on 1 January 2001 condemned as 'silly and boring' an appeal by the Gulf Cooperation Council for Iraq to comply with UN resolutions demanding the elimination of its weapons of mass destruction. The GCC position had failed to win support from other Arab states; and France, Russia and China – three Permanent Members of the UN Security Council – were giving support to the Iraqi request for a portion of the oil revenues to be channelled to the Palestinian victims of Israeli violence in Gaza and the West Bank.[16] Baghdad was also winning support from a surprising source: Turkey, committed to frequent military attacks on northern Iraq, had agreed to open a rail link with Iraq that would run through Syria and would link Mosul with Turkey. An Iraqi Transport Ministry source was claiming also that Iraq and Jordan were discussing the building of a rail project that would link Haditha, 260 km west of Baghdad, to the Jordanian port city of Aqaba. On 16 January, Taha Yassin Ramadan, Iraq's Vice-President, arrived in Cairo to sign the negotiated free-trade agreement with Egypt.

There was still no possibility of a pan-Arab consensus. Kuwait and Saudi Arabia, ever sensitive to Washington whim, were determined to block any Iraqi attempts to break out of the sanctions straitjacket. In this, they could rely on the support of most, but not all, of the other Gulf states. Now Uday, Saddam Hussein's older son, was proposing through his *Babel* newspaper that parliament change the Iraqi map on the legislature's emblem to show Kuwait as part of Iraq – a reversal of the earlier Iraqi pledge that Iraq would respect the UN-demarcated border. The paper declared:

> Iraq's map that represents the symbol of the assembly does not include the full borders of Iraq as known to the various segments of the Iraqi people, that is Kuwait City. Recommendation: Putting the full map of Iraq including Kuwait City as part of a larger Iraq as an emblem of the representatives of the people.[17]

Such a suggestion was unlikely to endear Baghdad to the Emirate.

The Uday proposal was promptly denounced by the Kuwaitis. Sabah al-Ahmed al-Sabah, Kuwait's foreign minister, said that the Emirate had submitted protests to the UN Security Council and the Arab League in response to Uday's 'Greater Iraq' claim. The *Babel* proposal was 'aggressive and infringing on Kuwait's sovereignty'; it was 'a clear violation of Security Council resolutions'. If Uday was antagonising the Kuwaiti Emirate, his father was continuing to irritate the United States. On 15 January 2001 it was announced that a certain S. Hussein of Baghdad had donated $100 million to impoverished Americans, following the decision of President-elect George W. Bush to cut government aid to the poor and to let private philanthropists shoulder the burden.[18] Doubtless Mr Bush was grateful for the contribution of his Iraqi benefactor.

On 22 January Kuwait, in a surprise move, reportedly welcomed a call for the UN sanctions on Iraq to be lifted. Thus Jassem Boodai, editor of the Kuwaiti newspaper *al-Ra'i al-'Aam* wrote a full-page leader (21 January) calling for an end to the economic embargo, saying that it hit ordinary Iraqis and was only serving to strengthen the Baghdad regime: 'Iraq's regime will not fall unless it is directly targeted, and not by providing it with a fortress to use Iraqis as human shields.' The following day, Sheikh Sabah al-Ahmed al-Sabah claimed to have been the first to congratulate the paper's editor-in-chief for his article. Here it was suggested that the sanctions should be lifted and that the UN should set up war tribunals to try President Saddam Hussein and members of his regime. At the same time Baghdad was conducting its own multifaceted campaign for an end to sanctions. Iraq and Syria had opened a 50-year-old oil pipeline in December, but now there were plans for a new pipeline to link the Kirkuk oilfields to the Syrian port of Baniyas. Syria had denied importing Iraqi oil but was thought to be using it for domestic consumption, enabling more Syrian oil to be exported. Thus a senior official of one multinational oil company acknowledged the changed situation: 'We are increasing our buying of Syrian crude.' Major Western oil companies, including BP and ExxonMobil, were resuming their purchases of Iraqi oil on the open market, despite evidence that Somo, the Iraqi oil marketing organization, was demanding illegal kickbacks.[19] Both BP and Exxon were claiming that their Iraqi oil deals complied fully with UN requirements.

In early February the ruling Ba'th Party in Baghdad, perhaps following Uday's lead, issued warnings that it could withdraw recognition of Kuwait if the Emirate continued to provide military support for US and British bombing raids on Iraqi territory. The official *al-Thawra* newspaper declared that Baghdad would take the appropriate decisions if Kuwait insisted on maintaining its support for US–UK military incursions into Iraq. Baghdad was now claiming that 320 Iraqis, mainly civilians, had been killed in raids by war jets using air bases in Kuwait and Saudi Arabia. At the same time Iraq was announcing that the first regiment of volunteers in the 'Al-Quds Al-Sharif Army' had been formed to liberate Palestinian 'from the river to the sea'. More than 5.6 million Iraqis had supposedly volunteered to fight on behalf of the Palestinians; and Ali Hassan al-Majeed, a member of Iraq's Revolutionary Command Council (RCC), announced that other volunteer regiments would be formed.

The Building of Links

On 12 February, Iraq's state airline resumed scheduled flights to Syria, after a break of more than two decades. The first flight of the Iraqi Airways jumbo jet to Damascus meant that Baghdad had now succeeded in establishing regular flights to three countries (Syria, Egypt and Jordan), despite UN sanctions. The Boeing 747, the first of what was expected to be two round trips to Syria every week, carried Mohammed Mehdi Saleh, Iraq's trade minister, and six other Arab passengers to Damascus. It seemed clear that Saddam Hussein was gradually undermining the harsh sanctions regime. A week later, a United Arab Emirates (UAE) firm, then operating a weekly ferry service to Iraq, announced that it would increase the sailings to three a week. Sultan bin Sulayem, the owner of Naif Marine Services, claimed that the trips had been approved by the UN Sanctions Committee.

The gradual establishment of Iraq's links with other Arab states and non-Arab states was doing little to mitigate the appalling suffering of the Iraqi civilian population. In February 2001, according to the Iraqi Health Ministry, more than 10,000 people, mostly children, had died because of diseases caused by the decade of sanctions. Few observers could doubt that the sanctions were continuing to have a genocidal impact. Some 7270 children under the age of five had died, with 3255 deaths of older people in the same month. The new fatalities brought to 1,471,425 the number of Iraqi civilians who had been killed by the US-maintained sanctions regime since August 1990. Hints that things were slowly becoming more normal were scarcely beginning to address the catastrophe that had been created by Washington to decimate the Iraqi people.

Kuwait was insisting that the sanctions and the US–UK air strikes had nothing to do with the Emirate. Thus Mohammed Sabah al-Salem al-Sabah, foreign affairs minister, remarked – in obvious ignorance of the relevant illegalities – that the air strikes and sanctions against Iraq were strictly within the jurisdiction of the Security Council. Thus the 'halting of air strikes and lifting of United Nations sanctions . . . are not matters that require Kuwait's intervention'. There must be an immediate release of Kuwaiti prisoners-of-war and an end to Iraqi threats against 'peaceful neighbouring countries'.[20] The Iraqi government newspaper *al-Jumhouriya* declared that Iraq was 'determined to retaliate' against Kuwait and Saudi Arabia for helping the US and Britain to bomb Iraq; and the Ba'th newspaper *al-Thawra* reinforced the point: 'It is not only American and Britain that are responsible for the criminal aggression on Iraq . . . Kuwait and Saudi Arabia are also to blame.' To Iraqi commentators the issue was simple: 'Iraq has the right to take military measures and plans to retaliate against the aggressors and those who give them facilities in the event of future attacks' (*al-Jumhouriya*). The fresh bombing campaign launched by President George W. Bush (see Chapter 8) was dismissed: 'He knows his aggression is a failure and it will increase our determination to defend our rights' (*Babel*).[21]

On 23 February Italy's Foreign Ministry blocked the departure of a humanitarian aid flight from Rome to Baghdad for 'technical issues'. One suggestion was that Cyprus did not want planes flying through its airspace after the US–UK bombing of Iraq the previous week. At the United Nations, the Kuwaiti Ambassador denounced the Baghdad leadership for not complying with UN resolutions, and urged Iraq to heed the 'sincere efforts by brothers' in the GCC states to break the stalemate over sanctions. At the same time Ambassador Abulhassan expressed anxiety about the attempts being made to exploit the suffering of the Iraqi people, and rejected earlier reports that Kuwait had changed its attitude to sanctions: the suffering of the Iraqi people could only be lessened 'in accordance with relevant Security Council resolutions'. The suffering of Iraqis was the fault of Iraq. It had nothing to do with what Kofi Annan had acknowledged were the shortcomings of the UN humanitarian programme, nothing to do with ridiculous bureaucracy of the sanctions regime, nothing to do with the vast number of 'holds' imposed on humanitarian contracts, and nothing to do with the obvious malice of the US and UK representatives in the Security Council. Abulhassan declared also that Arab countries were firm against Iraq – obviously untrue.

The United States, in the shape of Colin Powell, Secretary of State, was now struggling to buttress Arab support for what seemed to be an increasingly shaky sanctions system. Prince Saud, Saudi foreign minister, had recently signed a joint statement with Syria denouncing the recent US–UK bombing strikes around Baghdad, with the interior minister, Prince Naif, keen to deny that the kingdom had played any role – 'direct or indirect' – in the bombing campaign. In Syria, Secretary of State Powell received a cool reception, with the Ba'th Party newspaper asking why the United States had not launched air strikes against Israel for failing to comply with UN resolutions, and why Israel was allowed to possess nuclear weapons. After his talks in Damascus, Powell said that Syria had agreed to put its pipeline from Iraq, and the oil flowing through it, under UN control. President Bashar al-Assad had reportedly assured Powell three times that Syria did not want to break the sanctions. It remained to be seen: Arab outrage at the recent US–UK bombing of Iraq continued to mount. Arab parliamentarians meeting in Abu Dhabi issued a final communiqué calling for an end to sanctions, denouncing the 'no-fly' zones, urging the UN to discuss with Baghdad how to ease the suffering of the Iraqi people, calling for the creation of an international court to investigate Israeli atrocities against Palestinians, and condemning Washington's 'policy of double standards'.[22]

On 11 March 2001 Lebanon indicated that it was reversing its 1994 decision to break ties with Iraq: commercial and consular staff had been exchanged and the remaking of other links would soon follow. Then the Committee of the Families of Lebanese Detainees in Iraqi Prisons provided six names of Lebanese who had been arrested while studying religion at a Muslim Shi'ite school in Iraq, and urged the Beirut government to work to secure their release. In mid-March, it emerged that Saddam Hussein had been invited to attend the annual Arab summit in Jordan on 27 March, the first time since the 1991 Gulf War. Baghdad was now complaining that Jordan's commercial flights were doing nothing to end the embargo since Amman was insisting on obtaining prior UN permission before every flight. The important point, from Baghdad's perspective, was for the Sanctions Committee to be shown to be losing its grip on Iraqi affairs.

The Arab states, not all committed to pan-Arabism, well perceived that the antagonism between Kuwait and Iraq was preserving a permanent dislocation in the region. On 20 March King Abdullah of Jordan held two separate meetings in Amman with the foreign ministers of Kuwait and Iraq amid reports that he was searching for a 'reconciliation formula' that would satisfy both countries. Here Kuwait's Sabah al-Ahmad al-Sabah and Iraq's Mohammad Said al-Sahaf presented letters from their respective leaders explaining their two countries' positions regarding the scheduled (27 March) Arab summit. Al-Sahaf commented, following a meeting with the Jordanian Prime Minister Ali Abul

Ragheb, that there was no way that a reconciliation could be achieved during the two-day event: 'If the summit wants to review the Iraqi file, it should seriously discuss the lifting of the sanctions. Any issue that pertains to Iraq could be debated in the summit clearly and in a very objective way to find an Arab solution to this issue.' Kuwait declared that there could be no solution unless Iraq apologized for the 1990 invasion and released all the Kuwaiti prisoners-of-war.

The Jordanians seemed uncertain how to proceed. They wanted a solution to the sanctions issue, 'but this depends on the UN Security Council' (Abul Ragheb) – which in fact implied that no progress could be made without US approval. This was not 'a Jordanian summit, but rather an Arab gathering, and there should be a consensus to reach an agreement that would attain a balanced approach'. There was no Jordanian pressure for a solution to the sanctions issue, and it seemed likely that nothing could be achieved in Amman. There was a wide-ranging agenda, including the topic of economic integration for the creation of a common free-trade zone, but the ideological and political differences between the Arab states were sure to block any substantial agreement.

The Arab League Summit (March 2001)

Even before the Arab summit it was obvious that the foreign ministers remained divided over Iraq, but were in broad agreement on the Israeli-Palestinian matter. In a second day of talks the ministers struggled to devise a resolution that would satisfy Iraq on sanctions, while assuring other countries that Iraq was no longer a threat to stability in the region. Israel would be condemned for its aggression against the Palestinians, there would be a call for the resumption of Middle East peace talks, and steps would be taken to improve the flow of Arab funds to the Palestinians – but there was nothing in this that would disturb the Washington strategists, without whom Israel could not prosecute its policies.

A Jordanian official commented on 24 March that it was important that the issue between Iraq and Kuwait 'does not remain unresolved until the summit'. The vast majority of the 22 states meeting in Amman wanted progress to be made, but it was still not obvious how this could be achieved: 'The Iraqis are using a new language and logic: they are saying the sanctions were imposed on them because they entered Kuwait, and they should be lifted now they have exited Kuwait.[23] The Kuwaitis, on the other hand, are saying they need guarantees that the situation does not repeat itself . . . If Iraq wants it all and now, that is impossible to achieve.' The Palestinian matter offered less scope for controversy. The martyrs of the intifada would be applauded, it would be agreed that Israel had committed 'barbaric aggressions', Israel would be blamed for the stalemate in the peace process, the UN should provide international protection for the Palestinians, and Israeli officials should be treated as war criminals for torturing and killing Arabs in the Occupied Territories.[24]

The draft document, though largely predictable, made few observations that would not have been supported by independent sources:

> The draft appeals to the international community to request that Israel signs the [Nuclear] Non-Proliferation Treaty, as 'it owns nuclear weapons and weapons of mass destruction'. The draft resolution denounces 'the dangerous situation in which the Palestinian people are living, due to the continuing aggressions by the Israeli occupier . . . who is using all kinds of tools and weapons, including banned ammunition, as well as an economic blockade . . . continuation of its policy on settlements . . . home demolitions, and pollution of water and the environment contravening all signed agreements and international laws and accords.

The Arab leaders, the draft resolution continues, 'salute the Intifada, the martyrs and the Palestinian people in their brave struggle to achieve their legitimate rights and establish their State with Jerusalem as its capital'.[25]

In the event, as expected, the Arab states were unable to reach a compromise formula on the Iraq–Kuwait issue. Even before the opening of the summit (27 March), there had been marathon talks, informal contacts, mini-conferences and a plenary session. It was said that a draft wording had been accepted by Kuwait and Saudi Arabia, with Iraqi foreign minister al-Sahaf still insisting on three demands: a call for the lifting of sanctions, a call for the cancelling of the 'no-fly' zones in southern and northern Iraq, and a call for Arab countries to operate regular flights to Iraq.

A Jordanian official, asking not to be named, noted that even if the Arab states called for a lifting of the 11-year-old sanctions 'nothing would happen on the ground, nor would the lives of Iraqis change, because the embargo is a matter between Iraq and the Security Council'. Yet again, Washington was being allowed to shape the course of events. The official expected that the final document would say little about the Iraq–Kuwait issue: the communiqué would be 'very short and . . . use mild language'. The official text on 'the situation between Iraq and Kuwait' covered the usual items:

The Arab leaders

1. Reaffirming the need to respect the Arab League Charter and its goals and to observe Arab security on the basis of respecting the security of each state and sovereignty over its territories, resources, rights . . .

2. Reaffirming the respect of the independence and sovereignty of Kuwait and securing its security and territorial integrity inside internally-recognized borders and the non-interference in its internal affairs and the reaffirmation of Iraq's commitment to that . . .
   Reaffirming the independence and sovereignty of Iraq, its territorial integrity and its regional security and non-interference in its internal affairs and demanding an end to all that it is being subjected to in terms of actions and measures that are touching upon its sovereignty and threatening its security especially those taken outside the framework of . . . UN Security Council resolutions, especially the military strikes.
   Calling on Iraq to complete all commitments mentioned in the Security Council resolutions in order to find a speedy and final end to the problem of prisoners of war, missing Kuwaitis, and returning Kuwaiti properties.
   Demanding an end to all unresolved problems related to weapons of mass destruction and control means through negotiations between Iraq and the Security Council . . . in order to set up an area free of weapons of mass destruction in the Middle East.

3. Calling for the lifting of sanctions imposed in Iraq.
   Undertaking necessary measures to resume commercial flights with Iraq.
   Calling for cooperation regarding what Iraq has presented regarding missing Iraqis under the patronage of the International Committee of the Red Cross.[26]

No practical steps to resolve the dispute between Iraq and Kuwait or to secure the ending of sanctions and the illegal 'no-fly' zones were proposed. The validity of the UN resolutions and the authority of the Security Council – and so the dominant role of the United States – were upheld. The Arab League, including such Washington placemen as Saudi Arabia, Kuwait, Morocco, Egypt and Bahrain, was not about to upset the US-contrived subservience of the region.

The Kuwaiti foreign minister, Sabah al-Ahmad al-Sabah, subsequently addressed editors-in-chief of local newspapers and magazines in Kuwait City to indicate how keen Kuwait was to alleviate the plight of the Iraqi people. Kuwait had exerted its utmost efforts to mitigate such suffering, but Iraq had 'wasted another significant opportunity to assist its people'. The need to guarantee the safety and sovereignty of Kuwait must be upheld, as must the obligation of Iraq to comply with all the relevant UN resolutions: 'However, Iraq was calling on Kuwait to secure Iraq's safety, a matter which angered the Arab leaders ... I have told them it is hard to change my position.' Al-Sabah applauded the support offered by other Arab states, particularly Saudi Arabia, 'towards the just causes of Kuwait', and hailed the role played by the Kuwaiti press.[27]

On 1 April 2001 the trade agreement signed earlier in the year between Iraq and Syria took effect, with Damascus maintaining that the anticipated trade would fall within the scope of the United Nations framework. It was estimated that the Iraq–Syria trade could reach $1 billion in 2001. At the same time Iraq and Morocco were holding the 9th session of their Joint Commission in Rabat to explore ways of developing their trade and economic cooperation as a route to the creation of a free-trade zone in the region. An exhibition in Baghdad, attended by around 120 Moroccan companies, was showing made-in-Morocco food, pharmaceutical products and electronic and mechanical goods. On 3 April Iraq and Morocco signed a package of agreements covering cooperation in the fields of economics, trade, culture, media and science; and agreed also to develop their cooperation in oil, transportation and telecommunications. The commercial exchanges between the two countries was reckoned at around $267 million.

Iraq and Kuwait

Kuwait was now declaring that, because Iraq had rejected the Arab summit draft on the Iraq–Kuwait situation, Kuwait itself would not feel committed 'to any formula reached' at the summit. Thus Hamid al-Bayyati, Kuwaiti representative of the Supreme Council for the Islamic Revolution in Iraq (SCIRI), commented that 'every time that Arabs try to reconcile with Iraq, the regime becomes more stubborn and creates more problems and tension in the region'.[28] At the same time Saddam Hussein, speaking in a cabinet meeting, was hailing the closer ties between Iraq and other Arab countries: 'Several Arab countries have started to revise their position on Iraq following pressure from their people but also in their own interests.'[29] However, Iraq made little progress at the 105th Conference of the Inter-Parliamentary Union, held in Havana, Cuba. An Iraqi proposal of right of appeal before international legal authorities against Security Council resolutions won only five votes in the Arab group.[30] Again the pro-US faction in the Arab camp had prevailed.

On 11 April Iraq signalled its readiness to cooperate with Jordan to resolve its differences with Kuwait. Thus Sabah Yassin, Iraq's Ambassador to Amman, commented that Iraq had said 'it would bless efforts exerted by His Majesty King Abdullah who assumes the Arab summit rotating leadership', adding that Iraq had 'positively reacted to all notions floated in the Arab summit to reach a common ground on the Iraq–Kuwait situation'. The key to solving the problems lay in tackling them 'within an Arab perspective' away from 'foreign intervention or pressure'.[31]

Three Steps Forward, Two Backward

King Abdullah, having talked with President George W. Bush, was interviewed by the London-based *al-Hayat* newspaper. It was time 'to lift the sanctions imposed on Iraq and clear the outstanding problems between Baghdad and Kuwait', but beyond the Iraqi people's suffering because of the embargo, 'there are also very important questions for Kuwait like security, prisoners and the missing'. These problems 'must be settled', and there must be dialogue between Iraq and the United Nations regarding the relevant UN resolutions.[32] At this time, in April 2001, it seemed that Jordan was prepared to do little to help the Iraqi people break out of the US stranglehold. However, in July, Jordan was signalling its willingness to begin constructing its portion of a joint oil pipeline with Iraq, even though Amman needed to raise around $400 million to begin the project. There were also further signs that Baghdad was moving back slowly into the international community.

In July 2001 Arab and other banks were seeking permission to start businesses in various parts of Iraq, within the so-called 'free-trade zones' designed to attract foreign business activity. Here one significant provision allowed foreigners to transfer their hard-cash earnings back home without restriction. In June, Malaysia had sent a medical aid flight to Iraq to protest against the sanctions regime, and Jordan had resumed scheduled flights to Baghdad. Aboard the first scheduled plane were Ahmed Darsh, Egypt's Planning and International Cooperation Minister, and Abdullah Rahman Mohammad Ali Othman, Yemen's Minister of Trade and Industry, travelling to Baghdad to attend meetings of the Council for Arab Economic Unity, an affiliate of the Cairo-based Arab League. It seemed plain that there was growing support for Baghdad throughout much of the Arab world, and there were even new accommodations with Turkey, accustomed to bombing northern Iraq and hosting American and British military aircraft. On 20 July 2001 the first Iraqi passenger train destined for Turkey in two decades left Baghdad. There were hints of an Iraqi revival but the economic embargo was still largely successful in preventing the rebirth of a national people.

The divisions, disputation and heart-searching in the Arab world had done nothing to mitigate the desperate plight of the Iraqi civilian population. One million children, mostly under five, had so far been killed by the embargo, and there was no end in sight. Millions of the surviving children, most of them born long after the 1990 invasion of Kuwait, existed in bleak destitution. Some 80 per cent of all Iraq's beggars were children under twelve, with many children working in jobs beyond their physical powers, with thousands dying monthly. It seemed that even these appalling circumstances, quite apart from the Israeli abuse of the Palestinian people, could not generate a righteous solidarity of purpose in the Arab world. However, the political climate was changing. The economic siege of Iraq was largely discredited in world opinion, and the repeated Israeli aggressions were affecting public attitudes throughout the region.

The Arab League Summit (March 2002)

At the Arab League Summit in Beirut (end of March 2002), Naji Sabri, Baghdad's foreign minister, pledged that Iraq would never again invade Kuwait, and in a closed session Iraqi delegate Izzat Ibrahim shook hands with Sheikh Ahmed al-Sabah, Kuwait's Deputy Prime Minister. Bush and Sharon were bringing to the Arab League a degree of solidarity that it had not known for years. One result was a summit communiqué that 'categorically' rejected a strike against Iraq. In April 2002 it seemed that the Arab world, Kuwait included, was unanimous in its opposition to the planned US–UK war on Iraq. If Bush and Blair were to launch a new military campaign against the Iraqi people, they would do so against the declared opinion of the UN Secretary-General, three Permanent Members of the UN Security Council, the European Union and the Arab League.

EIGHT

The Bombing Campaign

'Doing the Lord's Work'

The first President George Bush was a principal architect of the sanctions campaign, helped to instigate the 1991 Gulf War, and was determined – along with his various presidential successors – to ensure that the economic embargo would be maintained in perpetuity. On 19 January 2000 he applauded US pilots at the Ahmad al-Jaber air base in Kuwait, saying they were 'doing the Lord's work' in continuing to bomb Iraq, and he further declared: 'We [the United States] are a moral country . . . and you [the US airmen] are making a moral statement.' It is useful to recall the moral universe inhabited by the George Bush who launched the long war against Iraq.

It was George Bush who as CIA chief, Vice-President or President dismissed the multi-part World Court judgement against US terrorism in Nicaragua; who directly supported the Indonesian mass murder of East Timorese; who aided the death squads of Guatemala; who congratulated President Ferdinand Marcos of the Philippines on his rigged elections; who committed aggression against Panama (killing thousands of civilians in the process); and who provided political and financial support to Saddam Hussein over many years. Perhaps such details should be remembered when Washington claims high virtue in rolling back a 'brutal dictator'.

President George W. Bush has already launched illegal bombing raids against Iraq (see below), violating the UN Charter and outraging most of the international community. Bush II is often depicted as an illiterate ignoramus (one Bushism will suffice – 'redefining the role of the United States from enablers to keep the peace to enablers to keep the peace from peacekeepers is going to be an assignment'),[1] but it was soon plain that he had a keen sense of what was needed to protect traditional American interests. It was obvious that the economic embargo and bombing of Iraq initiated by his father would continue under the new Bush administration.

'Shooting Fish in a Barrel'

In 1991 the American defence of decency and Christian values produced a host of memorable incidents that Western propagandists are keen to forget. We need only mention the Amiriyah inferno where the carbonized bodies of hundreds of sheltering Iraqi women and children were encrusted on walls and ceilings; and the 'turkey-shoot' massacre at Mitlah Ridge, where US aircraft destroyed more than 2000 military and civilian vehicles and unknown thousands of fleeing Iraqis, who had been told to leave Kuwait but who had now been caught helpless in the desert. The retreating Iraqis were nominally complying with UN demands that they end their illegal occupation of a sovereign state, but their manifest retreat did not save them – as it should have done in international law.

The Iraqis had no means of defence in the open desert, and soon the American planes were queuing to share in the slaughter. The US Air Force planes dropped their cluster bombs, napalm incendiaries, depleted-uranium ordnance and any other types of bomb that they could load when they returned to their ships to rearm. A CNN journalist, Greg La Motte, later described the results of the hours-long carnage:

> What we're seeing is bodies strewn all over the place, body parts . . . civilian cars . . . burned out tanks . . . trucks, you name it . . . Some were completely disintegrated, including the people inside . . . thousands of people possibly could have died given the number of vehicles involved. The pilots described their mission as shooting fish in a barrel . . . the most horrific thing I have ever seen in my life: bodies everywhere, body parts everywhere . . . some of them thought that they could get out of their cars and run – not to be.[2]

The Iraqis had been trapped by a ridge on one side and a minefield on the other, with allied armour ahead and the bombers above. Some had desperately struggled to hide under bridges but to no avail. The Iraqis had been blasted into bits, body parts strewn everywhere; or they had been incinerated into nothing. The *Newsweek* journalist Tony Clifton described the aftermath:

> I could see a lot of the [US] soldiers really taken aback because there were bodies all over the place . . . I remember at one point looking down at a car track and I was up to my ankles in blood . . . a lot of very white-faced young men were going round saying 'Jesus, did we really do this?'[3]

In October 1994 Mitlah Ridge, where Iraq's fleeing soldiers had been 'roasted out of existence',[4] was being used as a live-fire training ground of the

US 15th Marine Expeditionary Unit. Thousands of rounds of ammunition were being blasted into the dunes near to a large and unmarked mass grave containing the bodies of countless Iraqi conscripts. The US soldiers fired their machine-guns and 'charged through smoke grenades across the sand, whooping and shrieking . . . It was about as near as they were going to get to shooting Iraqis'.[5] But there had been many post-war military attacks on Iraq – by the United States, Britain, France, Turkey, Iran, Kuwait, etc. – and many of these were set to continue through the 1990s and into the new millennium.

On 17 January 1993 the United States fired 46 cruise missiles at targets around Baghdad, a largely pointless exercise that was well applauded in the Western media. An editorial in *The Independent* (London, 18 January 1993) was typical. Here we were told that the missile assault was a 'measured response . . . well chosen . . . in furtherance of UN resolutions'. If Washington had failed to take action, Saddam Hussein 'may be tempted to intensify his taunts, and to crow about his successful defiance'. So the United States had fired 46 cruise missiles, costing well over $1 million each, because of the threats of 'taunts' and 'crowing'. But about half of the designated targets had not been destroyed, so on 18 January, around 75 US and UK aircraft again bombed Iraq to 'finish the job'. The American pilots knew what it was all about. Saddam had 'got his ass kicked', civilian casualties were 'a function [sic] of war', and anyway 'maybe a dud anti-aircraft round came back on the Iraqis' (nothing to do with the US).

Some Civilian Casualties

Civilians have always been casualties of the US-led bombing raids over Iraq, from 1991 to the present. On 13 January 1993 four of six American Stealth planes missed their targets, with one aircraft hitting a block of flats in a village. On 17 January, during a cruise missile attack, one Tomahawk went off course, hitting the Rashid Hotel in central Baghdad, killing two female receptionists. One, the 24-year-old Amira, was walking by the cashier's booth when a missile crashed through the hotel's western wall and a piece of shrapnel severed her neck. In the neighbourhood of Karrada, Buthaina Saheb was killed instantly when a projectile destroyed her two-storey house. Her two daughters, Leila and Nadia, and their five-year-old niece Sara were also injured; Nadia's spine had been broken by flying shrapnel and collapsing masonry.

Assassination Plot or US Ploy?

In June 1993 an alleged Iraqi assassination plot against former US President George Bush was used as the pretext for more cruise missile attacks on Iraq. The Clinton administration did not wait for such minor matters as a Kuwaiti court reaching a verdict, and was not troubled by reports that the plot suspects had been tortured into giving confessions. On 26 June some 23 cruise missiles were fired at Baghdad from the USS cruisers *Peterson* in the Red Sea and *Chancellorsville* in the Gulf. Washington admitted that about seven of the missiles had missed their targets, killing more civilians. One of the dead was Layla al-Attar, the world-renowned Iraqi artist killed with her husband when a cruise missile hit their home. President Bill Clinton, on his way to church, commented on the bombing: 'I feel quite good about what transpired. I think the American people should feel good.'[6]

On 3 September 1996 the United States fired 27 cruise missiles from B-52 bombers and two warships in the Gulf at targets in southern Iraq. This strike was judged to be insufficient, since presumably a number of the missiles had again missed their targets. The following day, a second wave of 17 cruise missiles was launched at Iraq, achieving nothing apart from helping Clinton in the US opinion polls. *Al-Ahram*, the most prestigious Egyptian newspaper, asked why the United States never intervened when Turkey invaded the Kurdish 'safe haven' in northern Iraq or when Iran sent its artillery into the same region. A Qatari newspaper commented that Washington 'found in the Arabs an easy prey as it fires missiles against them, uses them as a field test for its . . . modern weapons'. Even Syria, still hating Saddam, denounced US 'interference' in Iraq's internal affairs.

Operation Desert Fox

On 16 December 1998 Washington and London launched Operation Desert Fox, the most massive bombing campaign against Iraq since the 1991 Gulf War. For four nights of terror, the whole of a largely defenceless country came under comprehensive military attack in the dark from an unseen enemy. The US Navy launched 325 cruise missiles, the US Air Force nearly a hundred – twice as many cruise missiles as were launched during the Gulf War. In addition, American and British bombers flew 650 sorties, with the RAF Tornadoes alone dropping fifty 200 lb bombs.

None of this had any UN authorization. France, Russia and China – all Permanent Members of the Security Council – were outraged; and Kofi Annan,

UN Secretary-General, issued a statement saying that his thoughts were with 'the people of Iraq, with the 307 United Nations humanitarian workers who remain in the country, and all others whose lives are in danger'. It soon emerged that Desert Fox was a propaganda and military disaster. Washington and London had won international condemnation for their illegal aggression; after the first two nights of bombing only a tenth of 80 targets had been destroyed; and there had been massive civilian losses. The *non*-military targets that had been completely or partially destroyed included:

- the Hail Adel residential area (outskirts of Baghdad)

- the Baghdad Teaching Hospital

- the main grain silo in Tikrit

- the Basra oil refinery

- the Baghdad home of Hala, Saddam's daughter

- the Ba'th Baghdad Academic Institute

- the Baghdad Museum of Natural History

- the Tikrit Teaching Hospital

- the Baghdad Ministry of Labour and Social Affairs (responsible for the distribution of food rations).

The US Pentagon had predicted that 'as a medium-case scenario' 10,000 Iraqi civilians would be killed in Operation Desert Fox. In Saadoun Street, Baghdad, massed coffins reported by Western journalists gave some indication of the accumulating civilian casualties. Tariq Aziz subsequently reported fewer than one hundred military casualties, with civilian casualties 'much, much higher'. After the bombing, Iraqi doctors in Baghdad were reporting hundreds of civilian casualties. On CNN's *Late Edition* (20 December 1998) Nizar Hamdoon, the Iraqi Ambassador to the United Nations, spoke of 'thousands' of civilian casualties throughout Iraq.

After Operation Desert Fox (16–19 December 1998), itself the biggest ever missile onslaught on Iraq, the aerial bombardment did not end. The United States and Britain, in gross violation of the UN Charter and international law, continued the frequent bombing of targets in the so-called 'no-fly' zones. On 25 January 1999 a US missile hit the Abu-Khasib residential neighbourhood of Basra, causing many casualties: a young girl, Isra, lost her right hand. In one estimate, the US–UK bombing over the five weeks since the end of Desert Fox had caused about 200 civilian fatalities and injured hundreds more. The American and British patrols had flown about 16,000 sorties and dropped 550 bombs in southern Iraq; 11,000 sorties and 1100 bombs in northern Iraq.

The Civilian Toll

In late January 1999 the Pentagon confirmed that American missiles may have hit the al-Jumhuriya neighbourhood on the outskirts of Basra, while Western journalists were reporting a dozen killed and 40 wounded. Mike Huggins, a CNN producer, commented:

> I would say that there were up to 10 to 12 houses completely devastated. It took out the top storey of most of the houses. It ruined most of the living quarters of the other houses. People were going through the rubble collecting their belongings.[7]

On 24 February US–UK raids on the outskirts of Baghdad killed and wounded a number of civilians, further evidence that Washington and London were running a continuous undeclared war. On 28 February, American bombers destroyed the oil pipeline between Turkey and Iraq, killing one Iraqi worker and wounding two others. On 1 March American jets flying from Incirlik in Turkey dropped more than thirty 2000 lb and 500 lb laser-guided bombs, with pilots now being given greater flexibility to decide when to use their bombs and missiles.[8]

The raids continued, producing a rising roll of death and destruction. Targets included: the main pumping station serving the Mina al-Bakr oil terminal in Basra province, destroying a communications installation, a radio relay station and two houses (2 April 1999); sites in southern and northern Iraq, injuring dozens of people and destroying 14 houses (29 April); the tent of Jirgis Ayub Sultan, an Iraqi shepherd at Bashiqa, north of Mosul, killing the family of six and many of his sheep (30 April); a farmer's house and other buildings, killing four and wounding five (9 May); sites in southern Iraq, 14 killed and 17 injured (18 July); targets in the provinces of Basra, Muthanna, Dhi Qar, Najaf and Meisan, killing 18 people and destroying several houses (19 July); an astronomical campsite (11 August); sites in the Muthanna province, destroying rice stocks, warehouses and administrative buildings (10 August); targets near the cities of Talil, Basra and Samawa, killing eleven civilians (10 September); a target near the Ur archaeological site, wounding a Swedish journalist (21 September); and so on . . .

In early 2000 the seemingly endless US–UK bombing campaign was earning international criticism from the UN, media pundits and dissenting politicians in America and Britain. In London, the Labour MP Alan Simpson talked of the 'hidden war' against Iraq that was 'almost akin to punishment beatings'. It was 'difficult to see what moral, ethical or military sense any of it makes'; the international community 'really needs to step back and ask itself what the hell is going on . . . we are currently spending a colossal amount of money peppering Iraq on a daily basis'. On 9 February US Secretary of State Madeleine Albright commented that the anti-Saddam policies had 'a long way to go'. The bombings, and the deaths, were continuing unabated.

On 10 March 2000, Nasr Mazi, who grew dates and vegetables, was following his usual routine – until the bombers came. The village was hit by seven missiles and he was knocked unconscious. Two missiles had exploded, slicing down rows of 100-year-old date trees, and killing a donkey and 10 sheep. Five people were wounded in an area that could not remotely have had any military purpose. On 20 April, after yet more bombing raids, Iraq claimed that air strikes since December 1998 had killed 295 people and injured 860, most of the casualties being civilians. On 17 May US and UK aircraft attacked targets in Najaf province, killing the 12-year-old Omran Harbi Hwayer and a number of cattle and sheep. In London, Menzies Campbell, Liberal Democrat foreign affairs spokesman, talked about the 'significant policy shift' on bombing Iraq, which had never been 'announced or explained' to parliament. In early June Sergey Lavrov, Russian UN Ambassador, and Shen Guofang, Chinese deputy UN Ambassador, both speaking to the Security Council, denounced the US–UK bombing of Iraq.

On 15 August Russia condemned the US and British air raids as a violation of international law, and urged an end to both the aerial bombardment and the crippling economic sanctions. In particular the Russian foreign ministry said that the recent bombing of Samawa had caused civilian deaths and destroyed food stocks and residential areas. A letter from the Iraqi UN Ambassador condemned the same bombing raid, which had killed two civilians and wounded 19 others. In addition, the bombing had destroyed warehouses, traffic installations, a catering centre, a grain processing facility, six residential houses, and two civilian motor vehicles. There had also been damage caused to refrigeration plant, power facilities and the Samawa water supply. The raid had brought to 18,645 the total number of armed sorties flown by US and British aircraft since Operation Desert Fox, sorties that so far had killed 311 civilians and wounded nearly a thousand more.[9]

'No-Fly' Zones – Another Illegality

On 6 October 2000 the US vice-presidential nominee Richard Cheney called for military attacks on Iraq if there was evidence that it was developing weapons of mass destruction. In a debate with Senator Joseph Lieberman he noted that the Coalition that as defence secretary he had helped to form in 1990–91, was now weaker. (Lieberman opined that the use of force against Iraq was too weighty to discuss during the heat of a political campaign.) It was now obvious that the new US administration would face fresh problems over Iraq. Many countries, including France and Russia, were sending planes to Baghdad in a show of solidarity with the Iraqi leadership and the civilian population that had suffered so tragically under ten years of sanctions. On 30 October Esmat Abdel-Meguid, Arab League Secretary General, condemned the 'continuing bombings by US and British planes of Iraqi civilian installations and the resulting human victims caused by this aggression'. At the same time, the Iraqi government was protesting at the frequent US and UK violations of Iraqi airspace.[10] Here Mohammad Said al-Sahaf reiterated the familiar Baghdad position, highlighting:

> . . . the bellicose attitude being maintained by the United States . . . and the United Kingdom towards Iraq . . . a fixed policy aimed at undermining the country's sovereignty, independence and territorial integrity and at the systematic and concerted destruction of Iraqi lives, infrastructure and civilian installations . . .

The 'no-fly' zones were imposed by a 'unilateral decision' of the US and the UK and they lack 'any legal basis'. Iraq rejected 'the flimsy excuses and pretexts' used to justify 'military aggression against our country'. Moreover, the United States and Britain were not the only guilty parties: 'The logistical support provided by Saudi Arabia, Kuwait and Turkey to the Americans and British makes these countries key partners in the aggression being committed against Iraq, so that they bear international responsibility for actions that are deleterious to the people of Iraq.'[11]

On 8 November Ken Bacon, US Defence Department spokesman, demonstrated his sublime ignorance in answering press questions. He wrongly asserted that the 'no-fly' zones had been imposed by the United Nations, when in fact they were in breach of the UN Charter and had no UN authorization whatever. Bacon commented that the resumption of commercial airline flights in Iraq would make no difference to the policing of the zones since 'US and British pilots flying under UN authority' [sic] were able to distinguish between civilian and military flights. He suggested that, if there were any danger to the civilian flights, it would be posed by the Iraqis, who had been 'firing wildly at times . . . there is some risk that, due to lack of communications or over-enthusiasm, that they might fire at one of their own planes'. By contrast, the US and UK pilots were very careful to 'deconflict' civilian from military planes. But could Bacon indicate the procedural changes that had been made to ensure that allied pilots did not accidentally shoot down a civilian plane? Bacon: 'No.'

There were now growing tensions in the UN Security Council between the US and the UK on the one side and Russia, China and France on the other. Peter Hain, a junior minister in the British Foreign Office, had gone so far as to call France's policy on Iraq 'contemptible' – and then was forced to apologize. London had been upset by the arrival of a large French delegation and two French flights in Iraq: 'Frankly, French policy in Iraq has been pretty contemptible. It will put back a resolution of the crisis. I think that the French have absolutely no illusions that we do not welcome their dabbling in this matter.' So Hain reckoned that the US and the UK could bomb Iraq at will, but France was not entitled to 'dabble'. Then Hain declared that his remarks had been 'unscripted'.[12]

The Undeclared War

With revelations that Britain had dropped 84 tonnes of bombs on Iraq since the end of Operation Desert Fox, there were further suggestions in the United Kingdom and elsewhere that Washington and London were waging an 'undeclared war'. Menzies Campbell, Liberal Democrat foreign affairs spokesman, commented: 'Ten years of sanctions have driven the Iraqi people into poverty, malnutrition and ignominy and have done nothing to bring Saddam Hussein to heel. Saddam Hussein exploits the existence of sanctions, and he uses them as an excuse. They are his justification for brutality and privations he has imposed on his own people.' And Campbell suggested that in Arab capitals 'there is much anxiety and a belief that the Iraqi people have suffered as much as they need to.' But there was no end to the sanctions, or to the bombing.

On 12 November, American and British warplanes attacked targets in Basra province, firing four missiles at Hmaidi village. One of the missiles hit the Ali al-Hayaini school and wounded Laith Khairallah, Ali Matroud and Amjad

Jassim, all 12 years old; and 13-year-old Taleb Jamil. Two days later, US aircraft were bombing targets in northern Iraq after the Iraqi defence forces allegedly tracked the planes with radar and then fired at them. The United States was continuing to claim that its planes only attacked military targets in self-defence but the Iraqis were constantly producing evidence, often supported by independent observers, that civilians and civilian installations were being hit. President Bill Clinton had deplored the bombing of 'innocent civilians' by the Sudanese government, but seemingly remained committed to bombing in Iraq despite the toll of civilian life.

There was now further evidence that the US pilots were highly aggressive in the illegal 'no-fly' zones. The rules of engagement supposedly prohibited any bombing unless the Iraqis fired on the aircraft first, but Mike Horn a US pilot flying F-15s in early 1999, declared: 'Sometimes we flew in such a way that we provoked them to fire at us.' And where deliberate provocation was not admitted, human error was claimed. Thus when US aircraft had bombed and strafed Iraqi shepherds, it was because 'analysis misrepresented satellite imagery and thought a water trough for sheep was a missile launcher.'[13] Washington had no objection to Turkish pilots bombing the Kurds in the so-called 'safe haven' in northern Iraq: 'You'd see Turkish F-14s and F-16s inbound, loaded to the gills with munitions. Then they'd come out half an hour later with their munitions expended.' When US pilots later flew over the Kurds, whom they had supposedly been defending, they would see 'burning villages, lots of smoke and fire'.[14] The American pilots were under orders not to interfere with the Turkish bombing, and in the same vein the British aircraft were grounded at times when the Turks wanted to bomb the Kurds: 'On a regular basis, the Turkish authorities ground our aircraft so that their own air force can attack the very Kurds that the RAF was protecting a few hours before. After the Turkish jets land, our own pilots get airborne to resume their mission over the still smoking craters.'[15]

On 7 December American and British planes bombed targets in southern Iraq, wounding three civilians; while the Turkish government was considering whether to renew the licence for US and UK aircraft to use the Incirlik air base. On 17 December the licence was duly renewed, whereupon Iraq declared that it held the Turkish government legally and internationally responsible for the destruction caused by aircraft flying from its territory. There was no prospect that the new US administration would relax sanctions or abolish the 'no-fly' zones. General Colin Powell, then nominee for Secretary of State, had declared: 'My judgement is that sanctions in some form must be kept in place' until Iraq fulfilled its commitments. The embargo would be strengthened: 'We will work with our allies to re-energize the sanctions regime.' An Iraqi spokesman pointed out that Powell was ignoring the collapse of the Coalition, and that only Britain supported the US policy on Iraq. Tariq Aziz predicted that there would be no change in American policy since the current deadlock served US military-industrial interests: the United States could 'sell arms to countries that don't need them'.

In early 2001 there were signs that Britain was tiring of the bombing campaign and was about to suggest to the new Bush administration that it be ended. Menzies Campbell was not the only British politician who believed that 'ten years of inertia is no substitute for effective policy'. But there were still problems over a US–UK loss of face if policy U-turns were to be made, and observers were still stressing that Iraq had made no effort to comply with Security Council Resolution 1284 (see Chapter 4). Soon the British government was denying that there were any intentions to modify current bombing policy. If changes to US–UK policy were to be made, they would have to originate in the Washington of the new Bush regime. On 11 January, Richard Holbrooke, then US Ambassador to the United Nations, declared that Iraq would be one of the major issues facing his successor, saying that the effort to contain Iraq over the past ten years, 'while it is far from satisfactory', had been better than nothing. Saddam Hussein was 'a clear and present danger at all times'.[16]

President George W. Bush, having pledged 'civility' in his new administration, celebrated by launching fresh bombing raids on Iraq. On 21 January 2001 some six civilians were killed in the residential area of al-Salman in Muthanna province, and the search was continuing for more bodies in the ruins of houses and farms in Samawa. Tens of thousands of demonstrators lined the streets of Washington to boo the Bush inauguration, chanting 'Shame, shame, shame' and 'Hail to the Thief' (in reference to how Bush and his supporters, despite losing the popular vote, had resorted to a raft of dubious methods to secure the presidency).[17] Now, amid new allegations that Saddam Hussein had rebuilt his chemical and biological weapons factories, Bush was being urged to take even stronger action against Iraq.[18] The Kuwaitis were growing increasingly alarmed at Saddam's new confidence,[19] and there was widespread debate about whether Iraq had managed to build atomic bombs.[20] All the alarmist rhetoric was serving the usual purpose: the ground was being prepared for a fresh wave of bombing attacks.

On 28 January there were more US–UK air strikes against Iraq, but this was not the substantial bombing campaign that was being anticipated. On 12 February, after yet more raids, an Iraqi spokesman said: 'American criminals committed yet another crime when their planes bombed residential quarters in southern Iraq, injuring one person in Meisan province and six citizens in Basra province.' Some 17 residential buildings had been damaged in Nahran Omar in

Basra, and a power grid had been destroyed in the same area. There was worse to come.

The Bush Escalation

On 16 February 2001 the United States and Britain launched the biggest bombing raid on targets around Baghdad since Operation Desert Fox (December 1998). This air raid involved at least 80 aircraft, including 24 American strike planes such as F-16s, and nine RAF aircraft, including six Tornado GRIs. Some of the strikes were launched from the American aircraft carrier USS *Harry S. Truman* in the Gulf. The official US–UK reports stated that command and control targets had been hit by the bombers using stand-off munitions from inside the southern 'no-fly' zone. It was claimed that no civilian areas had been hit but that Iraqi anti-aircraft artillery might have damaged civilian properties.

There was some ambiguity about President Bush's precise role in the new US-led aggression. All the Bush-friendly reportage suggested that he had authorized the new bombing campaign ('The son claims vengeance for the father'[21]), but an interview with Bush, shown on CNN television and other channels, suggested that he had simply been informed that the strikes were under way. (On 27 September 2000 Bush had declared in Redwood, California, that he intended to have a 'foreign-handed foreign policy', so perhaps he too was confused as to what had transpired.) Bush, in Mexico at the time of the bombing raids, declared: 'We're going to watch very carefully as to whether or not he [Saddam Hussein] develops weapons of mass destruction, and if we catch him doing so, we'll take the appropriate action.' Even this brief comment was at odds with what was soon being claimed as the purpose of the attack. Geoff Hoon, British defence secretary, explained that the bombing had been a 'proportionate response' to the increased threat to the American and British aircraft flying over southern Iraq. (It was seemingly no business of Hoon and his ilk to remember the illegality of such flights.) Hoon emphasized that the new bombing raids were purely a matter of self-defence: 'Saddam Hussein should be clear that we will not tolerate continued attempts to endanger the lives of our aircrew. But if he stops shooting at us there will be no need for the RAF to attack his air defences.'[22]

In the previous six months the Iraqis had reportedly installed fibre-optic cables into the main command-and-control facilities around Baghdad, dramatically improving the effectiveness of their air defences. British and American pilots were said to have experienced an increasing number of 'trips' in the weeks before the bombing campaign, incidents where air crews can 'feel' a hostile missile or anti-aircraft shell close to the aircraft. In such a scenario the Iraqi fire was getting closer to the US–UK aircraft, which in any case were violating the airspace and territorial integrity of a sovereign state. How long, it had been asked, would Washington and London tolerate the growing probability that the Iraqis would succeed in shooting down one of the attacking planes?

The Iraqi media reported that one woman had been killed and 11 other people, including three children, injured during the aerial bombardment. Television footage from a hospital showed three children, three women and two men, bleeding from various wounds though no details were given about the severity of the injuries. On 16 February, the day of the bombing, two Iraqi children, seven-year-old Muhammed Qassim Muhammed and eight-year-old Ahmed Hameed Firhan, were injured when a cluster bomb from the 1991 Gulf War exploded while they were tending sheep in the Habaniya district, west of Baghdad. This tragic event symbolized the futility and horror of the long US–UK war on Iraq, begun in 1991 (or earlier) – an Orwellian 'war without end'.[23]

The response, outside the United States and Britain, to the new bombing campaign was almost universally hostile. Some western media, of whom better might have been expected, found the first Bush II aggression 'encouraging' since it demonstrated that the new US President was less isolationist that the pre-election rhetoric had suggested.[24] None the less, the bombing had simply repeated 'the mistakes of the past'.[25] Some British commentators were pleased to see that Prime Minister Blair was supporting Bush in a more vigorous enforcement of American policy,[26] but there was much criticism of the US–UK posture as well. The idea that the air raids were a 'self-defensive' measure was widely regarded as absurd, since the US–UK aircraft had no lawful justification for flying patrols over Iraq. British journalist Robert Fisk noted the Orwellian nonsense of the Pentagon phrase 'protective retaliation' to describe the bombing campaign.[27] Criticism was focusing also on the extent to which Blair had been involved in the Bush decision (if it was a Bush decision):

The decision to mount the raid was personally approved by Tony Blair who was involved in discussion from the beginning . . .[28]

Unease about Britain's role in the raids grew last night [17 February] after it emerged the US President, George Bush, failed to call Blair on a special hotline before the strikes commenced.[29]

Downing Street was swift last night to credit Geoff Hoon, the Defence Secretary, as the man who authorized the airstrikes against Iraq.[30]

The Labour MP Clive Soley, chairman of the Labour parliamentary group, suggested that Britain needed to be careful about supporting a US President with a limited knowledge of foreign affairs. (Perhaps Soley was remembering Bush's 'foreign-handed foreign policy' or his perception that 'More and more of our imports come from overseas'.) In the United States the raids on Iraq were criticized by various people, including Edward Peck, former US Ambassador to Baghdad, and Scott Ritter, former head of the UN disarmament team. But most of the criticism came from abroad, with only Israel being prepared to back the bombing campaign.

Iraq, unsurprisingly hostile to US–UK aggression, issued a press release linking the bombing campaign with Israel's oppression of the Palestinians:

> The United States and the United Kingdom commit another monstrous aggression against the people of Iraq. US and UK warplanes today bombed the suburbs of Baghdad injuring at least 11 civilians and killing three others. This action is a clear aggression against the sovereignty and territorial integrity of Iraq . . .

> Iraq considers this action a part of a continuous war of aggression waged against Iraq with bombs and sanctions since 1991.

> This aggression is waged by three countries, two of which are involved directly . . . the third country is Israel, which has a direct benefit from such aggression . . . these two countries prepare the grounds for the Zionist entity to commit another aggression against Arabs and Palestinians.

The International Response

The Arab League commented that the bombing raids had violated international law and would fuel anger throughout the Arab world, and even the generally pro-US Gulf states had failed to endorse the fresh military action. Several hundred Iraqis and Palestinians in Baghdad marched in protest, burnt an Israeli flag, and chanted slogans in praise of Saddam: 'With our soul and blood, we defend you, Saddam!' Tamader Jassim, a 19-year-old student, said: 'All the victims were innocent people who did not mean anything to America. They expect us to hate our leader by doing this, but they are wrong. We have started hating anything American because of these strikes.'

Russia, China and France – all Permanent Members of the Security Council – were predictably outraged at the aerial bombardment of Iraq, with other European states equally hostile to the military initiative. (Blair had seemingly kept his bombing plans secret from his European allies: 'The Italians and Germans are said to be sulking, and the French are reported to be furious.'[31]) George Galloway, a pro-Arab Scottish MP in the UK Parliament, in Baghdad on a 'solidarity visit', compared the bombing to 'Hitler marching into Czechoslovakia' and commented: 'What the British and American governments are doing is reckless, lawless and murderous. For every bomb that is dropped, Saddam is getting stronger.' Premier Blair seemed undeterred. If Saddam would not stop 'attacking us', Blair would 'continue to take the steps necessary to protect our forces and to prevent Saddam from ever again wreaking havoc, suffering and death'. Tam Dalyell, another Scottish MP in the UK Parliament, demanded an explanation: 'Not only Russia and China but, for heaven's sake, France as well have condemned our country over this. Parliament should be recalled early next week. We need explanations and we need them at once.'

On 18 February Joschka Fischer, Germany's foreign minister, flew to Washington to condemn the bombing raids, with France expressing its 'incomprehension and discomfort' and Bulent Ecevit, Turkish Prime Minister, urging Washington to look again at its Iraq policy. Claudia Roth, the designated Green Party leader in Germany, declared that bombing 'is not the right way to democratize Iraq', while Rudolf Scharping, German defence minister, was now appearing remarkably receptive to Russian and Chinese criticisms of Bush's proposed anti-missile shield ('son of Star Wars'). Condemnation of the bombing was also voiced across the Arab world ('unjustified use of force' – Jordanian premier Ali Abu Ragheb; Saddam 'not a threat' to the world – President Mubarak of Egypt; need to halt 'aggressive actions launched against Iraq in violation of United Nations resolutions' and to end 'international sanctions against the people of Iraq' – joint statement from Libya and Tunisia). Cuba denounced 'the false arguments used, once more, to justify criminal actions in frank violation' of international law 'and condemns the policy of genocide maintained by the US government against Iraq'.

The American and British aircraft had resumed their flights over southern Iraq, two days after the bombing campaign, in defiance of Saddam Hussein's pledge to avenge the raids. There was no immediate retaliation, though it seemed too early to conclude that the air strikes had been successful. Washington and London were now asserting that more bombing raids might be necessary, despite US–UK isolation on the world stage. On 21 February

American officials conceded that the aerial bombardment had only been *at best* a moderate success. Rear Admiral Craig Quigley, a Pentagon spokesman, acknowledged that the bombing had not been perfect ('It never is'), with the bombing accuracy rating only 'a B-minus or a C-plus'. CBS News said that only eight of the 20 targeted radars had been hit, suggesting that the 'self-defence' raids by US and UK aircraft had been largely ineffectual.[32]

So the bombing campaign against Iraq had not worked, had made Saddam stronger, and had outraged the vast bulk of international opinion. Even Saudi Arabia ('feelings of denunciation and anxiety over the recent escalation' – Prince Saud al-Faisal) and *Newsweek* ('The . . . sanctions . . . have become unworkable . . . Some good US allies have broken ranks with Washington' – 20 February 2001) were voicing open criticism of the failed and illegal US policy on Iraq. But even now the bombing continued. On 22 February, American aircraft bombed sites in northern Iraq, earning yet more international condemnation. Thus General Leonid Ivashov, head of International Relations at Russia's Defence Ministry, referred to America's 'new defiance of world opinion' and the 'barbaric and inhumane' treatment of the Iraqi people: 'There was no military justification for the strikes.' President Bush was reiterating his 'primary goal' of making it clear to Saddam Hussein 'that we expect him to be a peaceful neighbour in the region' – as presumably indicated frequently by American bombs and missiles. On 24 February the Moroccan Human Rights Association (AMDH) joined the chorus condemning US–UK bombing raids on Iraq, terming them 'war crimes and collective extermination against humanity'. The AMDH urged that those responsible for the bombing be tried, and that the Arab League work towards the abolition of sanctions on the Iraqi people.

More Civilian Casualties

George Galloway visited bereaved families and relatives of the 22 people, mostly women and children, wounded by the US–UK bombing.[33] He also visited the residential areas that had been hit by the air strikes, and heard the stories of some of the Iraqi victims. Fourteen-year-old Munder had been kicking a ball along the street when the sirens sounded. He fled in terror but then a blast knocked him unconscious to the ground. When he awoke in Yarmouk hospital, he was being treated for two shattered ankles, a shattered wrist and shrapnel in his face and chest. A baker had survived the collapse of his shop, a labourer had been blown off his bicycle, and the abdomen of a 44-year-old woman had been penetrated by a massive shard of steel. The woman's 18-year-old son, his arm hideously mutilated, lay in the bed next to her.[34]

On 23 February 2001 George Galloway had an off-the-record conversation with a senior Whitehall source who said that he was speaking 'candidly and honestly'. The man gave his views on the recent bombing campaign (16 February):

> This was a cock-up from first to last . . . right down to killing Muslims on a Friday [the Muslim holy day] . . . It seems to have been something the military wanted, primarily the US military . . . We knew the targets were outside the zones by several degrees, but no one seemed to know the significance of those degrees.[35]

What was it all about? How were the targets selected? What was the real purpose of the bombing campaign? To degrade Iraqi air defences? To terrorize a civilian population? To give the US and UK aircraft something to do? To establish the macho credentials of George W. Bush? Who could doubt that Bush II needed all the public relations help he could get. On 30 August 2000, he had declared: 'Well, I think if you say you're going to do something and don't do it, that's trustworthiness.' But he knew that he was required to have views on authoritarian regimes and that the Israelis should be mentioned from time to time. On 13 March 2001 President Bush gave further insights into his foreign-policy thinking:

> But the true threats to stability and peace are those nations that are not very transparent . . . They're very kind of authoritarian regimes. The true threat is whether or not one of these people decide, peak of anger, try to hold us hostage, ourselves; the Israelis, for example, to whom we'll defend, offer our defences; the South Koreans.'

The US President presumably shared the belief that the 'no-fly' zones had been created, albeit without UN authorization, so that the US-sanctioned air forces could protect the Shi'as in southern Iraq and the Kurds in the north. But Washington was no nearer to explaining how the protection of Shi'as and Kurds was consistent with the frequent American, British and Turkish bombing of the areas where they happened to live. There was ample testimony, from UN and other independent sources, indicating thousands of Iraqis wounded, traumatized and killed by US, UK and Turkish warplanes in the southern and northern 'no-fly' zones. Was the bombing campaign of 16 February really launched as a necessary US-authorized exercise in self-defence? Was this new aggression a reliable indication of the shape of US foreign policy under the new Bush administration?

On 12 March 2001 the 12-year-old Naima Mashal Ahmed was killed when a bomb from the 1991 Gulf War exploded in the Qaim district of Anbar, west of Baghdad. She had been picking mushrooms with her sister Haneen, who was seriously injured by the bomb. Since the Gulf War Iraqi civil defence teams had managed to defuse some 56,483 missiles and cluster bombs, but the civilian casualties being caused by this lethal residue continued to mount. On 16 March a bomb planted in Baghdad killed two people and injured around 30 others.

The recent heavy bombing campaign had not been repeated, despite the humiliating fact that most of the targets had not been destroyed. Why had American and British aircraft not returned 'to finish the job'? Was the defence of the illegal US–UK aircrews no longer a priority? Were Washington and London smarting under the sheer weight of international condemnation? Isolated bombings were still taking place but there was no renewed onslaught. On 30 March a US Air Force F-15 fighter-bomber attacked a site in southern Iraq in response to what US officials called 'recent Iraqi attempts to shoot down US and British pilots'. Had the 16 February bombing campaign changed nothing? If that operation had been successful, why were further bombing strikes still necessary?

In early April there were reports of a new US-devised strategic ploy. US–UK planes had already been dropping concrete bombs 'to avoid collateral damage'. (Is it not unhealthy to be hit by fast-moving lumps of concrete?). Now they were apparently dropping leaflets on Iraq. On 2 April *Nabdh al-Shabab*, the newspaper, published one of the leaflets. It declared: 'We warn you, soldiers of the Iraqi anti-aircraft weapons, not to fire at the coalition's planes and not to open your radars against them.' (The use of the word 'coalition' was no more than propaganda: the anti-Iraq Coalition had dissolved years ago.) Then the newspaper, having acquainted its readers with the West's new strategic weapon, urged them to tear up the leaflets and to continue fighting. A US spokesman felt obliged to point out that there had only been one drop of such leaflets, on 16 February, when the heaviest recent bombing campaign had been waged. (Were the Iraqis really expected 'not to fire at the coalition's planes' when those very aircraft were dropping bombs on Iraq?) Iraq, for its part, had no worries about the new Western ploy: the leaflets had been 'ridiculed and dismissed by our brave fighters'.

On 6 April 2001, Thamir Zair, an Iraqi farmer, was killed when a bomb from the 1991 Gulf War exploded in Dhiqar province near the city of Nassiriya, and one week later American bombers were again attacking sites in southern Iraq. On 14 April, Baghdad appealed to the Arab League to persuade Saudi Arabia and Kuwait to stop granting facilities for American and British bombers to attack targets in Iraq. To much of the Arab world, and to many independent observers, it did seem remarkable that Saudi Arabia, site of the holy cities of Mecca and Medina, could continue conspiring with Christian aggressors against a brother Muslim country.

The Unending Aggression

The situation in mid-2001 was plain. The grand anti-Iraq Coalition, cobbled together by US bribery and threats in the early 1990s, had almost entirely dissolved. Many of the Arab states had been reluctant to support a Christian war against a Muslim brother, and it was not long before Russia, China, France and others were expressing criticism of the US–UK posture. For a time France helped the United States and Britain to patrol the so-called 'no-fly' zones but decided years ago to withdraw from the illegal charade. The United States, helped by a servile UK poodle, continued the flights over Iraq, dropping bombs, concrete or leaflets when it chose, having decided long ago that unprincipled arrogance was the best attitude to adopt. (On 16 February 2000 George W. Bush declared in Hilton Head, South Carolina: 'If you are sick and tired of the politics of . . . principles, come and join this campaign.')

Washington and London continued to defend the overflight and bombing policies, though much of the argument had now descended into farce and absurdity. The southern Shi'as were hardly being protected by high-flying aircraft that never attacked anything other than Iraqi air defences and civilian installations; and the northern Kurds were not encouraged to learn that the 'protective' overflights by NATO allies, America and Britain, were frequently suspended to allow bombing raids on the Kurds by NATO ally Turkey using US-supplied aircraft and munitions. Saddam could attack the Shi'as by means of armoured land forces; the Turks could attack the Kurds by means of both aerial bombardment and land invasion. 'Safe havens'? The US-led campaign of overflights and bombing has never focused on protecting anyone except American and British pilots – who had no ethical or legal right to be there in the first place.

The flights were useful in producing trauma and terror in a civilian population, and as a way of collecting surveillance data for subsequent military aggressions. And the frequent bombings were useful as practice 'in the field'. Thus a significant editorial in a prestigious London newspaper observed that the bombing gave American and British pilots '*a valuable form of live-fire training*'.[36] How useful to be able to bomb a distant foreign country, albeit a sovereign member of the United Nations, just for practice!

On 28 April 2001, there were further US–UK air raids on civilian targets, with an official from the Iraqi Ministry of Information declaring: 'A formation of hostile planes raided civilian and service establishments in Najaf province...' An American spokesman for the US European Command, based in Germany, claimed that only military targets had been attacked. But now there were signs that Washington was concerned that US pilots were becoming increasingly insecure in conducting their illegal flights over Iraqi territory, with the Pentagon suggesting that the pilots were at serious risk of being shot down. A British official commented that 'One day the Iraqis will get lucky'; and Steven Simon, of the London-based International Institute of Strategic Studies, observed: 'It is a tough dilemma. The argument against flying is that sooner or later an aircraft will be shot down, which would be a huge propaganda victory for Saddam. Equally, if you stop the patrols that is also a victory for Saddam.'[37] On 18 May American and British aircraft again bombed targets in southern Iraq.

In early June three American warplanes 'buzzed' an Iraqi Airways Boeing 707 civilian aircraft on a domestic flight carrying passengers between the Baghdad and Basra governorates. The warplanes trailed the civilian aircraft for 17 miles, with the American pilots demanding to know details of the civilian aircraft. Iraq immediately dubbed this event an 'act of aerial piracy' which 'constitutes a serious violation of Iraq's sovereignty and territorial integrity and endangers the life and safety of a large number of innocent civilians...'[38] On 23 May, American and British aircrafts fired missiles at wheatland in the Hamdaniyah district of the Ninawa governorate, causing an extensive fire that completely destroyed the wheat crop.[39]

On 19 June 2001 Iraqi sources reported that 23 people were killed and 11 injured when British American aircraft bombed a football field near the northern city of Mosul: 'The raids, which targeted a football field, martyred 23 citizens and wounded 11 others who were playing football' (Iraqi News Agency). American and British sources denied that bombs had been dropped, though admitting that allied aircraft had been in the region.[40] Nizar Hamdoon, Iraq's Deputy Foreign Minister, reiterated what was common knowledge: 'These bombings continue on an almost daily basis in violation of international law and in violation of Iraqi sovereignty... We have lost faith in the Security Council. Sanctions will never be lifted by the United States and Britain because they are politically motivated...' The Iraqi News Agency reported that the bombing of the Tel Afr soccer field had killed, amongst others, four brothers aged from four to 29 years: the Tel Afr residents 'buried their dead... shouting their anger against this American and British crime'.[41]

A month later, on 19 July 2001, a documentary film released in the United States by Scott Ritter, former US weapons inspector in Iraq, accused

Washington of having manipulated inspections to spy on Iraq and to provide a pretext for military strikes against Baghdad.[42] Ritter declared: 'They [the Americans] used UNSCOM in two ways – as a vehicle for information pertaining to the security of Saddam Hussein and to manipulate the process of information to create appropriate triggers for military action.' He claimed that the United States had sparked confrontations over access to sensitive areas that could provide an excuse for bombings. Saddam Hussein, claimed Ritter, had been fundamentally disarmed as early as 1995: 'Iraq is a defanged tiger.' And yet the sanctions, the illegal air patrols and the bombings were still continuing. Targets for air strikes – many of them confirmed by independent observers, including UN personnel – have included residential areas, oil pipelines, schools, hospitals, livestock, food warehouses, wheat fields and Bedouin tents in the desert.

There were no signs that the pattern, consolidated over more than a decade, was about to end. On 10 August 2001, American and British bombers carried out an extensive attack on Iraqi targets – allegedly a missile site, a radar installation and a military communications centre. Some 50 aircraft – 20 US and British strike aircraft and 30 support planes – were involved in the operation, the US aircraft flying from the carrier USS *Enterprise* in the Gulf and from bases in Saudi Arabia and elsewhere in the Gulf. Iraq reported that one person had been killed and 11 wounded. Four days later, American and RAF jets launched further strikes on Iraq, though there was allied reluctance to report the scale of the operation. Further attacks occurred over subsequent days and weeks. For example, on 26 August, US and British warplanes attacked civilian targets in southern Iraq: 'US and British warplanes violated our airspace, carrying out two sorties from Saudi Arabia and 16 sorties from Kuwait. The planes flew over the province of Basra, Dhiqar, Meisan, Qadissiya and Wassit, attacking service and civil installations in Wassit province.' The Iraqis subsequently reported that two people had been killed and several houses destroyed. Four days later, there were further raids in southern Iraq, killing two villagers.

On 31 August 2001, it was confirmed, by both Iraq and Western sources, that US and British aircraft had attacked and destroyed the radar installations at the civil Basra airport. An Iraqi transport official commented that the warplanes had 'committed a despicable crime by bombing the radar station of Basra International Airport, which guides civilian landings and take-offs'. The official noted that the equipment was registered with the International Air Transport Association: 'It was fully destroyed.' It was further pointed out that the international airport was important in Basra province, home to Iraq's main port on the Gulf and major oil installations, 300 miles south of Baghdad. A US official declared that the airport was 'dual use', with both civilian and military facilities: 'We used the right kind of bombs on the target to see to it that there would be minimum collateral damage.' The bombing continued, according to the United States and Britain, targeting only military installations, but according to Iraq causing frequent civilian deaths.

On 10 September American and British planes bombed farms in southern Iraq, killing eight civilians and injuring others in the al-Saliya area between al-Numinayah and al-Zubaidayeh in Wasit province, south east of Baghdad: 'The US and Britain committed yet another savage aggression that targeted Iraqi civilians . . .' The planes used missiles and cluster bombs, leading to the possibility that unexploded ordnance, a consequence of unexploded cluster bomblets, would cause fatalities in the future. Later in September, more bombing raids were carried out by Allied aircraft. On 2 and 14 October, for example, further raids were carried out against what the US–UK authorities claimed were military sites and what the Iraqis claimed were civilian installations.

The US–UK raids continued into 2002. Iraqi civilians were killed in January and February, and there were signs that the United Nations was growing uneasy about the illegal allied use of the 'no-fly zones', with Secretary-General Kofi Annan preparing to discuss the zones – which had already been criticized by his predecessor, Boutros Boutros-Ghali.

Iraqi children and adults were being killed by the frequent bombing raids and by the explosive residue from earlier US–UK strikes. Iraq remained a target nation, vulnerable to a seemingly endless bombing campaign from American and British warplanes. In early May 2002 allied aircraft flying from an air base in Turkey bombed targets in Ninevah province, killing one person and wounding three. On 28 May American and British aircraft dropped heat flares on crops of barley in the Ninawa governorate, burning large areas of the crops in the districts of al-Hamdaniya and Hamam al-Alil. It then seemed increasingly obvious that Washington and London were planning a drastic escalation of the military campaign against the Iraqi people.

On 5 July 2002 Kofi Annan ended a third round of UN–Iraq talks in Vienna designed to prepare the ground for a return of UN weapons inspectors to Iraq. It seemed that little progress had been made: Iraq wanted an end to sanctions but the UN officials, under US pressure, had insisted that the inspectors must first give a satisfactory report on the weapons issue.

The United States responded to the failure of talks by leaking a Pentagon war plan, *Centcom Course for Action*, to *The New York Times*. The document, drawn up by US Central Command in Tampa, Florida, gave details of how overwhelming military force would be used in a planned invasion of Iraq. A three-pronged attack involving air, land and sea forces would be launched to crush all Iraqi resistance and to topple the regime. Some 250,000 American soldiers and marines would be deployed in the invasion, while hundreds of aircraft flying from eight countries would bomb thousands of targets in Iraq, including airfields, roads, communication sites, bridges, warehouses and factories. In July 2002 the Pentagon had reportedly increased the production of ordnance and was stockpiling masses of military hardware in the Gulf and elsewhere. The document gave no details of timing for the planned invasion of Iraq.

NINE

Tightening the Sanctions

Losing the Propaganda War

The United States was losing the propaganda war on Iraq. There was a growing international perception, outside Kuwait, that Saddam Hussein was no longer a threat to the region and that the sanctions regime was having a devastating impact on the Iraqi civilian population. There were also mounting business pressures on Washington for a change in policy. Russia, France, China, some Arab states and others were manoeuvring for commercial advantage over Iraq, and US companies did not want to be left out. There was no prospect that the United States would be prepared to face the humiliation of abandoning the embargo, but the Washington strategists were increasingly aware that US policy had to be repackaged in propaganda terms. SCR 986, the oil-for-food provision, had been projected by the United States as a humanitarian device, whereas in fact it served to keep the sanctions in place, to provide a financial bounty to US-friendly 'compensation' claimants, and to secure US access to much-needed Iraqi oil. It was now necessary, judged Washington, to repackage the sanctions policy in a way that gave the appearance of compassion but which in reality resulted in a tightening, not a relaxation, of the punishing embargo.

The possible answer, we were first told in 2000, was 'smart' sanctions: that is, sanctions that could be cosmetically presented as being targeted on the Iraqi regime and Iraqi military capability, not on the helpless Iraqi people. But there were hidden agendas. Washington, under the George W. Bush administration, was determined to make the sanctions more effective while the strategists prepared the ground for a new war. 'Smart' sanctions would tighten the loopholes and cloak the war plans, while being hyped as demonstrating humanitarian concern.

By early 2000, the United States and Britain had been left almost totally isolated in the international community by insisting that the sanctions regime continue indefinitely. At the end of March, despite its months-long opposition to the proposal, Washington was forced to agree an increased revenue allocation for Iraqi oil-industry spare parts.[1] (The competence of presidential candidate Bush to handle such issues was being questioned: 'I think anybody who doesn't think I'm smart enough to handle the job is underestimating.'[2]) Now the US–UK position on sanctions was being widely criticized, even by the UN Secretary-General and the UN ambassadors of many countries.[3] Again it seemed clear that Washington was paralysing the Iraqi oil industry by using the UN Sanctions Committee to put essential spare parts on hold (see Chapter 3).

The US Response

In mid-2000, it was being emphasized that both the presidential candidates – the Democratic Vice-President Al Gore and Republican Texas Governor George W. Bush – would remain committed to existing US policy on sanctions. Both were determined that millions of innocent Iraqi civilians would continue to be punished for the real or alleged crimes of the dictator over whom they had no control. Thus Robert Pfaltzgraff, Professor of International Studies at Tufts University, commented: 'I don't see any fundamental change in US policy regardless of the outcome [of the presidential election]'. Neither Bush nor Gore was expected to ease the sanctions or to abandon the illegal 'no-fly' zones that provided a spurious justification for overflights, data collection, bombing and Iraqi deaths. At the same time Ken Katzman, Iraq expert at the Congressional Research Service, declared: 'Whoever is elected will order a review to see what steps are feasible. Both would look at the status of the exile movement . . . whether it has the capacity to shake up Saddam.' In any event it seemed obvious that both the sanctions and the overflight policy (this latter costing $1.8 billion a year) would continue.

On 4 August 2000 the United States was expressing public disagreement with the French interpretation of restrictions on flights to and from Iraq. Paris was now maintaining that a French charter flight to Iraq would not necessarily violate the sanctions regime – since the UN Security Council had never adopted a specific text banning all flights. Resolution 670 (25 September 1990) had essentially only banned aircraft carrying cargo, so it was possible that there was no intention to ban passenger flights. Thus a spokesman for the French foreign ministry commented: 'The refusal by some members of the Sanctions Committee to allow flights to and from Iraq may have led people to believe that there is an air embargo. There is no such thing.' Still a US State Department official insisted that it was up to the Iraq Sanctions Committee to determine that a plane was not carrying cargo. And there also had to be a 'determination of whether there's a commercial benefit' to Iraq. At the same time Hubert Vedrine, French foreign minister, was declaring that the sanctions on Iraq were 'cruel, ineffective and dangerous.'[4]

Various countries were now contemplating the possibility of sending humanitarian flights to Baghdad, a development that was alarming the United States. France and Russia were continuing to dispute the US interpretation of relevant UN resolutions, and Iraq itself was announcing the resumption of commercial flights through the 'no-fly' zones. In October 2000, Washington felt obliged to negotiate with the UN Sanctions Committee to revise the rules governing flights so that there would be no appearance that the sanctions were being violated.[5] Peter Hain, a minister in the British Foreign Office, seemed desperate to play down the significance of sanctions-busting flights: 'Any fantasy that flights going in, with or without UN approval, are going to undermine the fundamental structure of sanctions is precisely that – a fantasy.' Voices in the Wilderness observed that Hain was protesting too much: 'Perhaps he's just a little bit worried by the tide of public opinion.'[6] On 31 October Niall Andrews, Dublin MEP, flew from Ireland to Iraq on a flight loaded with humanitarian aid: 'I was in Iraq in May and I saw the horrific conditions – 500,000 young children have died in the country since 1990 and a third of all children under the age of five are seriously malnourished. My intention is to make a symbolic visit with humanitarian aid on board. Even if we sent 100 jumbo jets there with aid, it would not be enough. Andrews gave advance warning of his intention to fly aid to Iraq but did not wait for approval. Few observers could doubt that the authority of the sanctions regime was under serious threat.

Breaching Sanctions

There were dozens of flights into Baghdad's refurbished Saddam International Airport. For example, on 31 October 2000, seven flights touched down, including aircraft from Turkey, Lebanon, Russia and the United Arab Emirates, all carrying officials and business delegations for Baghdad's international trade fair. It was all a far remove from two years before when the airport was deteriorating and the frequent arrival of foreign flights could not be contemplated. Niall Andrews, Irish MEP, had arrived in an eight-seater aircraft carrying $15,000 worth of medicines for the children of Iraq, a symbolic gesture against a sanctions regime that he regarded as redundant and repellent. Another arrival was a giant TU-154 from Moscow with 50 parliamentarians and businessmen led by Pyotr Romanov, Communist Deputy Speaker of the Duma

– a plain statement that one of the Permanent Members of the UN Security Council was rejecting the long US–UK war against Iraq. And politicians and businessmen were not the only visitors: a host of intellectuals, soccer players, entertainers and others had been pouring into Baghdad to show their solidarity with Saddam Hussein in his stalwart support for the Palestinians and his robust stand against Western imperialism.

Since August 2000 dozens of humanitarian flights had landed in Baghdad, and it was far beyond the capacity of Washington and London to stem the flow. Many of the arrivals, having merely filed their flight plans, had refused to seek explicit permission from the Sanctions Committee (that is, from the US and Britain). While American and British planes were carrying out more bombing raids on Iraq, Saddam was hosting Ali Abu al-Ragheb, Jordanian Prime Minister, who had flown to Baghdad with 100 officials and journalists to 'promote good relations between the two countries'.

One authoritative survey indicated the extent to which foreign interests were courting an Iraq that was slowly moving out of the shadow of international isolation.[7] It was reported that ExxonMobil, Royal Dutch/Shell and BP were all seriously interested in the business opportunities in Iraq, and 'Total, Repsol and ENI have also kept in touch'. France's TotalFinaElf had secured exclusive negotiating rights for the huge Majnoon and Bin Umar oilfields and was close to signing contracts with the Iraqi authorities. Washington and London, with their own commercial agendas, were being outflanked by the rising tide of international commercial enterprise. Nor was the US–UK sanctions policy being helped by the universal perception of the devastating impact of the embargo on the lives of the Iraqi people.

Kofi Annan had spoken of the 'moral dilemma' posed by the genocidal sanctions regime, and had even conceded that the United Nations was in danger of losing the propaganda war – *'if we haven't already lost it'* – about who was responsible for the suffering of millions of innocent men, women and children: 'Is it Saddam Hussein or the United Nations?' Even the Iraqi opposition was being forced to recognize the abject failure of US–UK policy: 'The sanctions regime is helping to keep Saddam in power. They keep people poor and dependent on the regime. There needs to be an urgent reappraisal.'

The International Response

On 10 November 2000 the redoubtable George Galloway made yet another trip to Iraq to highlight the suffering being inflicted on innocent civilians by Washington and London.[8] He declared: 'The sanctions are morally wrong and have led to appalling misery and death among the Iraqi people. We have always said that they did not cover civilian flights and the British government will now be humiliatingly forced to accept that.' The bizarre mindset of Washington on such matters was well illustrated by an incident during the refuelling of the flight on its way to the Iraqi capital. The American authorities telephoned London about Father Noel Barry, a passenger on the plane, a former press officer to Cardinal Thomas Winning and a columnist with the *Catholic Times*. Washington was concerned that Father Barry was carrying cholesterol and angina medicine, for his own use but possibly banned by the Sanctions Committee. Barry patiently explained that he was taking medication to counter the formation of kidney stones.

There was now a groundswell of opinion against the sanctions regime. Even Iran, Saddam's traditional enemy, was recognising the genocidal impact of the embargo. On 13 November, Kamal Kharrazi, Iran's foreign minister, called for the sanctions to be lifted, saying that they were causing many sufferings to the Iraqi people. Three days later, the US State Department seemingly admitted that the sanctions policy had failed: they had not succeeded in toppling the Iraqi regime, which in any case had never been a purpose of the UN resolutions, 'but they have caused devastating misery to ordinary Iraqis'. One typical report summarized the emerging US attitude:

> Washington admitted that UN-imposed sanctions on Baghdad have not budged Iraqi President Saddam Hussein's regime. State Department officials said the crippling sanctions . . . have been more damaging to the middle class than the ruling élite.

In a rare admission, Washington said the suffering of Iraqis welcomed back Baghdad into Arab ranks, particularly in the wake of the violence erupting in the occupied Palestinian territories.[9]

Kofi Annan was again regretting the suffering of the Iraqi people under sanctions and hoped that they would soon be lifted. It was acknowledged that a growing number of Western and Arab countries wanted to see an end to the embargo. As one significant international move among many, the Islamic summit in Doha, in November 2001, had encouraged its 56 member states to ignore the sanctions. It seemed that soon the United States and Britain would be forced into a change of policy.

Igor Ivanov, Russian foreign minister, was now hinting at a new plan – 'agreed upon' within quarters of the UN Security Council – that might contribute to a solution of the Iraq problem. He declared that a halt to the US–UK air raids on Iraq was essential:

This condition is an important step towards the normalisation of conditions not only around Iraq but also in the Arab Gulf region. We believe this will be in the best interest for Iraq and its neighbours . . . we believe that we are able to offer support for the normalisation of relations.

On 18 November William Cohen, US defence secretary, met Sheikh Jaber al-Sabah and other Kuwaiti leaders to discuss sanctions and other matters. Already Cohen had been told by various Gulf leaders of their increasing concern that the embargo was hurting the Iraqi civilian population. The pressure was mounting. Peter Hain, the British Foreign Office minister responsible for the Middle East, was expressing his wish to see sanctions lifted: 'I want to see sanctions suspended so that everything can move forward. Iraq can move forward, the region can move forward.' This was no more than public-relations hyperbole. Hain had always been one of the most vigorous supporters of the genocidal sanctions system, and even now he was stressing that the only route to progress was Security Council Resolution 1284 (see Chapter 4) – a device for the indefinite prolongation of the embargo. But perhaps Hain's new tone was in response to the mounting agitation from 'moderate' Arab states. The case for sanctions was lost – in the Middle East, Britain, United States and elsewhere.

Washington was now concerned at the 'illegal' pumping of Iraqi oil, Basra light, to Syria. Richard Roth, US official for Near Eastern affairs, commented that as long as the new revenues came under UN control 'we don't have a problem', but there was still a question about whether the new conduit for Iraq exports would win UN approval.[10] The situation seemed increasingly uncertain. Saudi press reports were suggesting that Baghdad was willing to allow the return of UN arms inspectors, under certain conditions, but it seemed unlikely that the United States would agree to the new proposals.[11] China was reportedly agreeing with Kuwait on the need for Iraqi compliance with all relevant UN resolutions, but was keen to see an end to the sanctions regime. On 27 November, Tang Jiaxuan, China's foreign minister, declared on television: 'China sympathizes with the suffering of the Iraqi people under long-term sanctions' and criticized 'some Western countries for setting up no-fly zones in a sovereign country against the United Nations Charter and the norms of international relations'.

On 27 November 2000, Taha Yassin Ramadan, Iraq's Vice-President, arrived in India to discuss food supplies; and on the following day Tariq Aziz, Iraq's Deputy Prime Minister, was discussing the sanctions issue with officials in Moscow (Ivanov: 'The main task is to stabilize the situation on the Persian Gulf'). On 3 December, around 115 European politicians, clergymen and members of non-governmental organizations (NGOs) arrived in Baghdad from

Paris, yet another attempt to test the sanctions regime. Claude Cheysson, former French Socialist foreign minister, was part of the European delegation:

America has turned Saddam Hussein into the devil to justify its physical and military presence in the Middle East. President Hussein is more popular now than he was before the embargo was imposed. It's criminal. The poor and the young are suffering and they have no say. Britain has had a long relationship with the Middle East and it especially knows how valuable Iraq is for oil and how weakening a country's people in this way is historically a great mistake.

Gisele Halimi, former French Ambassador to UNESCO, echoed the sentiments: 'Two thousand children are dying every week because the European Union and the UN are under the menace of American dictates. We are going to tell the world – Listen, this has gone too far. We are going to end the embargo.'

US–UK Desperation

Washington and London were being pushed into a fresh scrutiny of the sanctions regime. A dramatic political U-turn would plainly be impossible but perhaps a fresh cosmetic packaging of the policy could be managed. Discussion of so-called 'smart' sanctions was imminent. In early December 2000 the United States and Britain were reportedly considering new sanctions on Iraq that would tighten the noose on the Saddam regime while at the same time easing the suffering of the Iraqi people. London, involved in discussions, was waiting for George W. Bush to take power on 20 January 2001 in order to coordinate with the United States on fresh sanctions being considered that would allow Iraq to import a wide range of humanitarian goods and to resume air flights.[12] This was all very puzzling. Iraq was already supposed to be allowed to import humanitarian goods, even at times under the terms of a 'fast-track' procedure (see Chapter 3), and many of the air flights had already resumed. The new sanctions would also freeze Iraqi assets, though many of them were already frozen, and ban Iraqi officials from being allowed to travel abroad – which would prevent Baghdad from presenting its case in other countries (and in the UN?). The new 'smart' sanctions, awaiting a smart George W. Bush for their implementation, were to be advertized as having a humanitarian purpose but were obviously being shaped to tighten the economic embargo.

On 4 December Benon Sevan, Executive Director of the Office of the Iraq Programme, was again urging the UN Security Council to readjust the work of the UN Sanctions Committee in order to expedite the delivery of humanitarian aid to Iraq. It was a forlorn hope since Washington and London were both committed to a policy of deliberate obstructionism. Sevan noted that the demands on the system had become more complicated: 'We cannot go on applying similar procedures which were valid at the time when it was only food and medicine.' (He emphasized that the United Nations was now also involved in the rehabilitation of the Iraqi infrastructure.) He was well aware that key Committee members (that is, the United States and Britain) were *politicising* the relief effort in Iraq: he urged such members to allow the Programme to 'maintain its distinct humanitarian identity'. UNMOVIC, the successor to UNSCOM, was now ready to begin the duties specified in Resolution 1284 (see Chapter 4), which meant nothing since the putative weapons inspectors had no access to Iraq.

The international pressure continued to mount for a realistic modification of a sanctions regime that was killing thousands of innocent Iraqis For example, the commentator Muqtedar Khan, criticising sanctions in general, observed:

> The United States and its allies have maintained sanctions against Iraq for nearly [sic] a decade. Thousands of Iraqi children have died out of hunger, malnutrition and lack of medical supplies. An entire nation has slowly receded into the Stone Age. The United States' objective was to get rid of Saddam Hussein or at least reduce his ability to threaten his neighbours. According to the White House and the State Department, sanctions have not accomplished this goal . . . If sanctions had worked, they would have been lifted to ameliorate the human tragedy of Iraq . . . sanctions, in spite of being devastating, have proved to be utterly ineffective.[13]

In the light of such criticisms, increasingly widely expressed, the UN Security Council moved to allow Iraq more flexibility in how it spent its oil revenues. The changes meant very little but created the impression that at least something was being done to ameliorate the suffering of the Iraqi people. Even at this stage, James Cunningham, US envoy to the Security Council, was prepared to utter the demonstrable absurdity that the existing 'food-for-oil program is meeting the needs of the Iraqi people while denying the Baghdad regime access to funds it would use to further threaten its neighbours'. Even Kofi Annan had repeatedly acknowledged that the UN humanitarian programme had never been intended to meet the full humanitarian needs of the Iraqi people – a truly lamentable admission that, even if the oil-for-food scheme had worked as intended, the Iraqi people would still have been expected to suffer through a plethora of humanitarian deprivations. Chen Xu, the Chinese representative, expressed the truth of the matter: 'The oil-for-food program cannot and will never completely address the humanitarian suffering of the Iraqi people and only an early lifting of the sanctions can achieve this objective.'

Hans Blix, head of UNMOVIC, noted Iraqi dissatisfaction with Resolution 1284: 'I think that Iraq is very interested in taking a step forward. They dislike many aspects of this resolution. They would like to have sanctions lifted immediately when they accept the resolution or at least suspended immediately' (see Chapter 4). There was growing recognition also, not only of the Iraqi dislike of the sanctions clauses in SCR 1284, but of the mounting international outrage at the social impact of the embargo. The talk about cosmetic 'smart' sanctions was continuing but it was obvious that the new Bush administration would not 'go soft on Saddam'. Secretary of State-designate Colin Powell, seemingly eager to dispel his 'dove' image, had said: 'We will work with our allies to re-energize the sanctions regime.' Could 'smart' sanctions be 're-energized' sanctions? The White House was facing big decisions.

There was renewed speculation about where sanctions were going. President Bush, one analyst judged, would take time to shift the American Iraq policy because the Republicans had promised to get tough on Saddam Hussein: 'But once they've spent a few months sounding and acting tough, I think they will come to the same conclusion: you can't oust Saddam with air power, sanctions or a feeble Iraqi opposition, and it's time to change policy.' (In fact one of the first foreign -policy acts of the Bush administration was to launch heavy bombing strikes on targets near Baghdad – 16 February, see Chapter 8.) The pressure to ease the embargo on Iraq was continuing to grow, not least from American companies eager not to miss out on lucrative oil-linked contracts and deals to rebuild the shattered Iraqi infrastructure. The Iraqis expected little change. Thus Sami Borhan, 48-year-old business manager, commented on Bush: 'Like father, like son. His policies will only be a follow-up of the policies of his father.' And the Iraqi weekly *Alif Ba* summed up the common Iraqi view: 'A change at the top of the American administration does not change the nature of Washington's policy. All American officials still wallow in the Zionist filth.' The daily Iraqi newspaper *al-Qadisiya* noted the Iraqi determination to break the embargo.[14]

Most of the international appeals for an end to sanctions intended no sympathy for the Saddam regime. Thus Human Rights Watch, one of the most prestigious human rights organizations, had sent a letter a year before to the United Nations, stressing the atrocities and war crimes committed by the Iraqi government but urging that the sanctions regime be restructured 'so as to minimize its impact on the civilian population'. Then it had been noted that there was 'a continuing degradation of the Iraqi economy' and 'an acute deterioration in the living conditions of the Iraqi population'.[15] A principal reason was 'the prolonged measures imposed by the Security Council'.[16]

The Failure of Sanctions

In early January 2001 the sanctions regime was being attacked from every quarter. For example, *The Gulf Today*, a UAE daily newspaper, declared that sanctions had outlived their purpose, hit the Iraqi people more than the government, and served Israel's interests. Hans von Sponeck, former UN Humanitarian Coordinator who had resigned in protest at the sanctions, was arguing that the infliction of such suffering on the Iraqi people was a violation of international law. (However, Israel had benefited by seeing the destruction of one of the principal threats to its security.)[17] Von Sponeck and Denis Halliday, his predecessor who had also resigned, published a letter in response to Peter Hain:

> Arguing for an end to economic sanctions is not at all about 'propping up a dictator'. Have sanctions targeted the proper parties? No. Have sanctions imposed in 1990 retained their legality? The UN Charter, the International Covenants on Human Rights and a host of other treaties allow only one answer: they have not.[18]

Now it was being noted that the flights over the 'no-fly' zones served no useful purpose: 'These flights of futility are symbolic of a failed war and a failed policy of sanctions and intimidation . . . They merely obstruct the dialogue necessary for ending the Iraqi people's suffering and gaining re-entry for the UN's exiled weapons inspectors.'[19] Moreover, as Saudi Arabia had reportedly made clear, Britain's solitary role in supporting America damage its role in the Middle East, stymie business, and undermine British and European Union attempts to mediate the Arab–Israeli conflict. And it did nothing to undermine the Iraqi regime: 'It actually helps Saddam who, careless of his people's lives, welcomes every foolish bomb.'[20]

Perhaps Britain really was considering a review of its Iraq policy and would in due course communicate fresh thoughts to the new Bush administration. A British official suggested that the Blair government had in fact been looking at the idea of 'smart' sanctions, though it was far from obvious how the Bush people would respond to a British overture. In fact US–UK policy on Iraq was usually shaped in Washington. Who could doubt that Bush II was happy with that arrangement?

Iraq was now declaring that it would be prepared to cooperate with the UN, but only on certain conditions:

> If the Security Council wants the continuation of cooperation, it should first lift, unconditionally and completely, the sanctions on Iraq. It should also stop and condemn the aggression against Iraq which has been going on for ten years and compensate Iraq for the damage that it has sustained.

Taha Yassin Ramadan, Iraq's Vice-President, urged such conditions in advance of the talks to be held in February with Kofi Annan. Now, Baghdad assumed, there would at last be an opportunity to express Iraq's legitimate grievances and the action that should be taken to address them. Again it seemed unlikely that Washington would permit the talks to reach a constructive outcome. American activists were now delivering around $250,000-worth of humanitarian supplies to Baghdad, in obvious defiance of President Bush's declared aim of tightening up the economic embargo. The 70 anti-sanctions campaigners, including Ramsey Clark, former US Attorney-General, had not asked Washington for permission to make the trip, though technically they had not broken sanctions because they had flown to Baghdad on an approved Jordanian aircraft.

On 16 January 2001 Shell, the Anglo-Dutch oil company, admitted that it had been holding talks with Iraq on the possibility of future oil exploration: 'We have had preliminary talks at a technical level which concerned one of several possible sites.' Shell, discussing the Ratawi oilfield, was just one of the many oil firms from France, Italy, Russia, China and elsewhere to have opened negotiations with Iraq, pending an end to sanctions. Iraq was known to have proven oil reserves of – about half of the Saudi resources; and it was anticipated that further exploration of the Western Desert would bring Iraq's known reserves up to the level of Saudi Arabia. And it was now clear that, even under the crippling sanctions and with a deteriorating oil industry, Iraqi production was having an impact on the global oil market.[21] BP and Exxon had begun buying cargoes of Iraqi crude, though insisting that such purchases did not flout UN rules.

Such developments, some only marginally within the terms of the sanctions regime, were providing further evidence that the multinational companies could be relied upon to put commercial advantage above the spirit of the embargo. Again it seemed plain that if the US–UK sanctions policy did not change, it would be gradually outflanked by the course of commercial affairs. Now Iraq was feeling confident enough to demand a surcharge on oil purchases, as a way of circumventing UN control over the entire revenues – a move that was exasperating America and Britain but none the less highlighting the need to examine the discredited sanctions policy. Saddam Hussein seemed to be slowly turning the embargo to his advantage, leading Sheikh Sabah al-Ahmad al-Sabah, Kuwaiti foreign minister, to urge a lifting of sanctions since it was the Iraqi regime that did not want the embargo to be removed.[22]

There was a growing international view that sanctions were crumbling despite US–UK efforts to maintain them. Anti-embargo activists were arriving, and many other flights; an international trade fair had been held in Baghdad and trade negotiations were under way with various countries. The regime was struggling to prise its oil revenues out of the grip of UN committees, and Iraq had recently signed an agreement in Cairo to launch an Iraq–Egypt free-trade area. And behind all such developments was the almost universal international condemnation of what the sanctions were doing to the Iraqi people: 'Around 1.65 million Iraqis, 700,000 of whom are children under the age of 18, have died as a direct result of the sanctions.'[23] Colin Powell had recently received a full briefing on Iraq policy from the State Department Bureau of Near East Affairs. Unidentified Department sources suggested that Powell had serious doubts about the continued maintenance of sanctions.[24]

The IAEA (International Atomic Energy Agency) inspectors were finding no irregularities in Iraq; the Baghdad regime was growing closer to such erstwhile foes as Syria and Iran; Britain was saying that the Iraqi threats to US–UK flights over the 'no-fly' zones had diminished;[25] and Washington and London were on the propaganda defensive. Colin Powell, despite his reported doubts, had instructed staff to devise ways of 're-invigorating' the sanctions, possibly by introducing an element of 'smart' targeting. At the same time, 'Washington has been watching in dismay as the sanctions gradually erode . . .'[26] Now it even seemed impossible for the United Nations to penalize oil firms that make illegal payments to the Saddam regime: 'If there is a violation – if it's among the oil buyers – it's up to their governments to take action' (UN official). With Iraq demanding that its customers pay 40 cents a barrel straight to the regime, many recent oil sales had been to obscure companies registered in Russia, Belarus, Liechtenstein, Ukraine, Sudan, Malaysia and South Africa; no company had admitted paying surcharges.

The United States, sensitive to the growing clamour for 'smart' sanctions, was struggling to resist any moves that would weaken the embargo. Kofi Annan remained concerned about the genocidal impact of the sanctions regime and was continuing to press, albeit with characteristic diffidence, for an amelioration of the suffering of the Iraqi people. A UN committee, set up by Kofi Annan, was expected to recommend 'smart' sanctions, a time limit on sanctions and majority voting on sanctions committees (these last two would be bitterly opposed by Washington). A draft of the report made suggestions that should have been quite obvious a decade before:

> Sanctions regimes, in particular the Security Council resolutions that enact them, must be carefully designed, clearly establishing their goals, identifying the targets, tailoring the type of sanctions imposed so that they are adequate to the situation, specifying clear criteria that need to be satisfied in order for the sanctions to be suspended or lifted.

Other suggestions, the 'smart' element, urged the targeting of the finances of leaders rather than the general population; and an effort 'to minimize the potential for adverse humanitarian impacts and to maximize the ability for humanitarian goods and services to reach civilian populations'. Such things as 'food, medicine and medical supplies' should 'be excluded from sanctions regimes'. Colin Powell, seemingly insensitive to such considerations, was now proposing that the sanctions on Iraq should be strengthened.[27]

It was already obvious that the sanctions system, as working, was killing tens of thousands of Iraqi civilians and continuing to erode the civic and industrial infrastructures of the country. However large the approved funds for the purchase of humanitarian goods, the United States and Britain were using the Sanctions Committee to sabotage the operation of the humanitarian programme (see Chapter 3). In fact, many of Iraq's trade partners were increasingly reluctant to negotiate contracts because of the associated bureaucracy and delays; and, even when goods were finally delivered, the contractors may not receive payment for months. Any scheme to introduce new types of sanctions, 'smart' or not, would be unlikely to address the persistent US–UK obstructionism at every stage of the process.

The messages from Washington were mixed, perhaps deliberately to add to the general confusion. In February 2001 American troops were training with the Kuwaiti army; Colin Powell was hinting that Iraq's diplomatic isolation might be ended if the UN weapons inspectors were allowed back into the country; and the possibility of 'smart' sanctions was again being considered. Now it was being acknowledged that Saddam Hussein had dramatically boosted the amount of oil revenue he was receiving outside the UN sanctions controls, partly by means of the newly reopened Syrian pipeline. And there was also the matter of the surcharge on oil sales and petroleum smuggling through Turkey, Jordan and Iran. In one estimate it was suggested the 552-mile pipeline connecting Iraq with Syria's Mediterranean port of Banias had been receiving 120,000 to 150,000 barrels a day since November 2000, with Leo Drollas, Deputy Directorof the Centre for Global Energy Studies, London, putting the current figure at around 200,000 barrels daily. This meant that, with Iraq offering Syria a sharply discounted price of about $15 a barrel, the shipments could be providing the Saddam regime with up to $3 million a day. Washington also knew that between 40,000 and 150,000 barrels of oil and diesel fuel were being shipped from northern Iraq to Turkey every day aboard hundreds of trucks that had travelled the route for years. The Americans had always ignored this sanctions-busting traffic because they needed access to the Incirlik air base.[28] US policy was slowly shifting, in part through the attitude of Colin Powell: despite the mixed messages, Powell did not then seem committed to using sanctions to achieve 'regime change' (that is, to oust Saddam) or to further wreck the Iraqi economy. Thus analyst Henri J. Barkey, formerly at the State Department, commented: 'Powell shifted the whole emphasis to the arms control aspect to de-emphasize the economic side.'[29]

The 'Smart' Sanctions Ploy

On 21 February 2001, the British government was reportedly preparing to discuss with the new US administration plans to impose 'smart' sanctions on Iraq. Now officials were confirming that the time had come to define a more 'clear-cut' sanctions policy thatwould focus on Saddam Hussein's attempts to acquire weapons of mass destruction and on the finances of leading members of the Iraqi regime.[30] Thus a Downing Street source declared: 'The mixture of measures – sanctions, military posture, oil revenues and enforcement around the borders – these are all elements that will be looked at again.' A fundamental reappraisal seemed about to begin, with US officials admitting that the alliance between the United States and Britain had begun to lose the public-relations war: 'With governments across Europe lining up to condemn the strategy, the Washington–London axis looks increasingly isolated.'[31]

US State Department officials had been given the task of 'retooling' the sanctions, so that Colin Powell would have new policies to offer the Arab states on his imminent tour of the region. At the same time, with Blair about to meet Bush, officials on both sides of the Atlantic were stressing that the reappraisal did not mean that there would be any softening of sanctions. Brian Wilson, the new Foreign Office minister responsible for Iraq, declared that there were two strands to British policy: 'The first is to minimize the human impact [of sanctions] and the second is to maximize the inability of Saddam Hussein to wage war on his own people, the region and the rest of the world.'[32] Did Wilson really believe that Saddam had ambitions to invade Chile, Mongolia and New Zealand?

The declared purpose of the US–UK review of the embargo was to scrap any of the sanctions that were hurting the Iraqi people, while strengthening those measures that were focused on the Saddam regime. The alleged Chinese involvement in helping Iraq to install fibre-optic communications systems suggested a need to tighten certain targeted sanctions, though it was by no means clear how this might be achieved. There was also a requirement for a more robust propaganda initiative to persuade doubting allies, such as France, that an abandonment of sanctions would increase the instability of the region. American and British intelligence services were expected to step up their covert operations against Iraqi agents approaching commercial companies to purchase components that could be used for building nuclear, biological and chemical weapons.

The overall need for a US–UK shift in sanctions policy was obvious. British diplomatic sources were quoted: 'In the Arab world we are the villains of the piece and many people are unhappy that we are struck with a policy that is not getting us any friends . . . *it is very easy for our critics to blame us for babies dying and we have to acknowledge that we have lost the propaganda war*' (my italics).[33] But there was still a rump of official opinion hoping that a fresh propaganda initiative was all that was required: 'It may be that all there will be is a change of presentation to re-focus domestic and international attention on Saddam.'[34] Perhaps 'smart' sanctions would be linked to a new propaganda drive.

It was plain that Washington and London had an uphill task. If so-called 'smart' sanctions could do the trick, why had they not been introduced three, six or eight years ago? Why were the United States and Britain so remorselessly committed to the genocide of the Iraqi people? What were the real agendas? To cut down the Iraqi population to Saudi levels, to install a tame puppet, and to dominate the Iraqi oil resource as Washington dominated the Saudi one?

On 22 February, a week after the fresh US–UK bombing campaign against Iraq, the Russian Duma overwhelmingly backed a resolution demanding that President Vladimir Putin tell the United States to lift the sanctions on Iraq. Thus a statement issued by the lower house of the Russian parliament declared:

Because of the multiple use of force against Iraq without UN authorization and the catastrophic humanitarian situation in the country, Russia believes that there is no need to preserve UN resolutions imposing economic sanctions against Iraq.

However, the Russian government – which, with China and France, had failed to veto the crucial resolution SCR 1284 (see Chapter 4) – had no appetite for ignoring the existing relevant UN resolutions. Thus Vasili Sredin, Russia's deputy foreign minister, commented: 'We are actively fighting for a fair political solution of the Iraqi problem on the basis of existing resolutions by the UN Security Council.' Despite all its complaints about the embargo, Russia was still prepared to let Washington run a totally discredited and genocidal policy.

On 24 February 2001 Colin Powell began his Middle East tour. Iraq staged a demonstration in protest: General Powell had 'blood on his hands' because of his involvement in the 1991 Gulf War. At a joint news conference in Cairo with Igor Ivanov, Russia's foreign minister, Powell said nothing new: the cause of the problem was in Baghdad, Saddam refused to abandon his pursuit of weapons of mass destruction, the UN and the US had an obligation, etc.: 'He threatens not the United States, he threatens this region, he threatens the Arab people, he threatens the children of Egypt, the children of Saudi Arabia, the children of Kuwait with these weapons.' *Rich – from someone whose country had killed around a million Iraqi children through the biological warfare of hunger and disease.*

Colin Powell was emphasizing that the US review of sanctions was at an early stage – typical procrastination in the absence of any humanitarian intent. In the West Bank city of Nablus, hundreds of Palestinians demonstrated in support of Iraq, burning photographs of Bush and Powell and, in reference to the recent US–UK bombing of Iraq, chanting: 'Stop the British and American aggression.' In Jenin, West Bank, pro-Iraq demonstrators set fire to pictures of Bush and Blair. Mouin Bashour, a protest organizer in Beirut, declared: 'We are here to ask Powell to listen to the people, not the leaders. The people's message is obvious: "No" to the bombing of Iraq, and "No" to US support for the Israeli crackdown on Palestinians.' Again Iraq was insisting on a total lifting of the UN embargo, and rejecting any US–UK scheme to introduce 'smart' sanctions that would do no more than preserve a demonstrably genocidal policy with minor cosmetic changes. In Baghdad Mohammed Mehdi Saleh, trade minister, declared: 'Whether they are smart or stupid sanctions, we will reject them.'

On 25 February, Colin Powell denounced the Israeli 'siege' of Palestinian areas: 'And now it is necessary for Israel to lift the siege as soon as possible so that economic activity can begin again in the region.'[35] Was the US Secretary of State about to recommend the bombing of selected Israeli targets if Israel refused to comply with UN resolutions? In Kuwait, Powell – along with the former President Bush, General Norman Schwarzkopf, Margaret Thatcher and others – contemplated elements of the 1991 Coalition, now largely dissolved. Again a British diplomat was on hand to admit the unavoidable truth: 'We have lost the propaganda war with Saddam. The perception today is that the UN sanctions are responsible for the deaths of children in Iraq.[36]

The search was still on for 'smart' sanctions – or at least for sanctions that might *appear* smart. President George W. Bush had memorably likened the existing sanctions to 'Swiss cheese – that means they are not very effective' (and he was impressed enough with this utterance to repeat it ad nauseam), but now was the time, meeting with Prime Minister Blair, to improve matters: 'We're going to work together to figure out a way to make them more effective.' It was left to Gary Sick, Middle East Institute at Columbia University in New York, to doubt that any sanctions could be devised that people had not already thought of in the last ten years. Neil Patrick, Royal United Services Institute in London, was just as sceptical about the search for 'smart' sanctions: 'What is proposed is not so much genuinely smart as an attempt to make sanctions appear smarter and more presentable.'[37] So again it was all about propaganda. Foreign Office sources were now acknowledging that smartness in presentation was at least as important as any new sanctions that might be invented – as if the genocide of a generation of Iraqi children could be glossed over by a new public relations initiative.

The aim was for Washington to have a revised sanctions scheme ready for the Arab summit scheduled for 27 March, though it was difficult to imagine what difference a few cosmetic changes would make. The US–UK posture was totally discredited and even Washington's erstwhile Arab allies were increasingly reluctant to support a policy that was killing a brother Muslim state. Colin Powell, in Kuwait City, was now trying to demonstrate macho credentials: 'Iraq, the aggressor, sits stranded, trapped in a prison of its own making, its people, children, put at risk by a regime that also puts at risk the people and children of the entire region by threatening to rebuild its army and manufacture weapons of mass destruction.' And Powell presumed to utter the familiar mantra that *the United States had no quarrel with the Iraqi people*, but it was important, he said, to continue the fight against evil.

Iraq had begun talks with the United Nations on the sanctions issue and related matters, while Washington was happy to report Arab support for its consideration of 'smart' sanctions. But, on his return to Washington, Powell conceded that his plan to allow modified sanctions that would ameliorate the plight of the Iraqi people was likely to run into opposition from hard-liners in the Bush administration. He argued that the existing sanctions regime was 'in a state of disarray, and that changes were needed: more civilian supplies could be allowed into Iraq while tightening up the controls on strategic materials'. It was a difficult distinction to make: even food is 'dual-use'.

The new bombing campaign (16 February 2001), what one Arab dubbed 'a fearless act of self-defence', further alienated even the moderate Arab states and pushed Washington and London into even greater international isolation. The search for 'smart' sanctions would continue, but the quest – like SCR 1284 – was widely being perceived as no more than an exercise in advertizing gimmickry. There was nothing in the proposed 'smart' sanctions that would address the massive problems of the human tragedy in Iraq: the increasingly malnourished and sick population, and the collapsing civil and industrial infrastructures. Colin Powell was intending to unveil a package of changes to the sanctions regime before the Arab summit took place in Amman, but it seemed unlikely that anybody would be listening. Various countries were tacitly breaking the spirit, if not the letter, of the embargo, and increasingly the US–UK policy was being seen as a foolish dogma whose time had passed.

On 7 March Secretary of State Colin Powell assured the House International Relations Committee that his plan to reshape sanctions would not let Baghdad off the hook. There would be no easing of the pressure on Saddam Hussein, but it was now essential to take steps to win international support for a more rational policy: 'I think the characterization that I have sometimes heard that we are easing up or giving up is quite incorrect. *We discovered a collapsing situation. We are trying to fix a collapsing situation with respect to the sanctions*' (my italics). Attempts to block Saddam Hussein's military ambitions had been 'hamstrung' because much of Europe and the Arab world was blaming the sanctions for impoverishing the Iraqi people. To refocus sanctions would make it possible to stem the Iraqi development of weapons of mass destruction: 'That gives us a new floor we can all agree to.' Powell did not have an easy ride, but many observers had expected it to be worse. Representative Benjamin A. Gilman (Republican, NY) expressed the common dissenting opinion: 'Loosening the sanctions against Iraq could provide Saddam Hussein with a greater ability to increase his weapon account.'[38]

In summary, the Powell proposals did not amount to much:

I discovered that we had an Iraq policy that was in disarray, and the sanctions part of that policy was not just in disarray, it was falling apart . . . It has nothing to do with regime change. That's US policy. That's US policy that let's put in basket two, the no-fly zone, or in basket three, Iraqi opposition activities.

My immediate concern was basket one, the UN basket and how it was falling apart . . . We were being accused and we were taking on the burden of hurting Iraqi people, hurting Iraqi children, and we needed to turn that around. The purpose of these sanctions was to go after weapons of mass destruction.

. . . it seems to me one approach to this was to go to those sanctions and eliminate those items in the sanctions regime that really were of civilian use and benefited people, and focus them exclusively on weapons of mass destruction and items that could be directed toward the development of weapons of mass destruction.

I found that our Arab friends in the region; as well as members of the Permanent five in the United Nations, as well as a number of my colleagues in NATO, found this to be a very attractive approach and that we should continue down this line . . .

So this wasn't an effort to ease the sanctions, this was an effort to rescue the sanctions policy that was collapsing. We discovered that we were in an airplane that was heading to a crash, and what we have done and what we are trying to do is to pull it out of that dive and put it on an altitude that's sustainable, bring the coalition back together.[39]

The 'Fast-track' Option – Again

What Powell was suggesting was an effective 'fast-track' facility for civilian goods – but this was already in place (did he know?), and it was not working. It was ridiculous to imagine that it could. In any modern economy there are literally hundreds of thousands of humanitarian items that are essential to the functioning of society. How could the Office of the Iraq Programme, or some equivalent, be expected to scrutinize hundreds of thousands of contracts every week to nod through the harmless civilian products and block anything that might have relevance to weapons production?

Why did nobody point out that the bureaucracy of the sanctions system was akin to the worst type of command economy – where every nut and bolt, every sock and shoe, every toothpick and ear swab, every loaf and bun, every cow and sheep, every window and door frame, every brick and tile, every scalpel and suture . . . has to be recorded, approved, stored, accessed, distributed, used, replaced, etc.? How on earth can a food industry, a national health service, a housing sector, a power network, a telecommunications system, and an oil industry be run with such a Kafkaesque regard for labyrinthine bureaucracy, endless procrastination and insane obsession? Kofi Annan had frequently remarked that the UN management of Iraq's access to supplies of every type could not be expected to replace normal economic activity. Colin Powell's fringe efforts were a nonsense, adding nothing extra, and conveying no hint that he even knew how the existing sanctions system worked.

The United Nations was recommending that civilian goods should be allowed to enter Iraq without needing approval by the Security Council or the Sanctions Committee. On 9 March Benon Sevan said that Kofi Annan was in favour of including non-military supplies on so-called 'green' lists for automatic review and approval for entry into the country. Again this was mystifying. How were the so-called 'green' lists expected to improve on the lists of humanitarian items allegedly rushed through under the terms of the 'fast-track' system? Washington was supposed to be thinking along the same lines, but what did it all mean? Just as the United States and Britain were blocking countless items from being 'fast-tracked', so they could prevent them from being added to the 'green' lists. The 'smart' sanctions of Washington and Kofi Annan were proving to be as stupid as the ones already in force.

On 21 March 2001 the US State Department was again claiming to have won Arab support in its efforts to modify the sanctions regime – as if such efforts had been a constructive US initiative instead of, as was the truth, a desperate public relations ploy forced on Washington by the rising international clamour against what the US–UK policies were doing to the people of Iraq. Richard Boucher, US State Department, said that the Arab countries wanted to loosen the blockade on consumer goods while strengthening the military restrictions. It had taken the United States nearly eleven years to decide that there might be some PR mileage in paying lip service to the radical notion that Iraqi children were entitled to eat. Even now the new sanctions proposals were no more than talk: nothing new was being done to mitigate the genocidal impact of the sanctions regime.

The 22 Arab states met in Amman on 25 March – to agree about the Palestinians and to disagree about the Iraqis (see Chapter 7). Washington was as happy as might be expected in the circumstances. There would be no impediments to the Israeli oppression and no radical challenge to the devastating embargo against the Iraqi people. There were plenty of signs that sanctions were crumbling, but Washington still had enough Arab friends – led by mercenary feudalists – to be content that there would be no overwhelming Arab-coerced breach in the crumbling sanctions wall. Amman had been mixed: yes, sanctions were a horror, but enough Arab leaders were keen to protect their standing in Washington.

The Bush administration was reportedly working on a revised sanctions plan for Iraq, though there seemed to be no concern for the suffering of the Iraqi people. A principal idea was that UN monitors would be posted outside Iraq's borders and at key airports, to prevent Saddam Hussein from importing military goods. Iraq's neighbours would be cajoled into accepting the plan by allowing them limited trade with Baghdad, including the purchase of Iraqi oil at discounted prices. Again it was interesting that Washington could presume to decide how UN personnel would be deployed under the new arrangements. And there was nothing in this that would alter the US grip on the Iraqi economy. All the proceeds from the sale of cheap Iraqi oil would continue to be deposited in special UN-administered accounts over which the United States would have complete control.

The new proposals were, by April 2001, no more than wish-list generalities. It was said that the specifics would be hammered out by June, when the Security Council was scheduled to review the sanctions issue. But observers who knew the grim history of sanctions were expecting little. Time after time, under international pressure, the United States had taken purely cosmetic initiatives to disguise its commitment to the sanctions regime. Thus, after the harrowing Ahtissari report (1991) on the state of the Iraqi civilian population, Washington declared that humanitarian goods might be excluded from the embargo, but there was little change in the humanitarian situation. The deaths continued to soar and the surviving population remained destitute. UN Resolutions 706, 712 and 986, all US-sponsored in an acquiescent Security Council, were no more than cynical attempts to counter the growing international perception that Washington was perpetrating a genocide against a helpless people. Similarly, SCRs 1284 (1999) and 1409 (2002), both nominally intended to accelerate the flow of humanitarian supplies while tightening Iraq's access to military equipment, were not designed to address the basic cause of Iraqi suffering – that the Iraqi people had lost control over their own national economy. Few independent observers imagined that the so-called 'smart' sanctions, still mired in the US-manipulated bureaucracy of the sanctions regime, would do much to alleviate the humanitarian plight of Iraqi civilians.

The new sanctions regime, if it were ever to transpire, would involve *more* bureaucracy – which would increase the scope for US obstructionism. A list of oil companies authorized to buy Iraqi petroleum would be compiled, in order to drive out the shadowy middlemen believed to be making illegal payments to the Saddam regime. Some of the new provisions would be administered solely by Washington – a sure recipe for covert sabotage of the scheme; and other aspects would be run by UN bodies, but only with American approval. States bordering Iraq would be given financial incentives to block oil smuggling, and efforts would be made to tighten the controls on oil revenues. One European diplomat commented: 'These are the directions so long as the front line states play ball.' Another remarked that Western officials were already haggling with various countries about the incentives (that is, financial bribes) they would be offered for agreeing the changes to the sanctions system.[40]

There would be a revised list of banned items. Some obviously benign items, now banned as 'dual-use', would be allowed. Banned items would be described in detail to clarify the situation for would-be suppliers. Holds had been placed on $3.3 billion-worth of contracts for imports to Iraq, with $3.1 billion-worth of these placed by the United States. Now a State Department official was suggesting that the new arrangements 'would remove the need for the United States to put so many goods on hold'.[41] (In fact the value of holds was set to rise drastically – see Chapter 3.)

So the sanctions system would remain intact, Washington would still be able to pick and choose what contracts it blocked, and Iraq would have gained no new element of control, essential to addressing the needs of the Iraqi nation, over the management of its own economy. Thus a fully accredited UN member, whose sovereignty and territorial integrity were explicitly stated in Security Council resolutions, would be endlessly maintained as a US protectorate, a quasi-colony. The 'smart' sanctions being developed by the Bush administration would do nothing to mitigate the suffering of the Iraqi people. Instead, *the prevailing sanctions system would be preserved while 'front line' countries would be bribed into helping the United States to tighten its grip on all aspects of Iraqi affairs.*

It was now emerging that even this new attitude to sanctions, grossly hypocritical as it was, was too much for the hawks in the Bush administration to swallow. Anything that even hinted at relief for the Iraqi people was to be instantly dismissed as appeasement ('and look what happened in the 1930s', etc.). So there was no guarantee that the Powell proposals, shaped to expand US control, would be adopted. For example, Donald Rumsfeld, US defence secretary, believed it would be much more productive to fund anti-Saddam terrorism and to bomb the Iraqi regime out of existence.[42] It was far from certain that any new sanctions arrangements would be implemented. Russia and other states were continuing to suggest that the sanctions should be lifted if Baghdad allowed UN weapons inspectors back into the country, but that was too much for Washington: the United States would never be willing to contemplate a radical move that would sacrifice its control over the Iraqi economy.

The UN Office of the Iraq Programme was now reporting (31 March–6 April 2001) that the Sanctions Committee had placed on hold $3.43 billion-worth of contracts, about $3 billion-worth of these for humanitarian supplies and put on hold mainly by the United States. It was clear that US obstructionism, far from showing any sensitivity to international demands for change, was being intensified in response to mounting American frustration at the resilience of the Saddam regime and the abject failure of the years-long US propaganda war. Iraq, for its part, was working to consolidate its trade links with other countries wherever possible. Thus on 7 April 2001, Taha Hamud Yasin, Secretary of the Iraqi Oil Ministry, announced that it would soon be possible to sign a joint contract for the building of a natural gas pipeline to Turkey, giving scope for future linkage into the European gas network.

Iraq was continuing to circumvent the UN controls in its quest for revenues from oil sales[43] – an anomaly that Washington's 'smart' sanctions were intended to address. At the same time the Iraqi casualties from sanctions were continuing to mount, for every age range and in almost every disease category. The American efforts to address the Iraq issue did not focus on such problems, in reality caused almost entirely by US policy.

On 12 April 2001 the US State Department, knowing its priorities, warned the American oil companies not to purchase Iraqi oil that had been obtained with an 'illegal' surcharge payment to Iraq. Greg Sullivan, the Department's Near Eastern Bureau spokesman, reported that the United States had distributed a letter to 25 American oil firms, urging them to determine the sources of their oil. It was thought that the major American oil companies were taking steps to prevent Saddam from gaining access to the surcharge, but that smaller oil firms might be circumventing the UN rules – buying Iraqi oil, paying the surcharge, and then selling the oil to the larger companies: 'The Iraqi ploy is not new. The letter is only an effort to alert these companies that Iraq is once again trying to subvert the sanctions regime and the oil-for-food sale' (Sullivan).

On 17 April Muhamed Salem al-Sabah, Kuwait's foreign minister, visited Washington and discussed matters, including 'smart' sanctions, with Secretary of State Colin Powell. The Kuwaiti minister prudently observed that 'he came while carrying the love and respect of Kuwaiti people and leadership to your great country'; and Powell responded by promising to protect Kuwait from any aggression it might face in the future. Iraq was not mentioned, but already the mantra had been routinely intoned on the previous day by a State Department official: 'smart' sanctions would ease the suffering of the Iraqi people, while tightening the grip around Iraq's military establishment.

On 18 April 2001, Russian President Vladimir Putin again declared his support for an end to sanctions. Speaking with Taha Yassin Ramadan, Putin again asserted that the sanctions should be lifted if Iraq allowed UN weapons inspectors to resume their work in the country. Putin, committing crimes against humanity in Chechnya and keen to abolish any semblance of democracy in Russia, was no more than a cynical opportunist. But on Iraq, he was part of an international consensus. Washington and London were admitting that they had lost the propaganda war against Saddam Hussein – it had always been difficult to promote the starvation of children as a righteous Christian act – and there were signs that Iraq's international isolation was being gradually eroded.

It was soon clear that the idea of 'smart' sanctions did not represent an easing of the embargo, with humanitarian concerns in mind, but a toughening of the sanctions to make them more effective. There would be talk of facilitating the provision of humanitarian supplies, with no promise that the number of contract holds imposed by the US and Britain would be reduced, while states such as Jordan and Turkey, tolerating many porosities in the embargo, would be expected to firm up the restrictions on the illicit traffic in goods. In such circumstances, it was not surprising that Iraq and many other states quickly perceived 'smart' sanctions as a device for increasing the privations of the Iraqi people. On 17 May 2001 Iraq declared that it would reject a British presentation of the US–UK-contrived plan to make sanctions more effective.

The United States and Britain announced that a draft resolution on smart sanctions would be circulated to the Security Council members with a view to gaining international approval for the new scheme. The hyperbole was predictable: it was said that the restrictions on civilian goods would be relaxed while the bans on weapons-related materials would be tightened. Thus Charles Duelfer, formerly a top US weapons inspector in Iraq, commented: 'I think what we are seeing is an effort by the international community to separate those steps which are being taken to try to constrain the weapons activities of the regime from unintended effects on the Iraqi population . . . it will free up things to the civilian sector.' The cosmetic gloss was convincing few observers. While US spokesmen were striving to sell the new idea to a sceptical international community, a meeting of around 300 Christian leaders and clerics held in Baghdad declared that the continuation of the economic embargo in any form would be 'tantamount to the extermination of an entire people'.[44]

On 23 May 2001 Russia expressed its hostility to the new US–UK embargo plans.[45] At the same time Iraq was declaring that, if the Security Council adopted the new scheme, it would immediately stop supplying oil to the international markets, and would punish any Turkish or Jordanian efforts to tighten the controls on sanctions.[46] It was now widely perceived that the concept of smart sanctions was a mechanism for strengthening the embargo, while Western propagandists were intent on representing the new plans as essentially humanitarian in purpose. A British diplomat at the United Nations admitted that the control of goods would be 'more effectively enforced' under the proposed arrangements.[47]

Iraq continued to insist that it would not sell any oil through a revised system that continued to channel oil revenues to a UN escrow account over which Baghdad had no control. Moreover, the Security Council seemed split on the new proposals. Russia and China were arguing that they had not been given any notice of the list of 'military' items that would be embargoed, and France was urging new compromises in the US–UK plan. It seemed that the Council might argue for months before taking any decision, during which time Baghdad would have succeeded in punching fresh holes in the embargo.

In the event, the Security Council adopted Resolution 1352 on 1 June 2001 – with no negative votes and no abstentions. The surprising unanimous vote was secured only because the resolution had been purged of any controversial proposals. The absurd commitment of 'all Member States to the sovereignty and territorial integrity of Iraq' was reiterated, at a time when Iraq sovereignty was being violated in countless ways; and the Security Council declared its intention to do no more than 'consider' new arrangements for the supply of goods to Iraq, and to implement such new (undefined) arrangements for a period of 190 days beginning on 4 July 2001. Washington and London had laboured hard to produce a resolution that would not be vetoed in the Council. The result was a statement of the intention to 'improve the controls' on the supply of items to Iraq but hardly providing a firm basis for a comprehensive system of smart sanctions. The petty and vague SCR 1352 had been passed unanimously, but there was no guarantee that international agreement would be forthcoming for the detailed 'new arrangements' that were being hatched by the Washington strategists.

On 10 June 2001, Saddam Hussein was warning of a 'new confrontation' if Britain and the United States attempted to impose a new system of 'smart' sanctions. He had no doubt about the US–UK objectives:

> The basis of the enemy plan is to break Iraq's national will and colonize it by new technical methods . . . through controlling its money and preventing Iraq from development. If the aim was to prevent Iraq from importing weapons, why do they not simply issue a resolution banning other countries from exporting weapons to Iraq and punishing any country that violates this resolution?

The five Permanent Members of the Security Council continued to discuss the concept of smart sanctions, but little progress was evident. Moreover, it was plain that various other countries were concerned at the likely impact of a tightening of the embargo on their own economies. Jordan, for example, at risk of losing its entire oil supply, opposed the new scheme but conceded it would be forced to observe it. One pressure on the Jordanian government, pushing it to ignore its pro-Iraq public opinion, was a free-trade agreement signed with Washington and still awaiting congressional approval.[48] On 26 June 2001, Russia announced that it would oppose any detailed US–UK plans for the implementation of a smart-sanctions scheme. It seemed obvious that any Security Council resolution drafted to put meat on the bare bones of SCR 1352 would face a Russian veto.[49]

On 1 August, Amir Muhammed Rasheed declared that Baghdad would favour Russia, Syria, Jordan and Turkey in striking oil deals because of their support for Iraq against the US–UK smart-sanctions resolution being prepared: 'Russia is in the first place, then neighbouring countries, and cooperation with these states will be reflected in all economic and political spheres.' And now it seemed that the tepid French support for the draft resolution was jeopardising the TotalFinaElf negotiating rights for the huge Majnoon and Bin Umar oilfields in southern Iraq: 'Iraq condemns negative stances and it will behave in its economic and trade dealings in accordance with such stances.'

The devastation of Iraq by sanctions continued through 2001, with no prospect of desperately-needed reconstruction in the social and industrial sectors. The Economist Intelligence Unit (London) placed the cost of such reconstruction at between $30 billion and $60 billion, with the Save the Children Fund commenting that 'the deterioration in Iraq's civilian infrastructure is so far-reaching that it can only be reversed with extensive investment and development efforts.' The *Financial Times* judged that the so-called smart sanctions 'would not revive Iraq's devastated economy while control over Iraq's oil revenues remains in the hands of the UN and foreign investment and credits are still prohibited'. In the same vein *The Economist* concluded: '*Iraq needs massive investment to rebuild its power grids and its schools, and needs cash in hand to pay its engineers, doctors and teachers. None of this looks likely to happen under smart sanctions*' (my italics).

The September 11 attacks on America shifted the emphasis. There was already mounting pressure in Washington for a new and decisive military campaign against Iraq, but this was boosted enormously by the terrorist strikes against the twin towers and the Pentagon. The option of smart sanctions was being given increased attention by US planners, but with diminishing public exposure and discussion. Much of the talk now, even during the planning and waging of war against Afghanistan, was about how the US and its supine British acolyte could achieve 'regime change' in Iraq. It remained possible to refine or tighten the sanctions system, but it was obvious that the American priority was to topple the regime of Saddam Hussein. Washington strategists had been driven to admit that sanctions, smart or not, would not achieve that objective.

In October 2001, it was judged that the United States, while preparing for war on Iraq, was not ready to launch a new military campaign beyond Afghanistan. At the same time, Washington was continuing to develop plans for a more effective sanctions regime. On 19 November Kofi Annan again said that the cumbersome bureaucratic processes and the 'inordinate delays', as well as problems with the Iraqi authorities, were continuing to damage the humanitarian programme. The holds placed on contract applications, then running at more than $4 billion, remained at an 'unacceptably' high level.

New UN Resolutions, Old Policies

On 29 November the Security Council adopted Resolution 1382, scheduled to come into effect on 30 May 2002 and designed to indicate that Washington was trying to improve the sanctions regime. The SCR 1382 preamble routinely declared that the Council was determined to improve the humanitarian situation in Iraq and reaffirmed the commitment of all UN Member States to the sovereignty and territorial integrity of Iraq – sentiments that were at best ironic in view of the fact that the United States was then planning to launch the most devastating military onslaught on Iraq since the 1991 war.

The notional aim of SCR 1382 was to provide a Goods Review List and Procedures for its implementation in order to simplify the operation of the sanctions regime. It was easy to see that the new resolution would do nothing to improve the predicament of the Iraqi people. The list of banned items, intended to supplement prohibited items in other resolutions, was not exhaustive – which meant that 'refinements' could be made (to both the List and the Procedures) 'in light of further consultations'. Moreover, most contracts would still pass through the Sanctions Committee for approval, preserving the bureaucratic delays that had come to characterize that body's deliberations. Appeals against decisions of the Office of the Iraq Programme to refer contracts to the Committee were to be allowed, but only if they were registered within two days, and with no time limit on how long the appointed 'experts' might take to reach a conclusion.

It seemed obvious that Resolution 1382 would do little to streamline contract applications, that the characteristic US–UK obstructionism would persist, and that the Iraqi civilian population would continue to be denied humanitarian supplies in adequate quantity. It seemed clear that SCR 1382 had failed in its primary purpose – that of giving Washington a boost in the propaganda war, and that in these circumstances yet another cosmetic Security Council resolution would have to be produced.

On 14 May 2002, the Security Council unanimously adopted Resolution 1409, with Mikhail Wehbe, for Syria, none the less recording grave reservations:

> Syria believed it was high time to lift the sanctions to which the Iraqi people has been subjected for 12 years . . . the Council had lost its credibility as a result of the position of some permanent members in encouraging Israeli to defy international legitimacy, while Syria was required to vote for a resolution that would cause further suffering to a fellow Arab people . . . Syria totally rejected the policy whereby Israel had conducted naked aggression against the Palestinian people, despite claims of war crimes carried out in refugee camps. The Council had failed to enforce respect for its Resolution 1405 (2002), thus engaging in double-dealing.

The United States, chief architect of SCR 1409, claimed that the new resolution would ease the flow of humanitarian goods to the Iraqi people, so removing one of Saddam Hussein's principal propaganda weapons.

Under the new system, supposedly effective on 30 May 2002, contracts for supplies not referenced on a revised Goods Review List, were to be processed speedily by the UN Office of the Iraq Programme instead of having to be approved by the Sanctions Committee (see Chapter 3). The Office was required to forward the contracts for evaluation by experts from the UN Monitoring, Verification and Inspection Commission (UNMOVIC, set up by SCR 1284) and from the International Atomic Energy Agency (IAEA). The experts were required to pay particular attention to so-called 'dual-use' items, those that might have both civilian and military applications.

The new Procedures are set out in 18 dense paragraphs appended to Resolution 1409. The revised Goods Review List (S/2002/515) of prohibited military items runs to no less than 345 pages. Here, as with the earlier sanctions resolutions, there remains massive scope for bureaucratic complication and malicious obstructionism, but for the most part the Western media echoed the American propaganda position – 'UN relaxes sanctions to aid Iraqi civilians' (*The Times*, 15 May 2002). Informed observers were unconvinced. Thus Denis Halliday, former UN Assistant Secretary-General and former head of the UN Humanitarian Programme in Iraq, commented:

> The new 'smart' sanctions regime . . . is dangerously misleading . . . The reality is that we will continue to punish the innocent populace . . . As intended, UN hands will look cleaner as the children of Iraq continue to die from the ongoing loss of fundamental human rights due to the Security Council.[50]

In the same vein, Voices in the Wilderness noted the reality of the matter: 'The resolution [SCR 1409] is not designed to solve the humanitarian crisis in Iraq. It is designed to undermine the growing anti-sanctions movement.'[51]

The new resolution grew out of its predecessors and made reference to them. They, like it, had done nothing to address the central humanitarian problem facing the Iraqi people – that the national economy was in the hands of foreigners committed to the exploitation of Iraqi oil, the preservation of Iraq in a pre-industrial condition, and the overthrow of the political regime. The plight of the Iraqi civilian population would not be adequately addressed until Iraq was again allowed sovereign control over its own national economy. How deeply ironic it was that Resolution 1409, denying all realistic Iraqi sovereignty, could cynically repeat the mantra of so many earlier Security Council resolutions:

> *The Security Council . . . Reaffirming* the commitment of all Member States to the sovereignty and territorial integrity of Iraq . . .

The United States and Britain were then adopting yet another ploy to deny Iraq the full benefits from oil revenues administered by the United Nations. Under US–UK pressure the UN had adopted a policy of pricing Iraqi oil at the end of each month instead of at the beginning – a deliberate delaying tactic that was scaring away customers. In one estimate it was suggested that this policy could cost Iraq $4 billion in revenues during the six-month phase that would end in December 2002. This of course made a nonsense of all the other planned 'reforms' to the sanctions system. A massively reduced sale of oil would drastically curtail Iraq's capacity to contract for the supply of humanitarian and other essential supplies.

None of this was sufficient for the United States. The Bush administration remained committed to the policy of 'regime change' in Iraq. While Washington was earnestly proclaiming its concern for the welfare of the Iraqi people, the strategists were preparing for a new war – without any semblance of United Nations authorization and in the teeth of world opinion.

TEN

Compensation or Theft?

The Framework

There is evidence that the United States had been contemplating an economic embargo against Iraq *before* Saddam's invasion of Kuwait – perhaps because of pressure from Jewish opinion, Israel had been viewing Iraqi solidarity with the Palestinians with growing alarm, knowing that the rest of the Arab world was largely under the control of the US–Israeli axis, but that Saddam Hussein had not been so easily bought and subdued. Syria, still prepared to maintain a large force in Lebanon, was none the less a defeated nation licking its wounds. Libya had been bombed by the United States and had no stomach for further trauma. Egypt and Jordan, having made peace with Israel, were in thrall to the Jewish–American strategy for the region, and Morocco was in the pocket of the US State Department. Kuwait and Saudi Arabia – medieval feudalisms that still relied on slavery, torture, forced confessions, the suppression of women, and frequent head-choppings after prayers – relied on the United States to protect their democratic credentials. The other states in the Gulf Cooperation Council (GCC), with little clout, could be relied upon not to disturb the tranquil justice of the region. Iraq was the problem. Perhaps the answer was to lure Saddam Hussein into a foolish gamble and then to destroy his capacity to endanger the 'Zionist entity'.

The Question of Law

Law was a crucial consideration. Aggressive states, conspiring states, victim states – all have always recognized the power of law to sanctify conquest and to authorize redress. Worlds such as 'legal', 'lawful' and 'law-abiding' carry a strong connotation of approval. But law, always susceptible to mercenary and other blandishments, is not always principled; and, when principled, is often impotent.

Saddam Hussein, in his persecution of ethnic groups and his invasion of Kuwait, violated international humanitarian law and the UN Charter. The US, in its response to Saddam, violated the Hague Conventions, the Geneva Conventions, the UN Charter, the 1977 Protocol 1 Addition to the Geneva Conventions, the Genocide Convention, the Convention on the Rights of the Child, the UN social and political Conventions, and many other instruments of international law. Law, in the shape of ambiguous UN resolutions adopted by a US-dominated Security Council, could be invoked against Saddam, because he was relatively weak, but not against the United States, because it was a superpower.[1]

The Mercenary Motive

The US motivation behind Washington's Iraq policy derives in part from the plutocratic and mercenary character of the United States. This is unremarkable: the expansion of imperial hegemony has always been linked to command of economic resources. But with the United States this condition is developed to an unprecedented degree. The United States claims to be a democracy, but no serious observers doubt that money buys power, that corporate influence is the most significant political factor in the country. This had led some commentators – trying hard to square the circle – to term the United States a 'pluto-democracy'. The facts were plain in the last (2000) presidential election. Bush, attracting nearly $200 million in campaign donations (almost twice the amount given to Gore), had the support of oil and other energy interests ($12.7 million), agribusiness ($7.8 million), transport interests ($7.1 million), pharmaceutical companies ($7.7 million) and other corporate interests. The same factions, hedging their bets, also made donations to the Gore campaign, but on a smaller scale. It is important to realize that this plutocratic and mercenary ideology fed through into the punitive UN resolutions against Iraq.

The crucial UN Security Council Resolution 986 (14 April 1995, see Chapter 3) made provision (in Paragraph 8) for the channelling of oil revenues into a so-called Compensation Fund, whereby companies and other oganizations that had suffered damage and loss from the Iraqi invasion of Kuwait could claim financial redress. Thus in March 2000 Kofi Annan, UN Secretary-General, reported that some $6,418.9 million of Iraq's oil revenues had been transferred directly into the UN Compensation Fund, enabling – literally – hundreds of thousands of companies, other organizations and individuals to claim payment.[2] In November 2000 Kofi Annan reported that $10,472.9 million of the oil revenues had been transferred to the Compensation Fund.[3]

This meant that a vast 'gravy train' had been constructed for the benefit of an immense number of claimants, including US and Kuwaiti contractors delighted to be granted such easy pickings. In one estimate it was suggested that sanctions would have to remain on Iraq *for more than a century* if all the compensation claims were to be met.[4] Thus in June 2000 some $276 billion-worth of claims were in the pipeline at the Geneva-based UN Compensation Commission,[*] with more claims being added every week. Kuwait alone, having already received substantial payments, had a new claim in for $21.5 billion – at a time when nearly 10,000 Iraqis, mainly children, were dying every month for want of food, clean water and medical attention. In this context it was estimated that at the current rate of payment it would take 58 years (from June 2000) for Iraq to pay off its principal debt, but then Iraq would have to begin paying off the accrued interest levied by the UN authorities under guidance from Washington. At a modest rate of 3 per cent annual interest, the additional debt would amount to around $320 billion – which meant that Iraq would still be paying for the invasion of Kuwait in the year 2125.[5] It was plain that the United Nations would have no way of enforcing the payment of compensation and the accrued interest if the sanctions were to be lifted. Iraq would again have control over its own revenues and UN officials would no longer be able to manage the disbursement of funds to US-friendly claimants. *So of course Washington has a massive financial incentive to maintain the current structure of the sanctions system.*

The Abuse of Sovereignty

Iraq has been allowed no voice in any of this. The UN Security Council established the Compensation Commission, inevitably staffed by US-friendly officials, with the Commission itself financed entirely from Iraqi oil revenues. The Commission, controlled by the US-dominated Security Council, receives the claims, evaluates them, determines the sums to be paid from the

---

[*] The UN Compensation Commission, a subsidiary organ of the Security Council, has panels of Commissioners to evaluate six categories of claims ('A' to 'F') and a 240-strong Secretariat to administer the Compensation Fund. The Commissioners report to a Governing Council that makes decisions on the validity of claims in all the categories. One illustrative decision (S/AC.26/Dec.126, 2001, 21 June 2001) concerned 'part one of the ninth instalment of individual claims for damages above $100,000 (Category 'D' claims)'. Here 225 payments to 14 countries and two UN organizations were recommended: Australia (3 claims), Canada (4), Germany (1), India (22), Jordan (22), Kuwait (142), Netherlands (1), Pakistan (1), Slovenia (1), Sudan (7), Sweden (1), Syria (2), UK (9), US (7), UNDP Washington (1) and UNRWA Gaza (1). This single decision, one of scores, specified a total of $25,615,019.69 to be paid out of Iraqi oil revenues.

Compensation Fund, and informs Iraq of the outcome. The Commission is essentially a political body working to an ideological and mercenary agenda determined by the United States. Iraq is allowed no appeal against any Commission decision, however blatantly unfair or partisan.

It is possible to question the very legal basis of the Commission. The Security Council is a political body responsible for the maintenance of international peace and security. Its mandatory resolutions have the force of law in relation to its specifically political decisions and judgements. It has never been customarily a body that both receives and judges claims for financial redress in what should be a judicial rather than a political context. In fact this was recognized as a totally innovatory approach in January 1994 when, at an extraordinary session of the Compensation Commission, the UN Secretary-General observed: 'This is, in fact, an unprecedented project. As, for the first time in history, the international community shall bear by itself the responsibility for securing the processing of claims of compensation for war victims and taking decisions thereof.'[6]

The government of Iraq is rarely allowed to see the relevant claims documentation, which is processed in conditions of top secrecy. No Iraqi official is allowed to appear before the commissioners in order to present Iraq's pleas or to comment on individual claims. Iraq is not allowed to comment on the methods of assessing the claims or the documentary evidence submitted in their support. The entire compensation system, administered in secret by US-approved officials, is open to the grossest forms of abuse, which the appointed officials have no interest in detecting or discouraging. Where information *is* given to Iraq it is done so at the whim of particular officials, not because of any legal obligation to inform Iraq of its likely financial liabilities.

This is an extraordinary situation, vulnerable to legal – though impotent – challenge at many levels. Washington would not want to admit that the operation of the Commission was a purely political matter, designed to advance the US strategic and financial agendas, so it must be argued that the Commission is a judicial body. If so, Iraq is entitled to the normal protections afforded by judicial rights: namely the right to hear evidence, the right to challenge witnesses, the right to examine judicial protocols, the right to appeal decisions, etc. Why is such protection, manifest in natural justice, so plainly absent in the case of Iraq? Washington here as elsewhere, has committed a gross abuse: depriving a national people in a fully accredited member state of the United Nations of its political and judicial rights.

On 10 October 2000, Saeed H. Hasan, Iraq's UN Ambassador, sent a letter to the Secretary-General recording Iraq's appeal for:

A review of the compensation regime in the light of international law and for the acknowledgement of Iraq's right to claim compensation from the countries engaged in aggression against it for the consequences of that aggression . . . the United States, the United Kingdom and the countries that provide the logistic facilities for their aggression, namely Saudi Arabia, Kuwait and Turkey, should be made to bear full responsibility, including responsibility for the payment of the compensation to Iraq.[7]

An annex to the letter, from Mohammed Said al-Sahaf, Iraq's foreign minister, noted that the compensation regime imposed on Iraq bore 'no relation to international law, to say nothing of justice, truth and fairness . . . this would not have come about if the issue had been handled on the basis of international law and in accordance with the principles of justice and fairness'. He charged further, as already acknowledged by the UN Secretary-General in 1994, that the Compensation Commission 'established a precedent that had no counterpart in the history of the United Nations'. Iraq's right in law had obviously been violated:

Iraq has . . . been deprived of the right to be informed of all claims and to comment . . . Even in the rare cases where claims have been referred to it, Iraq has not been given sufficient time . . . no genuine hearings are held that Iraq is invited to attend . . . The decisions reached . . . can therefore only be characterized as biased and unjust . . . as not complying with the norms of international law and the principles of justice. They have been formulated in accordance with Machiavellian political principles based on a narrow vision of opportunism and power.[8]

In short, the compensation regime nominally a just imposition, had in fact been designed to exploit the Iraqi oil resources for ideological and financial purposes. For example, vast Kuwaiti claims were being supported by Washington and London, and then approved by the Commission. Iraq was allowed no right to scrutinize the documentation, to discuss the claims before the commissioners, or to appeal the decisions on the sums awarded. Iraq's other point is obviously substantial: if compensation is due following illegal aggression against a sovereign state then were not the United States and other countries liable to pay compensation to Iraq in the light of the illegal bombing campaign that had been sustained over the years? The so-called 'no-fly' zones were authorized in no UN resolution, and Operation Desert Fox (December 1998) had been vigorously condemned by three of the UN Permanent Members.

Al-Sahaf summarized the Iraqi position on both aspects of the compensation issue:

There should be a review of the compensation regime . . . in the light of international law.

The countries involved in aggression against Iraq should bear full responsibility . . . Iraq's right to claim compensation . . . for all the damage it has sustained as a result of their aggression should be acknowledged.

In view of the fact that the establishment of the two no-fly zones was an illegal act . . . both duty and legal responsibility require the Security Council to adopt a resolution condemning the action.[9]

If, as was inevitable, Washington or London were to veto such a resolution, the other members of the Security Council and the rest of the world should 'condemn the wanton, daily aggression on the part of the United States and the United Kingdom'. This would require the two countries to bear responsibility for their aggression and for the payment of compensation; just as it would require Saudi Arabia, Kuwait and Turkey, aiding the aggression, to bear the same joint responsibility.

Iraq cannot have imagined that any notice would have been taken of the letter (10 October 2000). Kofi Annan seemed incapable of taking any action without US approval, and Washington would be certain to prevent any such resolution being drafted, much less being voted on in the Security Council. The character of the compensation scheme is plain. It is an 'extortion scheme' designed to rob Iraq of hundreds of billions of dollars.[10] By 2001, the Compensation Commission had received $320 billion of claims, with $180 billion of them coming from Kuwait. The private claimants numbered 2.6 million, in addition to the vast claims made by corporate and government bodies. Israeli business – including florists, greengrocers, cinemas and hotels – have received millions of dollars from Iraqi oil revenues to 'compensate for loss of income during the crisis';[11] and cash has even been paid out to compensate for damage caused by US bombing and the sanctions regime.

'Cherry Picking' from International Law

This entire bizarre situation is sustained by virtue of one simple fact: the unassailable military power of the United States. Washington 'cherry picks' the international laws it wants to observe, and ignores the rest; and it imposes 'legal' obligations on weaker states who are allowed no judicial right of appeal. The Vienna Convention on the Law of Treaties, itself an instrument of international law, declares that a treaty procured by 'coercion . . . through acts of threats' is 'without any legal effect' (Article 51) and a treaty 'procured by the threat or use of force' is 'void' (Article 52). Yet Washington constantly uses force or the threat of force to manage its relations with what it chooses to dub 'rogue' states, making the resulting treaties or UN resolutions 'without any legal effect' and 'void'. This means that substantial elements of current 'international law', secured through US coercion, have no legal validity – an observation that is unhelpful when legal appeals against American interest are lodged with a manifest superpower. There is no power to restrain the bully in the international playground, to confront the thug on the global street corner.

There are countless ways in which the United States chooses to manipulate or to ignore international law. Washington can effectively dismiss a UN Secretary-General (as it did Boutros Boutros-Ghali) and other senior UN officials, compel the United Nations to reduce US financial dues to the organization (as Washington has done), determine what business is on the UN agenda, decide which UN members shall serve on the Security Council (just as it banned Sudan),[12] and veto food aid, financial assistance and other help to impoverished states who dare to disagree with US policy. Washington can support terrorists wherever it wishes, as in Iraq, Palestine or the Balkans[13] – even to the point of shamelessly introducing overt domestic laws for the purpose.[14]

The Superpower Campaign

The war against Iraq is not being fought on a level playing field: the brutal heavyweight, in public soft spoken and sweetly reasonable, endlessly pounds the lightweight, enough to keep him hurting but still able to pay obeisance. In the West the lies about Iraq tumble off the mass-production propaganda line.[15] The Kuwaitis, constantly obstructionist, demand details of imaginary prisoners-of-war, while refusing to provide information about missing Iraqis; and demand the return of Kuwaiti property, ignoring the exhaustive lists of property already sent back to Kuwait. For example, one listing of returned property makes reference to 'All the equipment and tools belonging to Kuwaiti Airways', 'All the equipment and ammunition belonging to the Kuwaiti Air Force', 'All the military equipment and ammunition belonging to the Kuwaiti land and naval forces', and many other items. It is true that the Iraqi authorities have lied to UN staff and the world, as have all the parties to the protracted dispute. But if a government and a people are constantly threatened with extinction, with the years-long promise of annihilation, are they likely to be cooperative and compliant with their persecutor? Lies are a common currency of war, exploited by the United States in all its foreign wars, including the 1991 conflict and the sustained anti-Iraq campaign that followed.

The United States continues to wage a massive propaganda against Iraq, discounting the US role in building up Iraq's military power, discounting the early CIA cooperation with Saddam Hussein (when he was reliably anti-leftist), and discounting the US–Iraq military alliance in the war against Iran (1980–88). Iraq has been denounced for its frequent bouts of obstructionism in its dealing with the UN, but has been given no credit by Washington for its massive cooperation with UN officials over the years – to the extent that Iraq has suffered a substantial erosion of its industrial base and that the vast majority of its banned weapons have been destroyed. This degree of Iraqi compliance, often in circumstances of humiliation and military threat, is copiously reflected in UN documents: for example, 'excellent cooperation' from 'the Iraqi State Oil Marketing Organization . . . the Iraqi authorities have accorded . . . full cooperation' (letter from UN committee to Security Council, 19 May 1999); 'It went well, and we had good collaboration with our Iraqi counterparts' (Ahmad Abu-Zahra, IAEA team leader, 25 January 2000).

The propaganda continues[16] while innocent Iraqis, many of them born years after the 1991 war, die by the thousand every month. The Washington lie machine gathers pace to invent a humanitarian motive behind 'smart' sanctions, and to prepare the ground for yet another massive military onslaught on the Iraqi people. The American spokesmen talk of the UN inspectors 'thrown out of Iraq' in 1998, when in fact they were withdrawn by Washington as a prelude to the Desert Fox bombing campaign. The same spokesmen declare that Saddam Hussein 'must have something to hide' if he will not allow inspectors to return, when these spokesmen know full well that at least some of the UN inspectors were consorting as spies with Mossad and feeding surveillance data back to Washington in preparation for further military attacks. If the United States, in defiance of international law, will not let UN inspectors examine its chemical, biological and nuclear weapons plants, why should Iraq – constantly threatened with military aggression – be more helpful? And when will US apologists realize that to threaten a people with a hideous destructive arsenal – cruise missiles, napalm, depleted-uranium ordnance, cluster bombs, 'daisy cutters' as powerful as atomic bombs, and all the rest – is itself a terrorist posture?

American and British warplanes bomb Iraq when it suits current tactics or presidential whim, while the Washington war planners prepare a more comprehensive destruction. The United States and Britain conspire with fellow NATO-member Turkey in its air and land aggressions against northern Iraq,[17] while ignoring Kuwaiti and Iranian attacks on Iraqi targets in the Gulf. Washington, conducting an alleged 'war against terror', funds anti-Iraq terrorists and works hard – in violation of copious instruments of international law – to strengthen the long economic siege of an entire civilian population.

At the same time Israel, equally immune to international law and prodigiously armed by the United States, razes Palestinian crops and homes;[18] invades Palestinian territory by land, air and sea;[19] conducts assassination campaigns;[20] expands its colonial annexation of Palestinian land; steals Palestinian taxation revenues; and subjects entire Palestinian communities to economic blockade. The American President, George W. Bush, visits the Washington Holocaust Memorial Museum to show US solidarity with Israel as it constantly expands its illegal theft of Arab land, and denounces Palestinian resistance as Ariel Sharon perpetrates a huge terrorism against the Palestinian people, dispossessing thousands of families, pushing whole communities into destitution, and mutilating and killing tens of thousands of Arabs who dare to protest at such a terrible abuse of their human rights.[21]

The suffering of the Iraqi people and the linked plight of the Palestinians continued, while the United States planned a new and massive war against Iraq that would inevitably involve thousands of civilian deaths. Through 2002 it was obvious that Washington was developing its military agenda in almost total international isolation.

With France, Russia and China opposed to a new war, there was no prospect of the United States securing an enabling resolution in the UN Security Council. It was equally plain that the regional states – Israel and some Kuwaiti opinion apart – did not consider Iraq to be a threat to their interests. Indeed the reverse was true. Saudi Arabia and Iraq had reopened their border at Arar and Saudi businessmen were trading in Baghdad. Iran and Iraq were exchanging refugees, and Syria and Lebanon had normalised their relations with Baghdad. Regular air flights were taking place between Iraq and other Arab states, and even Iraqi Kurdistan was developing its cultural and sporting links with the Iraqi people.[22]

Saudi Arabia had refused to allow its territory to be used as a launching pad for a new American assault on Iraq; Iran's president, Mohammad Khatami, warned the United States to abandon its military plans ('We have never witnessed war being so much promoted in the US');[23] and even Kuwait's Minister of Information, Sheikh Ahmad Fahd al-Sabah, was emphasizing that Kuwait was opposed to American plans for a new war against Iraq.[24] Similarly, opinion in Britain, normally a predictably supine US ally, was less robust than the Bush administration would have wished. Dr Rowan Williams, appointed to

241

be Archbishop of Canterbury, signed an open letter condemning any possible attack on Iraq; and even Tony Blair, too uncertain to risk a vote on the Iraq issue in the House of Commons, appeared to be wobbling. Thus King Abdullah of Jordan, urging against war, said that Prime Minister Blair had confided to him his 'tremendous concerns' about an invasion of Iraq, which he thought a 'bad idea'.[25] At the same time Kofi Annan, UN Secretary-General, was emphasizing to the Arab newspaper *al-Hayat* that US plans for 'regime change' in Iraq went beyond United Nations policy.[26]

Even the US military was divided, with Pentagon debates on the matter reported, to be 'increasingly fractious'.[27] One problem for the United States was that – in the absence of international support (in contrast to the 1991 Gulf War) – America would be forced to fund the war itself, likely to cost around $80 billion.[28] This would inevitably have a substantial impact on other US spending and on the budget deficit.[29]

None of these considerations – US isolation, financial profligacy, the prospect of carnage and destruction on a vast scale – seemed to weigh with the belligerent Bush administration. When, in late July 2002 the Iraqi government invited Hans Blix, head of UNMOVIC, to visit Baghdad for discussions on weapons inspection, the United States immediately rejected the offer – as if Washington had an automatic right to speak for the United Nations. Colin Powell dismissed the possibility of talks, and on 3 August President George W. Bush declared that the issue of weapons inspections had nothing to do with American policy on the necessity of action to overthrow the Iraqi government: 'We owe it to the future of civilization' to topple Saddam Hussein. The United States wanted war – in Bush's words, 'no matter what the cost'.

Notes

Introduction

1. Edward S. Walker, *Near East,* US Department of State, Washington D.C., 15 March 2000.
2. Andrew Marshall, 'Take Iraq apart, says Bush advisor', *The Independent,* London, 21 May 2000.
3. Letter dated 6 June 1999 from the Chargé d'affaires of the Permanent Mission of Iraq to the UN addressed to the Secretary-General, S/1999/651.
4. Letter dated 6 July 1999 from the Chargé d'affaires of the Permanent Mission of Iraq to the UN addressed to the Secretary-General, S/1999/757.
5. Robert Fisk, 'The voices of protest find an unexpected audience in the US', *The Independent,* London, 14 July 2000.
6. *Ibid.*
7. Robert Fisk, 'Allies blamed for Iraq cancer torment', *The Independent,* London, 4 March 1998.
8. Jon Swain, 'Allied shells linked to Iraqi child cancer', *The Sunday Times,* London, 8 March 1998.
9. Stephen Bamtes, 'Britain's guilt on Iraq bombing', *The Guardian,* London, 14 February 2000.
10. *Report of the Commission of Inquiry into the Events at the Refugee Camps in Beirut,* chaired by Yitzhak Kahan, President of the Supreme Court Commission, 8 February 1983 ('The Commission recommended that the Defence Minister resign, that the Director of Military Intelligence not continue in his post and other senior officers be removed.')
11. John Casey, fellow of Gonville and Caius College, Cambridge, England, 'There is no justification for waging war against Iraq', *The Daily Telegraph,* London, 21 March 2002.
12. Said K. Aburish, *Saddam Hussein: The Politics of Revenge* (London: Bloomsbury, 2000), pp.109–10.
13. *Ibid.,* pp. 54, 56.
14. Ian Brodie, 'FBI admits its Waco teargas was flammable', *The Times,* London, 27 August 1999.
15. 'United States of America: Use of electroshock stun guns', Amnesty International, AMN 51/45/96, 12 June 1996; 'Ill-treatment of inmates in Maricopa County jails – Arizona', AMR 51/51/97, August 1997.
16. '"Not part of my sentence" – Violations of the human rights of women in custody', Amnesty International, AMR 51/19/99.

17. Ben Macintyre, 'Killing of black ignited years of racial tension', *The Times*, London, 13 April 2001; Martin Kettle, 'Cincinnati mayor declares curfew after second night of rioting', *The Guardian*, London, 13 April 2001.

18. Eve Goldberg and Linda Evans, 'The prison industrial complex and the global economy', *Nexus*, Australia, June–July 1999, pp.17–22; Duncan Campbell, 'Anger grows as the US jails its two millionth inmate – 25% of world's prison population', *The Guardian*, London, 15 February 2000.

19. 'United States Supreme Court rulings allow execution of juvenile offenders and the mentally retarded', Amnesty International, AMR 51/27/89, June 1989; 'United States of America – Death penalty developments in 1996', Amnesty International, AMR 51/01/97, March 1997.

20. This Cuban territory is itself occupied by US troops in violation of international law. After the Spanish–American War of 1898, Washington resolved to maintain its local hegemony over Cuba without the burden of a permanent troop presence throughout the entire island. In 1903 it imposed the Platt Amendment on a helpless Cuban government. This device, imposed under US military threat, coerced Cuba into leasing land. The Vienna Treaty on the Law of Treaties specifies in Articles 51 and 52 that treaties secured by coercion are 'without any legal effect', 'void' in international law.

21. Iraq's human rights record has been well documented over the years, not only by the United States and other hostile states. For example, on 15 August 2001, Amnesty International called on the Iraqi authorities to end 'the systematic torture and ill-treatment of political prisoners' and 'to improve the human rights situation in the country'. On 24 April 2002, the Foreign Affairs Committee of the European Parliament adopted a resolution condemning 'the serious, repeated violations of human rights and international humanitarian laws by the Iraqi government . . .' See also Samir Al-Khalil, *Republic of Fear* (London: Hutchinson Radius, 1990), and Sarah Graham-Brown, *Sanctioning Saddam: The Politics of Intervention in Iraq* (London: I.B. Tauris, 1999), pp.121–27.

Chapter 1

1. There is much commentary on how George W. Bush and his supporters subverted the US constitution to facilitate a Republican victory. See, for example, Vincent Bugliosi, *The Betrayal of America: How the Supreme Court Undermined the Constitution and Chose Our President* (New York: Thunders Mouth Press, 2001). ('In the 12 December, 2000 ruling by the US Supreme Court handing the election to George W. Bush, the court committed the unpardonable sin of being a knowing surrogate for the Republican Party instead of being an impartial arbiter of the law.') See also Jake Tapper, *Down and Dirty: The Plot to Steal the Presidency* (Boston: Little, Brown & Co., 2001).

2. Walter Lagueur, *The Age of Terrorism* (Boston: Little, Brown & Co., 1987), p.11.

3. Title 18, 2331, US Legal Code.

4. The Pentagon event later generated controversy, stimulated by the book by French author Thierry Meyssan *L'Effroyable Imposture* (The Frightening Fraud). The Associated Press first reported that a booby-trapped bomb had caused the explosion. Why did the photographs show such few signs of aircraft wreckage?

5. At first it was estimated that perhaps as many as 6000 people had lost their lives in Washington and New York, a figure that was later scaled down by about half.

6. Geoff Simons, *Vietnam Syndrome: Impact on US Foreign Policy* (London: Macmillan, 1998), pp.9–12.

7. *Ibid.*
8. On 28 September 2001 the UN Security Council adopted Resolution 1373, again condemning the terrorist attacks on the United States and calling on all states to work together to combat terrorism. SCR 1373, more substantial than the hastily adopted SCR 1368, specifies many practical measures to be implemented.
9. The attacks were announced on the same day that the former White House intern Monica Lewinsky testified for a second time to the grand jury investigating her affair with Clinton. Janet Reno, US Attorney General, questioned whether the evidence linking Osama bin Laden to the August (1998) bombings in Kenya and Tanzania was strong enough by the standards of international law to justify the US missile attacks.
10. In one estimate, some 21,000 bombs and missiles were used against Afghanistan between October 2001 and April 2002.
11. Richard Beeston, 'Saddam should not be ruled out, says US Intelligence', *The Times*, London, 15 September 2001.
12. Anton La Guardia, 'US dilemma over which rogue states to take on', *The Daily Telegraph*, London, 15 September 2001.
13. In March 2002, there were reports that a new American cruise missile, the Tactical Tomahawk, able to loiter over enemy territory and choose its own target, was to be brought into service later in the year.
14. R. James Woolsey, former CIA Director, 'Saddam may be target Americans are looking for', *The Daily Telegraph*, London, 17 September 2001.
15. *Ibid.*
16. Jessica Berry, Philip Sherwell and David Wastell, 'Army alert by Saddam points to Iraqi role', *The Sunday Telegraph*, London, 23 September 2001.
17. William Safire, 'Bite the bullet and target Iraq', *The Guardian*, London, 26 September 2001.
18. Julian Borger, 'Washington's hawk trains sight on Iraq', *The Guardian*, London, 26 September 2001.
19. Amberin Zaman, 'Turkey signs up, but fears Iraq is next US target', *The Daily Telegraph*, London, 29 September 2001.
20. *The Times*, London, 9 October 2001.
21. *The Guardian*, London, 9 October 2001.
22. Stephen Pollard, *The Daily Telegraph*, London, 10 October 2001.
23. *Ibid.*
24. *Ibid.*
25. Scott Ritter was urging people not to 'blame Saddam for this one' ('. . . no evidence to suggest Iraq is behind the anthrax attack'), *The Guardian*, London, 19 October 2001; and Richard Butler, admitting there was no hard evidence, was stressing the need to inspect Iraq for a bioweapon capability, *The Times*, London, 20 October 2001.
26. Hala Jaber, interviewing Tariq Aziz, 'Attack on Iraq "will be grave mistake"', *The Sunday Telegraph*, London, 28 October 2001; Hala Jaber and David Wastell, 'Tariq Aziz: we are ready for war', *The Sunday Telegraph*, London, 28 October 2001.
27. UN Charter, Article 2(4): 'All Members shall refrain in their international relations from the threat or use of force against the territorial integrity or political independence of any state . . .'
28. Martin Woollacott, 'Saddam will be the next US target, one way or another', *The Guardian*, London, 16 November 2001.
29. M. Engel, 'Iraqmania grips the US', *The Guardian*, London, 5 December 2001.

30. Peter Green, 'Iraq link to Sept 11 attack and anthrax is ruled out', *The Daily Telegraph*, London, 18 December 2001.
31. Charles Moore, editor of *The Daily Telegraph*, London, 20 December 2001.
32. Bronwen Maddox, 'Bush Jr wants to settle an old score', *The Times*, London, 15 February 2002.
33. Martin Woollacott, 'Saddam's destruction is now a matter of honour', *The Guardian*, London, 15 February 2002.
34. *Tehran Times*, Tehran, 14 February 2002.
35. *Morning Star*, London, 15 February 2002.
36. *The Daily Telegraph*, London, 15 February 2002.
37. *The Guardian*, London, 15 February 2002.
38. *Middle East News Online*, 15 February 2002.
39. *Bahrain Tribune*, Manama, 15 February 2002.
40. *Jordan Times*, Amman, 15 February 2002.
41. *The Daily Telegraph*, London, 19 February 2002.
42. *The Times*, London, 19 February 2002.
43. *The Times*, London, 20 February 2002.
44. David Graves and Neil Tweedie, 'RAF ready as US puts pressure on Saddam', *The Daily Telegraph*, London, 8 March 2002; Ewan MacAskill, 'From Suez to the Pacific: US expands its presence across the globe', *The Guardian*, London, 8 March 2002.
45. House of Commons, Early-Day Motion 927, 'Military action against Iraq', 4 March 2002 (Alice Mahon): 'That this house is aware of the deep unease among honourable Members on all sides of the House at the prospect that Her Majesty's Government might support United States military action against Iraq; agrees with Kofi Annan that a further military attack on Iraq would be unwise at this time; believes that such a course of action would disrupt support for the anti-terrorism coalition among the Arab states; and instead urges the Prime Minister to use Britain's influence with Iraq to gain agreement that UN weapons inspections will resume.'
46. Kamal Ahmed, Jason Burke and Peter Beaumont, 'Bush wants 25,000 UK Iraq force', *The Observer*, London, 10 March 2002.
47. Julian Borger, Richard Norton-Taylor, Ewen MacAskill and Brian Whitaker, 'Iraq: the myth and the reality', *The Guardian*, London, 15 March 2002.
48. Communiqué, The Arab League, Beirut Summit, 28 March 2002.
49. Nicholas Rufford, 'Blair refuses to release dossier on Iraq threat', *The Sunday Times*, London, 31 March 2002.
50. Kenneth R. Timmerman, *The Death Lobby: How the West Armed Iraq* (London: Fourth Estate, 1992); Michael White, 'UK anthrax strains "sold to Iraq"', *The Guardian*, London, 3 March 1998.
51. Peter Williams and David Wallace, *Unit 713* (London: Hodder and Stoughton, 1989), Chapter 17; Stephen Endicott and Edward Hagerman, *Biological Warfare: Secrets of the Early Cold War and Korea* (Bloomington and Indianapolis: Indiana University Press, 1998), Chapter 1.
52. Sheldon H. Harris, *Factories of Death: Japanese Biological Warfare, 1932–45, and the American cover-up* (London and New York: Routledge, 1994), p. xi.
53. Peter Pringle, 'Retarded boys used in US test on radioactivity', *The Independent*, London, 30 December 1993.
54. Simon Tisdall, 'US admits years of atomic radiation tests on people', *The Guardian*, London, 30 December 1993; Tim Cornwell, 'Life under the cloud of America's "Nazi"

tests', *The Observer*, London, 2 January 1994.

55. Jonathan Leake, 'MoD admits 40 years of human radiation tests', *The Sunday Times*, London, 24 November 1996. See also Rob Evans, *Gassed: British Chemical Warfare Experiments on Humans at Porton Down* (London: House of Stratus, 2000).

56. Paul Lashmar and Tom McCarthy, 'How Britain cast plague on paradise', *The Observer*, London, 15 December 1996.

57. Andrew Gilligan and Rob Evans, 'City dwellers exposed to biological warfare tests', *The Sunday Telegraph*, London, 22 February 1997.

58. Associated Press, 'UK's "secret mustard gas test"', *The Guardian*, London, 18 April 1998.

59. Harris, *op cit*, p. xi.

60. Harris, *op cit*, p. xii.

61. Ed Vulliamy, 'US law blocks weapons inspectors', *The Guardian*, London, 13 February 1998.

62. The United States has consistently ignored UN General Assembly Resolution 32/84 (12 December 1977) which prohibits states 'from developing new weapons of mass destruction' ... such as 'radioactive material weapons' and weapons with 'characteristics comparable in destructive effect to those of the atomic bomb'. Depleted-uranium munitions, fuel-air explosives and 'daisy cutter' bombs – all developed by the United States – clearly fall within the definition of prohibited weapons.

63. Boutros Boutros-Ghali, UN Secretary-General, *The UN and the Iraq-Kuwait Conflict, 1990–1996* (New York: Department of Public Information, UN, 1996), p. 5.

64. *Ibid.*, p.95. See also Tim Trevan, *Saddam's Secrets: The Hunt for Iraq's Hidden Weapons* (London: HarperCollins, 1999).

65. 'Scott Ritter's private war', *New Yorker*, 9 November 1998; 'Israel a contribué au desarmement de l'Irak', *Le Monde*, 30 September 1998, quoting *Ha'aretz*, Tel Aviv, 28 September 1998.

66. 'The anthrax hunter', *The Guardian*, London, 10 April 2002; Julian Borger, 'US hawk "tried to sully Iraq arms inspector"', *The Independent*, London, 16 April 2002; Rupert Cornwell, 'Bush hard-liners order CIA to report on US', *The Independent*, London, 16 April 2002.

67. Brian Whitaker, 'America wants Saddam out even if he gives ground', *The Guardian*, London, 6 May 2002.

Chapter 2

1. Washington's celebrated 'green light' for Saddam's invasion of Kuwait has been much discussed (see, for example, Geoff Simons, *Iraq: from Sumer to Saddam*, Macmillan, London, 2nd edn, 1996, pp.345–51).

2. The United States supported a pro-Saddam coalition in the Iran-Iraq War (1980–88) and became an active Saddam ally, to the point of sinking Iranian shipping in the Gulf.

3. See, for example, Kenneth R. Timmerman, *The Death Lobby: How the West Armed Iraq*, Fourth Estate, London, 1992; and the *Report of the Inquiry into the Export of Defence Equipment and Dual-Use Goods to Iraq and Related Prosecutions*, Richard Scott, London, 15 February 1996.

4. For a profile of Saudi human rights abuses, see Geoff Simons, *Saudi Arabia: the Shape of a Client Feudalism*, Macmillan, London, 1998, Chapter 1, pp. 3–68.

5. It is interesting that the first American report on Halabja judged that it was the Iranians, not the Iraqis, who had used chemical weapons against the Kurds (see Stephen C. Pelletiere, Douglas V. Johnson II and Leif R. Rosenberger, *Iraqi Power and US Security*

in the Middle East, Strategic Studies Institute, US Army War College, Carlisle Barracks, Pennsylvania 17013–5050, 1990).

6. For a detailed survey of the relevant reports and studies, see Geoff Simons, *The Scourging of Iraq: Sanctions, Law and Natural Justice*, Macmillan, London, 2nd edn, 1998, Chapter 3, pp. 105–72.

7. See *Ibid.*

8. Denis Halliday, *Economic sanctions on the people of Iraq: first degree murder or manslaughter?*, Paper for the International Conference, Madrid, November 1999.

9. Patrick Cockburn, 'Poisoned Tigris spreads tide of death in Iraq', *The Independent*, London, 23 April 1998.

10. Felicity Arbuthnot, 'Death of a nation', *Tribune*, London, 12 February 1999.

11. George Alagiah, 'Starvation: the West's weapon of mass destruction against Iraq', *The Independent on Sunday*, London, 28 February 1999.

12. Bert Sacks, 'Scenes from Baghdad, illusions from America: why do Iraqi children have to starve because we want to punish Iraq?', *Washington Law and Politics*, February/March 1999.

13. Hans von Sponeck, UN Humanitarian Coordinator in Iraq, press briefing, 26 October 1999.

14. Tom Campbell (Republican, CA) and John Conyers (Democrat, MI), US Representatives, new congressional letter to President Clinton on Iraqi sanctions, 23 November 1999.

15. Halliday, *op cit.*

16. *Ibid.*

17. This appeal for legal constraints on the behaviour of a 'dangerously out-of-control Security Council' is comparable to the suggestion made by Marc Weller, international legal expert, St Catherine's College, Cambridge, England, that the behaviour of the US-dominated Security Council over the Lockerbie affair should be referred to the World Court 'if the constitutional system of the UN Charter is to recover from the blow it has suffered in this episode' (see Marc Weller, 'The Lockerbie case – a premature end to the "New World Order"', *African Journal of International and Comparative Law*, 1992 [4], pp. 1–15).

18. 'Ministers ban vaccine for Iraq', *The Guardian*, London, 9 December 1999.

19. Michael Minnig, ICRC representative in Iraq, Agence France Presse (AFP), 8 May 1999.

20. 'Explanatory Memorandum Regarding the Comprehensive Embargo on Iraq: Humanitarian Circumstances in Iraq', Human Rights Watch, New York, 4 January 2000.

21. *Ibid.*

22. Report of the Group of United Nations Experts Established Pursuant to Paragraph 30 of Security Council Resolution 1284 (2000), February 2000. (NB: Resolution 1284 was adopted in December 1999 and so elsewhere is denoted by 1284 [1999].)

23. *Ibid.*, p. 4.

24. Beat Schweizer, ICRC head in Iraq, Agence France Presse (AFP), 23 January 2000.

25. Richard Norton-Taylor, 'Human rights advice to Iraq blocked', *The Guardian*, London, 18 February 2000.

26. Ewen MacAskill, 'Victims of West's almost forgotten war in Iraq receive daily reminder that death is waiting', *The Guardian*, London, 21 March 2000.

27. Report of the Secretary-General Pursuant to Paragraph 28 and 30 of Resolution 1284 (1999) and Paragraph 5 of Resolution 1281 (1999), S/2000/208, 10 March 2000.

28. *Ibid.*, Paragraph 50.

29. *Ibid.*, Paragraph 56.
30. It should be stressed that these recommendations were not for additional UN expenditures but simply to allow Iraq to use its own oil revenues.
31. Report S/2000/208, *op cit.*, Paragraphs 58–64.
32. *Ibid.*, Paragraph 72.
33. *Ibid.*, Paragraphs 128, 132.
34. *Ibid.*, Paragraph 149.
35. Sarah Boseley, 'UN sanctions "are killing Iraq's children"', *The Guardian*, London, 27 May 2000; Brian Denny, 'UNICEF underlines children's suffering in Iraq', *The Morning Star*, London, 15 June 2000.
36. Letter dated 9 July 2000, from the Permanent Representative of Iraq to the UN addressed to the Secretary-General, S/2000/668, 10 July 2000.
37. *Ibid.*, Section 3.
38. *Ibid.*, Section 6.
39. Yasmin Alibhai-Brown, 'Ten years of sanctions have failed to oust Saddam. But they're killing Iraq', *The Independent*, London, 31 July 2000.
40. *Ibid.*
41. Felicity Arbuthnot, 'Silent Hiroshima culls a nation's children', *The Sunday Independent*, Dublin, 6 August 2000.
42. Jeremy Hardy, 'Degraded policy', *The Guardian*, London, 18 November 2000.
43. Report of the Secretary-General Pursuant to Paragraph 5 of Resolution 1302 (2000), United Nations, S/2000/1132, 29 November 2000, Paragraphs 3 and 5.
44. *Ibid.*, Paragraph 135.
45. 'United Nations sanctions against Iraq: the destruction of an entire population', Media Monitors Network (MMN), Centre for Balanced Development (CBD), 12 January 2001.
46. *Ibid.*
47. *Ibid.*
48. 'The ten-year assault on the people of Iraq', Islamic Association for Palestine, Chicago, USA, 17 January 2001.
49. *Ibid.*
50. 'Sixteen arrested at UN Mission to Iraq marking the years of war on the Iraqi people', Voices in the Wilderness, *Middle East News*, Press Release Network, 17 January 2001.
51. Patrick Cockburn, 'If Saddam doesn't get you, the UN sanctions will', *The Independent*, London, 20 January 2001.
52. Jim Addington, 'Ten years suffering – enough is enough', *Morning Star*, London, 13 February 2001.
53. Report of the Secretary-General pursuant to Paragraph 5 of Resolution 1330 (2000), S/2001/186, 2 March 2001.
54. Report of the Secretary-General pursuant to Paragraph 5 of Resolution 1330 (2000), S/2001/505, 18 May 2001. See also the discussion of this report in Chapter 2, in connection with the US imposition of 'holds' on many humanitarian and other contracts.
55. *Ibid.*, Paragraphs 59 and 60.
56. *Ibid.*, Paragraphs 61 and 62.
57. *Ibid.*, Paragraph 64.
58. *Ibid.*, Paragraph 67.
59. *Ibid.*, Paragraphs 71 and 75.
60. *Ibid.*, Paragraph 80.

61.   *Ibid.*, Paragraphs 97–8.
62.   *Ibid.*, Paragraph 100.
63.   *Ibid.*, Paragraphs 126 and 136.
64.   Hala Jaber, 'I have seen good days and beautiful days in this hospital – these are the bad days', *The Sunday Telegraph*, London, 4 November 2001.
65.   Hans von Sponeck and Denis Halliday, 'The hostage nation', *The Guardian*, London, 29 November 2001.
66.   Residents were saying that key equipment was being removed from power stations in anticipation of US military strikes. The dismantling of weapons factories and key installations was also under way.
67.   Letter dated 11 April 2002 from the Permanent Representative of Iraq to the United Nations addressed to the Secretary-General, S/2002/424; Annex to letter, signed by Iraqi foreign minister Naji Sabri; Enclosure lists drugs and equipment on hold that relate to the treatment of various cancers.
68.   *Ibid.*

Chapter 3
1.   Peter Hain, 'I fought apartheid, I'll fight Saddam', *The Guardian*, London, 6 January 2001.
2.   *Procedures Established by the 661 Committee for the Oil-for-Food Programme*, Office of the Iraq Programme, UN.
3.   *Ibid.*
4.   *Guidelines on the completion of applications under oil-for-food programme*, similar versions of the *Guidelines* are offered for both manual and electronic formats; earlier versions of the *Guidelines* have been entitled 'Guidance on the Completion and Notification to Ship Goods to Iraq', Office of the Iraq Programme, approved by the Security Council 661 Committee on 3 September 1999.
5.   According to Article 23 of the UN Charter.
6.   Kais al-Kaisy, 'The sanctions that bring death', letter, *The Guardian*, London, 3 July 1994.
7.   *Ibid.*
8.   'Sanctions against Iraq', World Chronicle (recorded 20 May 1992), Information Products Division, Department of Public Information, UN, New York; Guest: Peter Hohenfellner, Chairman of Committee on Sanctions against Iraq; journalists: Bruno Franseschi, Raghida Dergham, Ian Williams; moderator: Michael Littlejohn.
9.   *Ibid.*
10.   Examples are given in Geoff Simons, *The Scourging of Iraq: Sanctions, Law and Natural Justice*, Macmillan, London, 2nd edn, 1998.
11.   *Ibid.*, pp. 121–21.
12.   *Ibid.*, pp. 121–22.
13.   David H. Harmon, Warning letter from US Department of the Treasury to Voices in the Wilderness, 22 January 1996.
14.   Response of Voices in the Wilderness (A Campaign to end the US/UN Economic Sanctions Against the People of Iraq, 1460 Carmen Ave, Chicago, IL 60640).
15.   Report of UN Secretary-General, S/1999/896, 19 August 1999.
16.   Edith M. Lederer, 'Official: UN delays aid to Iraq', Associated Press (AP), 22 July 1999.
17.   Letter from UN Secretary-General to President of the Security Council, S/1999/1086, 23 October 1999.
18.   *Ibid.*

19. *Explanatory Memorandum Regarding the Comprehensive Embargo on Iraq: Humanitarian Circumstances in Iraq*, Human Rights Watch, January 2000.

20. *Ibid.* Reuters (18 November 1999) cited UN sources as stating that of 389 contracts on hold the US accounted for 337, the UK for 29, and the US and the UK together 23.

21. *Ibid.*

22. Letter dated 14 January 2000 from the Secretary-General addressed to the President of the Security Council, S/2000/26, 14 January 2000.

23. *Ibid.*

24. Report of the Secretary-General pursuant to Paragraphs 28 and 30 of Resolution 1284 (1999) and Paragraph 5 of Resolution 1281 (1999), S/2000/208, 10 March 2000.

25. *Ibid.*

26. *Ibid.*

27. Briefing by Benon Sevan, Executive Director of the Iraq Programme, UN Office of the Iraq Programme, 20 April 2000.

28. *Ibid.*

29. Report of Secretary-General, 10 March 2000, *op cit.*

30. Letter dated 22 May 2000 from the Permanent Representative of Iraq to the United Nations addressed to the Secretary-General, S/2000/467, 23 May 2000; plus annex.

31. *Ibid.*, annex.

32. Introductory statement by Benon Sevan, Executive Director of the Iraq Programme, at the informal consultation of the Security Council, 6 June 2000.

33. *Ibid.*

34. Letter dated 11 June 2000 from Permanent Representative of Iraq to the United Nations addressed to the Secretary-General, S/2000/563, 12 June 2000; plus annex.

35. *Health Update Iraq*, World Health Organization (WHO), 24 November 2000.

36. Report of the Secretary-General pursuant to Paragraph 5 of Resolution 1302 (2000), S/2000/1132, 29 November 2000.

37. *Ibid.*, Paragraph 40.

38. Report of the Secretary-General pursuant to Paragraph 5 of Resolution 1330 (2000), S/2001/186, 2 March 2001.

39. *Ibid.*, Paragraph 45.

40. *Ibid.*, Paragraphs 59–60.

41. *Ibid.*, Paragraph 76.

42. *Ibid.*, Paragraphs 80, 84, 87.

43. *Ibid.*, Paragraphs 89, 91, 95, 107, 111.

44. *Ibid.*, Paragraph 112.

45. *Ibid.*, Paragraph 124.

46. *Ibid.*, Paragraphs 154, 159, 164, 168.

47. The 'fast-track' provision, authorized in Resolution 1284 (1999), Paragraph 17, is referred to as 'Accelerated procedures for the approval of contracts to specified humanitarian suppliers for Iraq', It was issued by the Office of the Iraq Programme. An approved list for housing items was added to the procedures on 26 February 2001.

48. 'Accelerated procedures…', *op cit.*

49. *Ibid.*

50. Report of the Secretary-General pursuant to paragraph 5 of Resolution 1330 (2000), S/2001/505, 18 May 2001.

51. *Ibid.*, Paragraphs 35, 61, 62, 64, 78, 80, 82, 103 and 107.

52. Weekly Updates of the United Nations Office of the Iraq Programme, 10 July, 17 July

and 24 July 2001: contract worths on hold (respectively) – 'over \$3.4 billion', 'almost constant at \$3.4 billion', and rising 'slightly to \$3.47 billion.

53.   Weekly Update, UN Office of the Iraq Programme, 8 January 2002.

54.   Weekly Update, UN Office of the Iraq Programme, 22 January 2002.

55.   See Weekly Updates, UN Office of the Iraq Programme, January to April 2002.

Chapter 4

1.   Geoff Simons, *Vietnam Syndrome: Impact on US Foreign Policy*, Macmillan, London, 1998, p. 333.

2.   Hans Blix was appointed head of the UN Monitoring, Verification and Inspection Commission (UNMOVIC), set up by Resolution 1284. Thus UNMOVIC became the successor to the discredited UN Special Commission (UNSCOM), but as yet has had no opportunity to fulfil its mandate.

3.   'Top UN inspector says Washington firm on Iraq sanctions', *Jordan Times*, Amman, 6 April 2001.

4.   See, for example, the discussion and details of the veto given in Anjali V. Patil, *The UN Veto in World Affairs 1946–1990: A Complete Record and Case Histories of the Security Council's Veto*, UNIFO/Mansell, Sarasota, Florida, United States, 1992.

5.   Simons, Geoff. *Iraq: From Sumer to Saddam*, 2nd edn. London: Macmillan, 1996.

6.   Evelyn Leopold, 'UN set to let Iraq sell oil worth \$2 bn', *The Independent*, London, 14 April 1995.

7.   See, for example, Seymour Hersh, *The Samson Option: Israel, America and the Bomb*, Faber and Faber, London, 1991.

8.   In early 2000, a five-member IAEA team ended a check of nuclear material in Iraq. Ahmad Abu-Zahra, IAEA team leader, reported: 'It went well, and we had good collaboration with our [Iraqi] counterparts.' It was emphasized that the IAEA personnel had no connections with the discredited UNSCOM teams.

9.   *Report of the Group of United Nations Experts Established Pursuant to Paragraph 30 of the Security Council Resolution 1284 (2000)*. NB: Resolution should be denoted 1284 (1999).

10.   On 9 February 2001 the Iraqi UN Permanent Representative commented in a Press Release: 'Many of Iraq's trade partners are increasingly reluctant to take part in the program's contracts due to the complicated mechanism and many delays in approving the contracts.'

11.   *Report of the Group, op cit*, Paragraph 5. The Report includes a 16-page table listing items of equipment placed on hold, mainly by the United States.

12.   *Analysis of Security Council Resolution 1284 (17 December 1999)*, Campaign Against Sanctions on Iraq (CASI), Cambridge, England, Briefing 2: 24 December 1999.

13.   Kathy Kelly and Jeff Guntzel, VITW (Voices in the Wilderness) letter in response to UN passage of Resolution 1284, 12 February 2000.

14.   Campaign Against Sanctions on Iraq (CASI), *Newsletter*, May 2000, p. 4.

15.   Andrew Marshall, 'Take Iraq apart, says Bush advisor', *The Independent*, London, 21 May 2000.

16.   Campaign Against Sanctions on Iraq (CASI), *Newsletter*, February 2001, p. 5.

Chapter 5

1.   See, for example, G. Edward Griffin, *The Fearful Master: A Second Look at the UN*, Western Islands, Boston, United States, 1972.

2.   Phyllis Bennis (*Calling the Shots: How Washington Dominates Today's UN*, Olive Branch

Notes

Press, Interlink Publishing, New York, 1996) has charted in detail how the United States manipulates UN institutions in its own interests.

3. The US decision to invade Iraq was taken weeks before the UN adoption of SCR 678 (29 November 1990).

4. This is a precedent for US military and diplomatic support for Turkey in its repeated invasions and bombings of northern Iraq.

5. This case is discussed in detail in Geoff Simons, 'Lockerbie: Lessons for International Law', *The Journal of Libyan Studies* (Oxford, England), Vol. 1(1), Summer 2000, pp. 33–47.

6. To secure international acquiescence for a US-led war against Iraq, Washington arranged bribes for various countries (some then on the UN Security Council), including Iran, the Soviet Union, China, Ethiopia, Zaire and Zimbabwe; tried (unsuccessfully) to intimidate Yemen; and tried (unsuccessfully) to cajole Cuba. Sudan, suffering famine, was punished for its attitude by a withdrawal of food aid. The characteristic US exercize in bribery and threat was only partially successful, but successful enough. The flawed SCR 678 was adopted, and used thereafter to justify a wholly disproportionate military onslaught on Iraq.

7. Boutros Boutros-Ghali, former UN Secretary-General, describes the ongoing tensions between Washington and the United Nations. (See Boutros Boutros-Ghali, *UNvanquished: A US–UN Saga*, New York: Random House, 1999.)

8. *Ibid.*, pp. 261–4.

9. *Ibid.*, pp. 296–7.

10. Robert Dole, Alan Simpson, Howard Metzenbaum, James McClure and Frank Murkowski.

11. Betsy Pisik, 'US rejects dialogue, Saddam's deputy claims', *The Washington Times*, 12 September 2000.

12. The provision of assistance to the Iraqi National Congress (INC) was pursuant to Section 575 of the Foreign Operations, Export Financing, and Relating Programs Appropriation Act of FY 2001 (PL 106–429). The report was mandated under this legislation. The political atmosphere for this act was shaped also by the Iraq Liberation Act of 1998.

13. *Report on Plans for Transfer of Humanitarian Assistance for the Relief of the Iraqi People, and for Radio and Television Broadcasting by the Iraqi National Congress.*

14. 'Text: Clinton Sends Report on Iraq to Congress', US Office of International Information Programs, 17 January 2001.

15. *Ibid.* The topics of administration and propaganda take up 3½ pages of the five-page text.

16. Stephen Farrell, 'UN officials round on Americans as "real villains"', *The Times*, London, 21 February 2001.

17. Tareq Ayyoub, 'Annan, Iraqi official discuss UN-Iraqi file', *Jordan Times*, Amman, 28 March 2001.

18. See Geoff Simons, *Iraq – Primus Inter Pariahs, A Crisis Chronology, 1997–98*, London: Macmillan, 1999, pp. 17–26 (sources given).

19. Jean P. Sasson, *Princess*, London: Bantam, 1993, pp. 264–5.

20. Derek Brown, 'Israel "making torture legal"', *The Guardian*, London, 23 October 1995.

21. Ramsey Clark and others, *War Crimes: A Report on United States War Crimes Against Iraq*, Washington DC: Maisonneuve Press, 1992; *US and its Allies: Crimes and Violations of Human Rights in Iraq*, A Report on: Part I: Crimes of the Military Aggression against Iraq, Part II: The Blockade and its Violations, prepared by A Panel of International Law

Experts in Iraq, The International Symposium, Baghdad, 5–8 February 1994.

22. George Monbiot, 'America's bioterror', *The Guardian*, London, 19 March 2002.

23. Quoted in *ibid.*

24. A. C. Grayling, 'The world's policeman cannot be above the law', *The Guardian*, London, 23 August 2001. On 8 May 2002, a spokesman for Kofi Annan said that the UN Secretary-General regretted the US decision not to ratify the Rome Statute of the International Criminal Court: 'The Secretary-General hopes that, in time, the United States will see it to be not only in its interest but in the global interest to support the new Court and actively participate in it' (Fred Eckhard). On the same day, Dato Param Cumaraswamy, the United Nations Special Rapporteur on the Independence of Judges and Lawyers, issued a statement: 'I am deeply concerned by the United States of America's action in "unsigning" the Rome Statute . . . By this unprecedented action . . . the US government has effectively forfeited its leadership role in the search for justice and the promotion and the protection of the role of law and human rights in the international sphere.'

Chapter 6

1. There was debate in the modern movement on whether the Jews would be liberated by their own political action or by divine intervention.

2. Today we often tend to focus on the Muslim-inspired hostility to Jews, but we should also remember the traditional Christian anti-Semitism, from the time of the early Church Fathers to the modern age. Thus St John Chrysostom stated that all Jews 'are drunkards, whoremongers and criminals'; in 1205 Pope Innocent III declared that Jews should be treated as 'damned slaves'; and the Nazi Julius Streicher, defending himself at Nuremberg, praised Martin Luther's 'On the Jews and their Lies' (in which people are urged to burn the synagogues, to deny Jews safe conduct and permission to use the streets, to reduce them to penury, and so on).

3. Andrew and Leslie Cockburn, *Dangerous Liaison*, London: Bodley Head, 1992, p. 27.

4. *Ibid.*, pp. 27–8.

5. The failure of Israel to obey, or the Security Council to enforce, SCR 465 led directly to the Hebron massacre of 1994.

6. Terms of Reference of the International Commission of Enquiry, *Israel in Lebanon*, The Report of the International Commission to enquire into reported violations of International Law by Israel during its invasion of the Lebanon, London: Ithaca Press, 1983. The prestigious Commission comprised Sean MacBride, Nobel Laureate; Richard Falk, Professor of International Law; Kadar Asmal, Senior Lecturer in Law; Brian Bercusson, Lecturer in Laws; Géraud de la Pradelle, Professor of Private Law; and Stefan Wild, Professor of Semitic Languages and Islamic Studies.

7. *Israel in Lebanon*, Commission Report, *op cit*, pp. 191–2.

8. *Ibid.*, p. 197.

9. *Ibid.*, pp. 162–86.

10. *Ibid.*, p. 182.

11. Anton La Guardia, 'Israel backs down over Palestinians', *The Daily Telegraph*, London, 2 February 1993.

12. Sam Kiley, 'No bangs, no smoking guns: victims just fell and bled', *The Times*, London, 17 October 2000. 'Dumdum' bullets were used by Britain in the Battle of Omdurman in 1898 and in the Boer War (1899–1902). In 1899 the Hague Conference, shaping international law, made them illegal.

13. *Ibid.*
14. Brian Whitaker, 'UN mediator tells Israel: lift blockade or risk war', *The Guardian*, London, 6 December 2000.
15. Sam Kiley, 'Army bulldozers flatten houses in Gaza', *The Times*, London, 7 December 2000.
16. Brian Whitaker, 'West rebukes Israel's assassins', *The Guardian*, London, 15 February 2001.
17. Lamis Andori and Sandy Tolen, 'Line of fire', *Morning Star*, London, 2 March 2001.
18. *Ibid.*
19. Uzi Mahnaimi, 'Sharon to push for torture law', *The Sunday Times*, London, 11 March 2001.
20. Ian Black and Suzanne Goldenberg, 'Europe turns heat on Israel', *The Guardian*, London, 14 March 2001.
21. *Ibid.*
22. 'In bed with Sharon, Bush succumbs to seductive advances', editorial, *The Guardian*, London, 22 March 2001.
23. Sam Kiley, 'Palestinians pay no attention to US call for calm', *The Times*, London, 31 March 2001.
24. Phil Reeves, 'Six dead after Israelis open fire with gas and guns', *The Independent*, London, 31 March 2001.
25. Suzanne Goldenberg, 'Arabs accuse US of betrayal', *The Observer*, London, 1 April 2001.
26. Dima Amr, 'Activists discuss unique crises of Palestinian, Iraqi women under threat of war', *Jordan Times*, Amman, 3 April 2001.
27. *Ibid.*
28. Sam Kiley, 'Israel flattens Palestinian camp in Gaza', *The Independent*, London, 12 April 2001.
29. Robert Fisk, 'Guns and bulldozers raze homes in Gaza', *The Independent*, London, 12 April 2001; Phil Reeves, 'Sharon's return to "old deeds" widens rift with moderates', *The Independent*, London, 12 April 2001.
30. Ghossam Joha, 'UN sanctions against Iraq long way off, linked to Israel's security', *The Star*, Amman, 29 April 2001.
31. *Ibid.*
32. Sam Kiley and Richard Beeston, 'Israel defends destruction of Arab homes', *The Times*, London, 12 July 2001.
33. Arieh O'Sullivan, *The Jewish Post*, 27 October 2000.
34. Ewen MacAskill, 'World leaders urge Israel to accept monitors', *The Guardian*, London, 20 July 2001.
35. Phil Reeves, 'Killing of baby by Jewish vigilantes ignites rural town', *The Independent*, London, 21 July 2001; Suzanne Goldenberg, 'Killers make funeral of wedding', *The Guardian*, London, 31 July 2001.
36. Sam Kiley, 'Sharon to challenge war crimes charges', *The Times*, London, 27 July 2001.
37. Richard Curtiss, *The Link*, AMEU, September 1997; cited again in John Mahoney, 'Israel's Anti-Civilian Weapons', *The Link*, AMEU, January-March 2001.
38. Phil Reeves, 'Aerial survey shows 34 new settlements built under Sharon', *The Independent*, London, 20 March 2002.
39. Sharm El-Sheikh Fact-Finding Committee, chaired by George J. Mitchell, Final Report, 30 April 2001.
40. The UN Human Rights Commission resolution was approved by 40 votes to 5, with 7

abstentions. Canada, the Czech Republic, Germany, Guatemala and Britain voted against the resolution. The United States, having lost its seat in 2001, was not a member of the Commission.

41. The fact-finding mission proposed by UN Secretary-General Kofi Annan would have had unique authority, but it is important to note the prestigious investigations that did take place. Thus Amnesty International delegates, having conducted a research mission to Israel and the Occupied Territories, 'compiled evidence indicating that serious breaches of international human rights and humanitarian law were committed [by the Israeli forces], including war crimes' (*Amnesty*, May/June 2002, Issue 113, p. 5). In the same vein, the US-based Human Rights Watch organization, followed detailed research (information collected from Jenin residents, international aid workers, medical workers, officials, etc.), concluded that 'Israeli forces committed serious violations of international humanitarian law, some amounting *prima facie* to war crimes' (*Israel, The Occupied West Bank and Gaza Strip, and the Palestinian Authority Territories*, May 2002, Volume 14, No. 3(E)). On 9 May 2002, Peter Hansen, Commissioner-General of the UN Relief and Works Agency for Palestinian Refugees in the Near East (UNRWA), commented on the situation facing the Palestinians in the Occupied Territories:

> After 18 months of closure and hardship the recent Israeli invasion has led to large-scale destruction of shelters, water supplies, electricity lines and sewage lines. There has been a large-scale destruction of civic infrastructure with a result that a large portion of the refugee population finds itself without the basic services and means of support for the minimum standards of life.

UNRWA estimated that an additional $70 million was needed to meet the emergency humanitarian needs of Palestinians resulting from the incursions by the Israeli military. Ariel Sharon had fulfilled his pledge of 5 March 2002:

> The Palestinians must be hit and it must be very painful. We must cause them losses, victims, so they feel the heavy price' (quoted in *Amnesty*, May/June 2002, Issue 113, p.4).

Chapter 7
1. Saeed H. Hasan, letter dated 7 August 2000 from the Permanent Representative of Iraq to the United Nations addressed to the President of the Security Council, S/2000/780, 8 August 2000.
2. Saeed H. Hasan, letter dated 11 October 2000 from the Permanent Representative of Iraq to the United Nations addressed to the Secretary-General, S/2000/982, 11 October 2000.
3. Report of the Group of United Nations Experts Established Pursuant to Paragraph 30 of Security Council Resolution 1284 (2000). (NB: Resolution 1284 was adopted in 1999). This report describes the progressive collapse of the Iraqi oil industry and indicates the relevance of contract holds to this process.
4. Richard Boucher, 'Regulations governing flights to Iraq', US Department of State, 6 November 2000.
5. Laila Shaheen, 'Qatar gift to Saddam may prompt curbs: "Arms" in Iraq schools, hospitals', *Kuwait Times*, Kuwait City, 20 November 2000.
6. Musa Keilani, 'Jordan – pioneer in lifting sanctions on Iraq', *Jordan Times*, Amman, 26

November 2000.

7. *Ibid.*
8. Iraqi Airways, grounded for a decade, had 37 planes: 15 Boeing jetliners and 22 Russian-built Ilyushin 76s. Four Boeing 727s and two 707s were in Amman, four aircrafts were in Tunis, and five Boeings and all 22 Ilyushins were in Tehran. One estimate suggested that the engines of the Boeings held in Jordan would need an overhaul costing around $14 million to make them airworthy.
9. The Council comprises Egypt, Jordan, Libya, Mauritania, the Palestinian Authority, Somalia, Sudan, Syria, Yemen and Iraq.
10. Sam Kiley, 'Saddam gives £6000 for every intifada "martyr"', *The Times*, London, 13 December 2000.
11. *Ibid.*
12. Dalya Dajani, 'Israel prevents humanitarian aid from Iraq reaching Palestinians – diplomat', *Jordan Times*, Amman, 15 December 2000.
13. Maryam Karami, 'No ban on Iraqi airliners crossing Iran's airspace', *Tehran Times*, Tehran, 20 December 2000.
14. 'Key paper to press Saddam's full compliance, back Iraqis', *Kuwait Times*, Kuwait City, 23 December 2000.
15. Moonirah Allen, 'Kuwait PoWs alive, in Qusay's charge', *Kuwait Times*, Kuwait City, 26 December 2000.
16. In a closed session of the Security Council, the United States and Britain blocked the request.
17. 'Uday seeks to add Kuwait to "full map": arms checks ruled out', *Kuwait Times*, Kuwait City, 15 January 2001.
18. Julian Borger, 'Saddam poses as fairy godfather to US poor', *The Guardian*, London, 16 January 2001.
19. Carl Mortished, 'Iraq plans new oil pipeline to Syrian port', *The Times*, London, 29 January 2001.
20. 'Peaceful neighbouring countries' that were conspiring with Washington and London in the frequent launching of bombing raids against Iraqi civilians.
21. Quotations in 'Iraq urged to obey UN', *Kuwait Times*, Kuwait City, 20 February 2001.
22. 'Arab parliamentarians support lifting Iraq sanctions', *Future News*, Beirut, 27 February 2001.
23. Caroline Faraj and Francisca Sawalha, 'Arab FMs agree on support for Palestinians, seek compromise on Iraq', *Jordan Times*, Amman, 25 March 2001.
24. *Ibid.*
25. *Ibid.*
26. 'Iraq-Kuwait proposal', Arab summit, unofficial translation obtained by *Jordan Times*, Amman, 28 March 2001.
27. 'We're keen on aiding the people . . . Iraq has wasted another chance', *Kuwait Times*, Kuwait City, 31 March 2001.
28. SCIRI, A Tehran-based organization and deeply hostile to Baghdad, was being courted by the United States to put further pressure on Iraq. SCIRI, approached by the INC's pro-US Ahmad Chalabi, was reluctant to serve as 'cover for US security services' that could increase regional instability.
29. 'Saddam hails closer Arab ties with Iraq', *Tehran Times*, Tehran, 10 April 2001.
30. It should be possible to use the International Court of Justice at The Hague (The World Court) for such a purpose.

31. Saad G. Hattar, 'Iraq ready to cooperate with Jordan to settle differences with Kuwait', *Jordan Times*, Amman, 12 April 2001.

32. *Ibid.*

Chapter 8

1. George W. Bush, interview in the *New York Times*, 14 January 2001.

2. Greg LaMotte, quoted in Philip M. Taylor, *War and the Media: Propaganda and Persuasion in the Gulf War*, Manchester University Press, Manchester, England, 1992, p. 253.

3. 'Tales from the Gulf', *The Late Show*, BBC2, 20 June 1991; see also Stephen Sackur, *The London Review of Books*, 4 April 1991, reprinted in Brian McArthur (ed), *Despatches from the Gulf War*, Bloomsbury, London, 1991, pp. 261–6.

4. Robert Fisk, 'Marines play at war in road of slaughter', *The Independent*, London, 14 October 1994.

5. *Ibid.*

6. Patrick Cockburn, 'Clinton acclaims Iraq strike', *The Independent*, London, 28 June 1993; Jurek Martin, 'US rallies behind Clinton's decision', *Financial Times*, London, 28 June 1993; 'Bodies among the wrecked streets', *The Daily Telegraph*, London, 28 June 1993.

7. Vijay Joshi and Ian Black, 'US planes "misfire" in Iraq', *The Guardian*, London, 26 January 1999.

8. Dana Priest, 'Allies escalate attacks on Iraqi air defences', *International Herald Tribune*, 3 March 1999.

9. Identical letters dated 15 August 2000 from the Permanent Representative of Iraq to the United Nations addressed to the Secretary-General and the President of the Security Council, S/2000/806, 16 August 2000.

10. Identical letters dated 28 October 2000 from the Permanent Representative of Iraq to the United Nations addressed to the Secretary-General and the President of the Security Council, S/2000/1056, 1 November 2000.

11. *Ibid.*

12. Richard Beeston, 'Hain apologizes for calling Paris "contemptible"', *The Times*, London, 9 November 2000.

13. 'Clinton condemns Sudan for bombing south but continues to bomb Iraq', *Crescent International*, 17 November 2000.

14. Mike Horn, quoted in Jeremy Hardy, 'Degraded policy', *The Guardian*, London, 18 November 2000.

15. John Nichol, 'Lift the sanctions against Iraq now', *The Observer*, London, 19 November 2000.

16. Judy Aita, 'Holbrooke: Iraq will be a major issue for Bush', US Office of International Information Programs', 12 January 2001.

17. Brian Denny, 'Bush celebrates with Iraqi bomb raids', *Morning Star*, London, 22 January 2001.

18. Richard Beeston, 'Bush faces Saddam weapons challenge', *The Times*, London, 23 January 2001.

19. Tom Raum, 'Bush inherits "whole new set of woes" over Saddam', *Kuwait Times*, Kuwait City, 26 January 2001.

20. 'The bomb and Iraq', *Mid-East Realities*, 28 January 2001. 'As war clouds gather in the Middle East public opinion is being prepared for a possible regional war that could likely include a combined Western/Israeli effort to take out the weapons of mass destruction of Syria, Iraq and Iran.'

21. Ben Macintyre, 'The son claims vengeance for the father', *The Times*, London, 17 February 2001.
22. Michael Evans, 'Bush and Blair bomb Baghdad', *The Times*, London, 17 February 2001.
23. Robert Fisk, 'Here it is – Orwell's war without end', *The Independent on Sunday*, London, 18 February 2001.
24. 'Mr Bush must not repeat the mistakes of the past', editorial, *The Independent*, London, 17 February 2001.
25. *Ibid.*
26. 'A reminder for Saddam', editorial, *The Daily Telegraph*, London, 17 February 2001; 'Saddam's reminder', editorial, *The Sunday Times*, London, 18 February 2001.
27. Fisk, *op cit.*
28. Evans, *op cit.*
29. Jason Burke, Kemal Ahmed and Ed Vulliamy, 'Blair and Bush defy world fury', *The Observer*, London, 18 February 2001.
30. Tom Baldwin, 'Downing Street quick to raise Hoon's profile', *The Times*, London, 17 February 2001.
31. Edward Luttwak, '"Eliminating Saddam is now both feasible and desirable"', *The Sunday Telegraph*, London, 18 February 2001.
32. Ben Macintyre, Michael Evans and Stephen Farrell, 'Raid partly failed, Pentagon admits', *The Times*, London, 22 February 2001; Michael Ellison, 'Most western bombs missed Iraqi targets', *The Guardian*, London 23 February 2001.
33. George Galloway, 'Shattered seconds', *Morning Star*, London, 26 February 2001.
34. *Ibid.*
35. *Ibid.*
36. 'Watch over Iraq', editorial, *The Times*, London, 22 August 2000.
37. Richard Beeston, 'Pilots' peril may force cuts in Iraq patrols', *The Independent*, London, 10 May 2001.
38. Mohammed Al-Douri, Iraq's Ambassador to the United Nations, Letter dated 3 June 2001 from the Permanent Representative of Iraq to the UN addressed to the Secretary-General; Tariq Aziz, Annex to letter.
39. Mohammed Al-Douri, Iraq's Ambassador to the United Nations, letter dated 5 June 2001 from the Permanent Representative of Iraq to the UN addressed to the Secretary-General; Tariq Aziz, Annex to letter.
40. David Usborne, 'Iraq claims air strikes kill 23 on football pitch', *The Independent*, London, 21 June 2001.
41. 'The US and UK commit a vile aggression against Iraqi civilians', Press Release, Permanent Mission of the Republic of Iraq to the UN, 20 June 2001; quoting the Iraqi News Agency (INA).
42. Scott Ritter, 'Shifting Sands: The Truth about UNSCOM and the Disarming of Iraq', documentary film, following Ritter, *Endgame: Solving the Iraq Problem – Once and For All*, New York: Simon and Schuster, 1999.

Chapter 9

1. It was not much of a concession because the United States could still block the oil contracts when they reached the Sanctions Committee – as indeed, according to investigating UN experts appointed by the Secretary-General, it continued to do.
2. George W. Bush, *US News and World Report*, 3 April 2000.
3. Ewen MacAskill, 'US and Britain retreat on Iraqi curbs', *The Guardian*, London, 1 April

2000.

4. 'US disputes French view of Iraqi air embargo', Reuters, *The Financial Times*, London, 5 August 2000.
5. *New Republic*, 30 October 2000.
6. Voices in the Wilderness, *Newsletter*, 12 November 2000.
7. Industry review by Deutsche Bank, October 2000.
8. Richard Beeston, 'MP breaks sanctions in first flight to Iraq', *The Times*, London, 11 November 2000.
9. 'US admits failure of Iraq sanctions', *Future News*, Beirut, 16 November 2000.
10. 'Iraq pumps oil to Syria as US watches closely', *Future News*, Beirut, 21 November 2000.
11. 'Ready to receive arms inspectors', *Kuwait Times*, Kuwait City, 23 November 2000.
12. 'Allies mull new curbs on Iraq', *Kuwait Times*, Kuwait City, 4 December 2000.
13. Muqtedar Khan, 'Valueless sanctions help no one', *Middle East News Press Release Network*, 5 December 2000.
14. 'More of the same expected from Washington in 2001', *Monday Morning*, Beirut, 11 January 2001.
15. Letter to the United Nations Security Council addressed to Ambassador Richard Holbrooke, President of Security Council, Human Rights Watch, 4 January 2000.
16. Humanitarian Panel set up by UN in January 1999, cited in *ibid.* Human Rights Watch emphasized its support for trials of the Iraqi leaders for war crimes, but stressed also the need to change the sanctions regime, known to be having a catastrophic effect on the Iraqi civilian population.
17. 'Sanctions on Iraq outlive their purpose, serve Israel's interests, daily', *Emirates News Agency* (WAM), 5 January 2001.
18. Hans von Sponeck and Denis Halliday, both former (resigned) UN Humanitarian Coordinators in Iraq, letter, 'Admit you have failed, Mr Hain', *The Guardian*, London, 8 January 2001.
19. 'Flights of futility. At last, Britain shifts ground on Iraq', *The Guardian*, London, 9 January 2001.
20. *Ibid.*
21. Richard Beeston and Damian Whitworth, 'Saddam may hold key to West's prosperity', *The Times*, London, 18 January 2001.
22. There was no doubt that the embargo made the Iraqi people more dependent on the regime and strengthened the domestic support for Saddam, but it was plain that the whole weight of Iraqi diplomatic efforts over years had been focused on the removal of sanctions.
23. 'Ten years on the Gulf War: ripping UN sanctions on Iraq continues', *The Star*, Amman, 22 January 2001.
24. *Ibid.*
25. Richard Norton-Taylor, 'Calmer tone on Iraq from MoD', *The Guardian*, London, 25 January 2001.
26. 'Bush administration takes steps to "re-energize" Iraqi sanctions', *Future News*, Beirut, 25 January 2001.
27. Ewen MacAskill, 'US tries to head off UN plan to reform sanctions', *The Guardian*, London, 9 February 2001.
28. Alan Sipress, 'More Iraqi oil evading sanctions', *The Washington Post*, 18 February 2001.
29. *Ibid.*
30. Richard Norton-Taylor, Julian Borger and Brian Whitaker, 'Allies repackage "smart"

embargo', *The Guardian*, London, 21 February 2001.
31. *Ibid.*
32. *Ibid.*
33. Michael Evans and Stephen Farrell, 'Allies to switch focus of sanctions', *The Times*, London, 21 February 2001.
34. Anton La Guardia, 'US-British talks aim to "sharpen" sanctions on Iraq', *The Daily Telegraph*, London, 21 February 2001.
35. Sam Kiley, 'Powell's peace call falls on deaf ears', *The Times*, London, 26 February 2001.
36. Richard Beeston, 'US faces uphill task to rebuild Gulf coalition', *The Times*, London, 26 February 2001.
37. Brian Whitaker, 'Allies struggle to find "smart" sanctions on Iraq', *The Guardian*, London, 26 February 2001.
38. Alan Sipress, 'Powell defends stand on Iraq', *The Washington Post*, 8 March 2001; Ben Macintyre, 'Powell out of step over sanctions', *The Times*, London, 9 March 2001.
39. 'Test: Powell explains changes in Iraq sanctions policy', *US Office of International Information Programs*, 9 March 2001.
40. Alan Sipress, 'US shifts attack on Iraq trade', *The Washington Post*, 26 March 2001.
41. *Ibid.*
42. Damian Whitworth, 'Europe fails to decipher White House code', *The Times*, London, 28 March 2001.
43. 'Iraq wins battle for own oil money outside UN control: Report', *Tehran Times*, Tehran, 10 April 2001.
44. 'Iraq sanctions go "smart"', *Emirate News Agency* (WAM), 18 May 2001.
45. Brian Whitaker and Amelia Gentleman, 'Russia blocks smart sanctions against Iraq', *The Guardian*, London, 24 May 2001.
46. One estimate suggested that Turkey was currently earning about $600 million a year from trade and transit fees on the oil pipeline that carried Iraqi crude to the Turkish Mediterranean terminal of Ceyhan under the UN-controlled oil-for-food deal.
47. Whitaker and Gentleman, *op cit.*
48. Brian Whitaker, 'Jordan first to lose when "smart" sanctions hit Iraq', *The Guardian*, London, 26 June 2001.
49. 'Russia issues warning over vote on Iraqi sanctions plan', *Morning Star*, London, 27 June 2001; Ian Traynor and Brian Whitaker, 'Russians oppose "smart sanctions"', *The Guardian*, London, 28 June 2001; Brian Whitaker, 'Russia blocks new sanctions on Iraqi arms', *The Guardian*, London, 3 July 2001.
50. Extract from correspondence with author.
51. *Voices*, newsletter of Voices in the Wilderness, No. 23, May 2002, p. 3.

Chapter 10

1. The US violations of international law in regard to Iraq have been widely discussed. See, for example, Ramsey Clark and others, *War Crime: A Report on United States War Crimes Against Iraq*, Washington DC: Maisonneuve Press, 1992; Geoff Simons, *The Scourging of Iraq: Sanctions, Law and Natural Justice*, London: Macmillan, 2nd edn, 1998; letter dated 9 July 2000 from the Permanent Representative of Iraq to the United Nations addressed to the Secretary-General, S/2000/669, 10 July 2000, dealing with 'war crimes committed against Iraqi forces by United States armed forces . . . in 1991; identical letters dated 10 July 2000 from the Permanent Representative of Iraq to the United Nations addressed to the Secretary-General and the President of the Security Council, S/2000/687, 13 July

2000, dealing with 'genocidal' and other crimes.

2. Report of the Secretary-General pursuant to Paragraphs 28 and 30 of Resolution 1284 (1999) and Paragraph 5 of Resolution 1281 (1999), S/2000/208, 10 March 2000, p.41. The revenue allocated to humanitarian supplies was nominally larger but, because of holds, procrastination, contractual breaches, etc., largely meaningless (see Chapter 3).

3. Report of the Secretary-General pursuant to Paragraph 5 of Resolution 1302 (2000), S/2000/1132, 29 November 2000, p.32.

4. Brian Whitaker, 'Gulf war reparations may take Iraq more than a century to pay', *The Guardian*, London, 16 June 2000.

5. *Ibid.*

6. Secretary-General, address to UN Compensation Commission Governing Council, S/1994/10, 14 January 1994.

7. Letter dated 10 October 2000 from Permanent Representative of Iraq to the United Nations addressed to the Secretary-General, S/2000/981, 11 October 2000.

8. *Ibid.*

9. *Ibid.*

10. 'Robbing Iraq under an extortion scheme billed as "compensation"', *Crescent International*, 5 December 2000.

11. *Ibid.*

12. Ewen MacAskill, 'US keeps Sudan off UN top table', *The Guardian*, London, 13 October 2000.

13. Peter Beaumont, Ed Vulliamy and Paul Beaver, '"CIA's bastard army ran riot in Balkans"', *The Observer*, London, 11 March 2001.

14. For example, the Iraq Liberation Act of 1998, which made $93 million annual provision for military equipment and training for Iraqi opposition activists. Two of President George W. Bush's appointees – John Negroponte (for UN ambassador) and Otto Reich (for senior Latin American post) – were associated with the illegal death-squad war against the Nicaraguans in the 1980s (Duncan Campbell, 'Bush nominees under fire for link with contras', *The Guardian*, London, 6 April 2001).

15. John Pilger, 'Iraq: yet again they are lying to us', *New Statesman*, London, 20 March 2000; George Galloway, 'You have mutilated the truth about Iraq', letter, *The Guardian*, London, 4 November 2000.

16. Jon Basil Utley, 'The seven big lies about Iraq', *Middle East News Online*, 9 March 2001.

17. John Pilger, 'Silence on the Turkish front', *Morning Star*, London, 21 April 2001.

18. Jason Burke, 'Homes razed in new Israeli attack', *The Observer*, London, 15 April 2001.

19. Sam Kiley, 'Israel tries to seize land and initiative', *The Times*, London, 18 April 2001.

20. Ross Dunn, 'Eight Palestinians die in airstrike', *The Times*, London, 1 August 2001.

21. Laura Peek, 'Bush visits Holocaust Museum in healing gesture to Israel', *The Times*, London, 20 April 2001. Sam Kiley and Richard Beeston, 'Israel defends destruction of Arab homes', *The Times*, London, 12 July 2001; Toby Harnden and Alan Philps, 'Bush and "good friend" Sharon turn up the pressure on Arafat', *The Daily Telegraph*, London, 8 February 2002; Justin Huggler, 'Six major West Bank towns in Israeli hands', *The Independent*, London, 5 April 2002; Janine di Giovanni, 'Children scream for water in the "City of Bombers"', *The Times*, London, 9 April 2002.

22. Hans von Sponeck, 'Go on, Call Bush's Bluff', *The Guardian*, London, 22 July 2002.

23. Simon Tisdall, 'Drop plans to attack Saddam, Tehran tells US', *The Guardian*, London, 24 July 2002.

24. 'Kuwait opposes strike on Iraq', *Kuwait Times*, 3 August 2002.

25. Tim Reid, 'Blair told me Iraq attack is bad idea, says King Abdullah', *The Times*, London, 2 August 2002.
26. *Ibid.*
27. Tony Allen-Mills, 'The gathering desert storm', *The Sunday Times*, London, 4 August 2002.
28. Roland Watson, 'War on Iraq "will cost US $80 billion"', *The Times*, London, 31 July 2002.
29. In a period of less than twelve months, to August 2002, the Bush administration had already managed to convert a $127 billion budget surplus into a $165 billion deficit.

Select Bibliography

Aburish, Said K., *A Brutal Friendship: The West and the Arab Elite*. London: Gollancz, 1997.

Aburish, Said K., *Saddam Hussein: The Politics of Revenge*. London: Bloomsbury, 2000.

Al-Radi, Nuha, *Baghdad Diaries*. London: Saqi Books, 1998.

Arnove, Anthony (ed.), *Iraq Under Siege: The Deadly Impact of Sanctions and War*. London: Pluto Press, 2000.

Aruri, Naseer (ed.), *Palestinian Refugees: The Right of Return*. London: Pluto Press, 2001.

Bennis, Phyllis, *Calling the Shots: How Washington Dominates Today's UN*. New York: Olive Branch Press, Interlink Publishing, 1996.

Butler, Richard, *Saddam Defiant: The Threat of Weapons of Mass Destruction and the Crisis of Global Security*. London: Weidenfeld and Nicholson, 2000.

CARDRI. (Committee Against Repression and for Democratic Rights in Iraq), *Saddam's Iraq: Revolution or Reaction?*. London: Zed Books, 1989.

Carey, Roane (ed.), *The New Intifada: Resisting Israel's Apartheid*. London: Verso, 2001.

Cockburn, Andrew and Leslie Cockburn, *Dangerous Liaison: The Inside Story of the US-Israeli Covert Relationship*. London: The Bodley Head, 1992.

Cockburn, Andrew and Patrick Cockburn, *Out of the Ashes: The Resurrection of Saddam Hussein*. New York: Verso, 2000.

Graham-Brown, Sarah, *Sanctioning Saddam: The Politics of Intervention in Iraq*. London: I.B. Tauris, 1999.

Halliday, Fred, *Two Hours that Shook the World – September 11, 2001: Causes and Consequences*. London: Saqi Books, 2002.

Hazleton, Fan (ed.), CARDRI, *Iraq since the Gulf War: Prospects for Democracy*. London: Zed Books, 1994.

Heikal, Mohamed, *Illusions of Triumph: An Arab View of the Gulf War*. London: HarperCollins, 1992.

Human Rights Watch, *Iraq's Crime of Genocide: The Anfal Campaign Against the Kurds*. New Haven and London: Yale University Press, 1995.

Israel in Lebanon. The report of the International Commission to inquire into reported violations of international law by Israel during its invasion of the Lebanon. London: Ithaca Press, 1983.

Ritter, Scott, *Endgame: Solving the Iraq Problem – Once and for All*. New York: Simon and Schuster, 1999.

Salinger, Pierre and Eric Laurent, *Secret Dossier: The Hidden Agenda Behind the Gulf War*. London: Penguin Books, 1991.

Simons, Geoff, *The Scourging of Iraq: Sanctions, Law and Natural Justice*, 2nd edn. London: Macmillan, 1998.

Simons, Geoff, *Iraq – Primus Inter Pariahs: A Crisis Chronology, 1997–98*. London: Macmillan, 1999.

Timmerman, Kenneth R., *The Death Lobby: How the West Armed Iraq*. London: Fourth Estate, 1992.

Trevan, Tim, *Saddam's Secrets: The Hunt for Iraq's Hidden Weapons*. London: HarperCollins, 1999.

Woodward, Bob, *The Commanders*. New York: Simon and Schuster, 1991.

Index

44

Index

444

235–238
Spain 130
Sponeck, Hans von 65, 72, 82, 96, 212
Sredin, Vasili 218
Stocker, Walter 149
Straw, Jack 42, 50, 52–53
Sudan 31, 37, 158, 214, 239
Sulayem, Sultan bin 169
Sullivan, Greg 225
Sultan, Jirgis Ayub 184
Sweidan, Daw 72
Syria 37, 43, 111, 162, 163, 167, 168, 169, 171,
175, 182, 208, 214, 215–216, 228, 230, 233,
241

Tactical High Energy Laser 153
Tactical Tomahawk missile 19–20
see also weapons, cruise missiles
Taliban 20, 31, 37, 44
Tehran 26
see also Iran
telecommunications 71, 75, 99–100
terrorism
against United States 25–28
by Israelis 143, 147, 152, 154
by United States 14, 126, 179, 240–241
see also bombing
Kosovo Liberation Army (KLA)
Lockerbie bombing
Thalaj, Hassan Ezba 36
Thatcher, Margaret 47, 218
al-Thawra 170
Tikrit Teaching Hospital 183
Titz, Miroslav 44
TotalFinaElf 206, 228
Trifani, Nicolas 157
Truman, Harry 138, 139
Tunisia 164, 193
Turkey 18–19, 46, 48, 128, 131–132, 159, 167,
176, 181, 182, 184, 186, 188, 197, 200, 205,
215, 216, 226, 228, 238, 241

Uday (Saddam's older son) 167–168, 169
Ukraine 214
Umm Qasr, deterioration of 74, 78, 104
UN Charter 40, 110, 112, 122, 123, 124, 125,
126, 137, 139, 159 (and note), 165, 179, 183,
212, 234
UN Commission on Human Rights
129–130, 154–155
UN Compensation Commission 127,
234–235, 236, 237, 238
see also Compensation Fund
'compensation' system
'gravy train' payments
UN Conventions, Covenants 29, 30, 58–59,

130, 212, 234
UN Department of Humanitarian Affairs
76
UNESCO 209
UN General Assembly 29, 61, 108, 123, 138
UN Human Rights Commissioner 146
UNICEF 81, 90
UN–Iraq talks 127–128, 200
United Arab Emirates (UAE) 157–158, 169,
205, 212
United Kingdom 28, 63, 65, 66, 68, 70, 71,
83, 88, 89, 90, 92, 93, 98, 102, 103, 138,
181, 197, 198, 203, 207, 215, 226, 231, 237,
238, 241, 242
United Nations 13, 14, 15, 29, 40, 56, 73,
121–122, 125, 127, 138
see also Economic and Social Council
(ECOSOC)
Security Council resolutions
UN Charter
UN Commission on Human
Rights
UN Conventions, Covenants
UN Department of
Humanitarian Affairs
UNESCO
UN General Assembly
UN Human Rights
Commissioner
UNICEF
UN Monitoring, Verification
and Inspection Commission
(UNMOVIC)
UN Office of the Legal Counsel
UN Population Fund
UN Relief and Works Agency
for Palestine and the Middle
East (UNRWA)
UN Sanctions Committee
UN Secretariat
UN Special Commission
(UNSCOM)
UN Special Commission on
Palestine (UNSCOP)
UN Population Fund 134
United States 14, 17, 18, 19, 20, 23–24, 25–28,
30, 31, 36, 55, 56, 58–59, 61, 63, 65, 66, 68,
70, 71, 83, 88, 89, 90, 92, 93, 95, 97, 98,
102, 103, 107–108, 121–128, 129–135, 138,
139, 147, 153, 157, 163, 181, 188, 198, 203,
207, 215, 226, 231, 233, 234, 237, 238–241,
242
Universal Declaration of Human Rights 130
UN Monitoring, Verification and
Inspection Commission (UNMOVIC)
115, 116, 129, 210, 211, 230, 242
UN Office of the Legal Counsel 89

44444

273